The FAMILY OUTDOOR BOOK

Georgina Heidi Drake of the Backpackers Club, who climbed Snowdon at the age of 3.

The
FAMILY
OUTDOOR
BOOK

edited by

Mike and Anne-Marie Edwards

Macdonald
Queen Anne Press

A Queen Anne Press BOOK

First published in 1984 by Arcady Books Ltd

Paperback edition published in 1985 by
Queen Anne Press, a division of
Macdonald & Co (Publishers) Ltd
Maxwell House, 74 Worship Street
London EC2A 2EN
A BPCC plc Company

BRITISH LIBRARY CATALOGUING IN PUBLICATION DATA

Edwards, Michael, *1932 –*
    The family outdoor book
    1. Outdoor recreation   2. Family recreation
    I. Title   II. Edwards, Anne-Marie
    796'.01'91   GV191.6

    ISBN 0-356-12012-0

Designed by Louise Burston

Typeset by Pauline Newton

Printed and bound in Great Britain by Butler and Tanner Ltd, Frome

Acknowledgements

First of all we thank our contributors who have worked splendidly with us throughout the making of this book. We would also like to thank Walt Unsworth of Cicerone Press, Rodger Witt of *Practical Boat Owner* magazine and Eric Gurney, the National Organising Secretary of the Backpackers' Club, for their help and encouragement. Our grateful thanks also to Geoff Gadsby, former editor of *Backpack*, Reg Lowe, and the Rewcastle family and the Drake family for some delightful pictures. Mrs Gavin, of Bramble Hill riding stables near Lyndhurst, kindly allowed us to take photographs. Brian James, administrator of the British Canoe Union, Araminta Webb, of the Royal Yachting Association, Robert L. Hovey, Chairman of the Lakeland Cross-Country Ski Club, and Eric Woolley, Class I British Ski Federation Instructor and Nordic Ski Coach with the English Council for Cross-country Ski-ing, helped us with advice and photographs.

We are grateful also for the help provided by the Ramblers Association, the Youth Hostels Association of England and Wales, the Scottish Youth Hostels Association, and the Island Cruising Club. We would like to thank Tracy Bourne of PGL Adventure Holidays, Ross-on-Wye, for supplying us with pictures including one for the cover, the Irish Press for their permission to reproduce the Derrynaflan chalice, the *Westmorland Gazette* for permission to reproduce their picture of Jennifer Hodkinson and Robert Hovey, Silva UK for permission to reproduce their compass, Alex Moulton for his photograph of the Moulton bicycle, and Simon Rowley for his photograph of Philippa Rewcastle.

A special word of thanks to all our friends for their support, especially Mary Chambers whose cheerful encouragement never fails, and Cecil Whitfield who helped with our photography. We are grateful also to Louise Burston who not only designed the book but helped and advised us throughout, Pauline Newton who typeset so patiently, and Beth Young whose suggestions on the editorial were invaluable. Finally, we thank our own outdoor family — daughter Julie and son Chris — for being such splendid members of our team.

Mike and Anne-Marie Edwards

Contents

Introduction

The family that shares an exciting outdoor interest which gets them out and about into the countryside at weekends and holidays is much more fun to belong to, for parents and youngsters alike. But how do you choose the most enjoyable activities for your family? How do you get started? How much will it all cost? And what does the future hold for the really adventurous family extending its horizons as the children grow older?

This book answers these questions and more. You share the enjoyment of each activity as you are guided by experts from the early stages right through to the time when you are ready to set off independently with your family.

And today there is a far greater choice of possible activities for everyone. For example, with the development of safe, modern equipment the whole family can enjoy a day together rock climbing or cross-country ski-ing, and new teaching methods have brought canoe touring within the range of all. For the less adventurous, pony trekking or back-packing may seem more attractive. Special courses with suitable accommodation are often run for families, and many clubs have family sections where information and ideas can be exchanged. You will find all the advice you need for your family in these pages. And the lists of useful addresses, books and magazines at the end of every chapter will help you in exploring your chosen activities further.

But the emphasis throughout is on enjoyment. After all, there is no prize for the first to climb a mountain or reach a ski hut! So, what are the rewards? You will have the satisfaction of passing on to your children the skills that bring you pleasure — handling a boat perhaps or riding a pony — and the children will develop a far greater sense of responsibility when they feel they are valued members of a 'crew'. What is more, they will learn to appreciate the countryside and its riches, an attitude which will stay with them forever.

Some activities can be undertaken even with toddlers, others will prove more rewarding with teenagers. But whichever you choose you will find yourself at the entrance to a new and exciting outdoor world which you and your family can enjoy together. This book is your key to the gate.

Roger Smith has been editor of the walkers' magazine *The Great Outdoors* since it was launched in March 1978. His job involves both testing new equipment and writing about the countryside, so he is able to enjoy the hills at all times of the year. This, coupled with the privilege of living and working in Scotland, makes him a lucky man.

Roger has walked in all parts of Britain and in several countries overseas. He often walks alone or with a chosen companion, but in recent years he has greatly enjoyed sharing the pleasures of country walking with his growing children (at the time of writing Becky is seven and Lindsay five).

An experienced writer and broadcaster, Roger is active in other recreations besides walking. He is a Grade One British Orienteering Federation event controller and has been involved with the sport of orienteering as competitor, organiser and administrator since 1970. Despite his advancing years he still runs regularly and has completed a number of marathons.

Roger is deeply concerned with the conservation of the natural environment, particularly in Scotland. This led him (with others of like mind) to form the Scottish Wild Land Group in October 1982, and he was the Group's first chairman. He is also a member of the Council of the National Trust for Scotland.

Roger Smith was born in London in 1938 and now lives in Alva, Clackmannanshire, with his wife Terry, two daughters, his father, and a varied collection of animals.

His books include:
The Spur Book of Orienteering (Spurbooks/Frederick Warne); *The Penguin Book of Orienteering* (Penguin Books); *Walking in Scotland* (as editor: Spurbooks); *The Winding Trail* an anthology for walkers (Diadem Books); *Weekend Walking* (Oxford Illustrated Press/Hamlyn); *A Visitor's Guide to the Scottish Borders and Edinburgh* (Moorland Publishing).

Walking

ROGER SMITH

Halfway up the hill, my six-year-old daughter stopped and turned to me. "Phew, I'm hot," she said. "How many hours have we been walking, Daddy?"

We had, in fact, been walking for all of 15 minutes, but it does serve to show how a child's ideas often differ from our own. Walking with children can be delightful, rewarding, or frustrating — but never dull.

That April day we had left our home at the foot of the Ochil Hills, not far from Stirling, with no real idea of where we were going. It was the first genuinely warm afternoon of the year and as we wandered up the hill my pack began to bulge with discarded clothing.

I managed to persuade Becky that it wasn't really time for a picnic yet and we went a little further along a lovely woodland track, with our springer spaniel, Cloud, scampering happily ahead of us. Before long Becky's imagination, which never descends to the level of the ordinary, was working at its vivid best. A small stream slipping into a culvert across the track led us to a genuine witch's cellar, and three leaves, each with a spell inside, were solemnly folded over and tucked into a pocket of the pack to take home.

I was half expecting to be turned into a toad at any moment but fortunately we left the wood before the magic could affect us too badly. Some of it may have become attached to Cloud: not long afterwards she cut her leg on something, possibly a sliver of glass. This meant that instead of walking home we went by bus, which for Becky seemed merely to add to the pleasures of the day.

By the time we got home she had a daisy-chain ready to give to her mother. Terry had been up the hill with younger daughter, Lindsay, looking for kestrels — without success on this occasion, though we can often find them. Inevitably, Becky wanted to know how far we had walked. Stretching it a bit, I allowed her four miles.

This seemed to please her enormously. "Soon I'll be able to walk 10 miles," she said, "and then I can come backpacking with you!" It pleases me that she wants to, but I am not too surprised, as we have encouraged our children to walk with us and enjoy the countryside since they were tiny.

NEVER TOO YOUNG

How soon can you start taking children out with you? Finding the right answer to this question is as important for the parents as it is for the children. If, like us, you walked regularly before your children were born, you will not want your activity to be interrupted for very long. Fortunately, there is no reason why it should be.

Baby 'slings' or front carriers, in which the baby is held against the chest, can be used safely from birth and as soon as the child can hold its head up (usually at five to six months) you can take it out using a baby-carrier, with the child on your back. There are several models available, all of which have the child supported in a sitting position and generally with some support for the head. Some have grab-handles which go some way to saving your hair, otherwise a prime target for inquisitive little hands! There is often a zipped pocket in which nappies, food, etc., can be carried.

These baby-carriers are comfortable for both parent and child and give you considerable freedom in planning your walks. The child is high up and thus has an excellent view of everything you pass. The steady motion of your walking will often combine with a good dose of fresh air to send the little one to sleep. If this happens, take care that the head cannot bang on exposed wooden or metal parts of the carrier — a towel or nappy strategically placed will solve the problem.

It is very important to remember that you are moving while the child is not. He must therefore be very adequately protected — children of that age lose body heat rapidly and good warm clothing is vital. If the child is happy, you will not need to worry and can enjoy the walk to the full. It is especially important to keep the head and hands warm, as that is where heat dissipates most easily.

My wife and I enjoyed many walks together with one or other of our children in a baby-carrier. On one occasion I had arranged to meet Terry on The Twmpa, a 'knob' on the Black Mountains ridge above Hay-on-Wye. I had been out for a training run along the ridge and Terry had come up from the valley with Becky, then aged nine months, on her back.

It was a fine August day, and we met as planned. We had our picnic in a little hollow near the summit, and I can still see the astonishment on the face of another walker as he came over the top to find this infant crawling happily about in the sunshine! One word of caution here — small children should only be taken into the hills in ideal conditions. It is too much of a risk to have them out at high level when the weather is poor. *You* can probably cope with rain or high winds, but the little one can't.

We found we could carry our children until they were about two years old. By that time, they were getting too heavy for us to feel comfortable with them on our backs, and were eager to walk short distances themselves, and to make their own explorations at ground level.

THE TODDLER STAGE

This is an awkward time for the parents who are keen walkers. Children must be encouraged to walk, and to explore their surroundings, but it can be frustrating for a fit adult who wants to cover 10 miles to be restricted to one or two miles in an outing. As with many things in life, a compromise is the best solution.

If you can slow your pace down to the child's, and try to see the natural world as he or she does, you will find a new delight in your surroundings. Tiny things, that we normally pass by without a glance, fascinate them; a stream becomes a magic playground in which boats of sticks and leaves are launched, dams are built, and the joy of getting wet *and* dirty is discovered. Insects and spiders are another source of fascination; ants and ladybirds have ways of their own which can be observed for hours, and caterpillars seem to have a particular attraction, I don't know why!

Being lucky enough to live in the country, we were able to find all these things without having to drive or take a bus, but for town-dwellers there are parks, canals and other open spaces within reach. Finding them can be the start of using a map, which I shall refer to in more detail later in this chapter.

Let small children have their walks, if they want to, and take the time to see what they see and to explain as much as you can to them. There are many excellent books on nature for small children. As soon as the child can recognise things from drawings or photographs, you can start relating what you see when you are out to the books at home. Colourful finds like flowers are particularly good for this, and you will soon get on to more identifiable birds like the robin (a regular visitor to gardens), ducks and swans on the pond or river, and cuckoos in the spring. These last are more usually heard than seen, and I find children take a great delight in recognising birds by their song, and of course in imitating them.

It is surprising how quickly children develop the strength and stamina to cover a reasonable distance on a walk. Lindsay got up her first 3000-foot mountain at the age of three. Well, all right, it was The Cairnwell, where the road is over 2000 feet at the highest point! It was still a fair climb for a little one, but at no time did she show signs of tiredness or of being fed up — if she had I would not have gone on.

Even so, parents may find themselves champing at the bit, and feeling the need for a 'real' walk. So a mixture of walks is perhaps the best idea — take the kids out whenever you can, but have an arrangement so that you can get out yourselves, either singly or together, if you have a kindly baby-sitter nearby. Walking with my wife is still a fairly rare pleasure for me, and the more enjoyable for that.

There will, of course, be occasions when your children don't want to go out. I don't advise forcing them; perhaps the weather is bad or they are simply not feeling like it. On the other hand, they shouldn't be stuck indoors all day either. Ours *have* been taken

Lindsay Smith makes friends with some ducks.

out under protest more than once, though only very locally. They've usually enjoyed it once we've made the effort to go.

FURTHER AFIELD

Christine Roche deals with family back-packing in the next chapter. I will just put in the thought that a camping holiday can be very successful. We've had several, usually with a four-person dome tent pitched at a 'base camp' and making explorations either on foot or with the help of transport from there, and they have been much enjoyed. In some ways, very small children are easier to deal with in camp, provided the weather is reasonable. We had a very easy week with Becky at a large campsite near Edinburgh when she was nine months old. She was able to crawl, and take an interest in things. There were lots of people about, most of whom seemed only too pleased to play with her, and at night she went at the bottom of our Vango ridge tent in her carry-cot.

Roger Smith's family tent the night before the blizzard.

You can't go too 'wild' with a child of that age because of the need to warm milk, wash nappies, etc., but we have tried one or two excursions with ours. I will tell you a story which shows what can go wrong on these occasions.

It was the first weekend of May and we had been promising the children we would go camping for some time. The weather seemed reasonably promising so on the Saturday we loaded the car and drove a short distance to a farm above Callander. We parked the car and set off up the glen, after getting permission to camp from the farmer's wife (aptly named Mrs Walker). My wife and I were carrying quite heavy loads; the children, then five and three, had small rucksacks with their waterproofs and a toy or two.

We took them a couple of miles up the glen at an easy pace, on a good track. There were lots of lambs about and it was a fine evening, so their interest was easily maintained. At a bridge we turned back down the stream to find somewhere to camp. After half a mile or so we found a likely spot, pitched, and had supper. After a short exploratory walk we turned in. We were about 1000 feet up and it was quite cool, but there seemed nothing to worry about.

Our dome tent is pretty stable, and we slept well. On the Sunday morning we awoke at about 7.30 and I opened the door zip a little way. I shut it again smartly — there was a blizzard blowing out there! During the night the wind must have changed and a big depression had come racing in. We were just at the point where systems of warm and cold air met, and the result, at our altitude, was wind-driven snow.

"Snow," cried Becky. "Goody, we can make a snowman!" My wife and I just

looked at each other. We had things other than snowmen on our minds. We had breakfast and got everything packed except the tent without going out. We all dressed in full waterproofs and made sure the kids had plenty on underneath. Then we dived out, dismantled the tent and packed it away in record time, and set off back to the car, our intended hill walk abandoned.

Back to the bridge was easy, with the wind behind us. Then we had to turn, to walk along the track. The snow was driving into our faces; it was uncomfortable enough for us, but for the children it was worse. I made some progress with Becky by getting her to walk behind me, and holding both her hands, awkward though this was. Lindsay had to be carried all the way, and Becky too for the last stretch (and we

Crossing the stepping stones at Hathersage, an exciting prospect for a child.

already had heavy packs).

It was a great relief to reach the car. Half an hour later we were down in Callander, sitting in a cafe with hot drinks. People in the town looked with astonishment at our white car — it was merely raining just those few hundred feet lower. And this was in May! It was only a little epic, but it does go to show that in hill country you must always be prepared for the worst.

As your children grow older, you will find that you no longer have to confine your walks to short excursions, and then comes another phase when *you* are holding *them* back! You then have to make a difficult decision. When should they be allowed to go off on their own? If they have been well trained in the basic skills of outdoor life — notably how to use a map and compass — you need have no fear about them surviving.

WHERE TO WALK

Where are the best places to take children walking?

Wherever you live, there will be somewhere enjoyable to walk not far away. Even in cities there are interesting places and a number of conurbations have set up 'Town Trails' linking places of historical and architectural interest. Walking round a town or city is by far the best way to see it, especially if there is a good guidebook available to help you.

Overall, your general guide will be the Ordnance Survey maps. The Ordnance Survey is our national mapping agency. Its origins lie in the government-of-the-time's alarm at the possibility of invasion or unrest from two quarters — France and the Scottish Highlands. The first properly surveyed and detailed maps were prepared by military teams in the latter part of the 18th century, under the supervision of the Board of Ordnance — a name which has stuck ever since.

A national triangulation survey using intervisible points to determine the 'lie of the land' followed, and most people will be familiar with the most notable evidence of that survey (which still continues) — the white stone pillars or 'trig points' that crown the summits of so many hills. These pillars are marked on the OS 1:50,000 maps — the 'Landranger' series frequently used by walkers — with a blue triangle, and reaching one of them can be a great incentive to a young walker.

The scale most commonly used by walkers was until recent years 1:63,360 — the classic one inch to the mile. Even those maps, though they used Imperial measurements and showed all heights in feet, used the kilometre as the basis for the squares representing the National Grid. This is a system whereby any point on the map can be easily identified by a 'grid reference'. The system is explained in the margin of OS maps. It is fascinating to remember that in 1945 there was a proposal that buildings should be identified by their six-figure grid reference for postal purposes. It never came to pass, but if it had my house would have been NS 882968 instead of FK12 5AH, its present postcode. I know which I prefer! Older readers will recall the fingerposts which stood at country crossroads in the 1950s and 1960s and which always bore

An inviting path near Wherwell in the valley of the river Test in Hampshire.

the grid reference of the place where they stood. An interesting little exercise would be to get the children to work out the grid reference for your house.

With the decision by Britain to go metric, the one-inch scale was modified to 1:50,000. This slightly larger scale, together with marked improvements in typography and layout, has given us very clear maps which are easy to read and follow. A first step, then, is to purchase the OS 1:50,000 map for your area. They are widely available and you should have no difficulty.

Study the map to see if you can locate interesting places to walk. In England and Wales all the *rights of way* (footpaths and bridleways where you are free to walk in law) are shown on OS maps — footpaths by red dots and bridleways, which are also open to equestrians and cyclists, by red dashes. (On 1:25,000 'Pathfinder' maps the colour used is green.)

See if you can work out a walk of say five miles from the map, making it circular so that you can return to your car or public transport at the end of the walk. Try to include a variety of countryside — farmland, woods, perhaps a river or lake. You can of course use roads to link footpaths — a road is as much the Queen's Highway for pedestrians as it is for vehicles — but off-road walking is generally more enjoyable. If you do choose to walk on roads remember to walk in single file facing the traffic.

If you get a walk worked out, take the map with you and use it frequently as you walk, checking every feature shown as you pass it, and explaining the map symbols to the children. It can be quite an exciting game to forecast what is coming up next. Simple things like buildings are easily spotted, then you can move on to water

Consulting the map on the Two Moors Way.

features, power lines, and contours — the brown lines which show the shape of the land and which will tell you, if you can read them accurately, whether you should be going uphill or down. Contour lines are marked at intervals with their height value, nowadays in metres. The higher the number, the higher the ground, so if you are walking from a 250-metre contour to a 300-metre contour, you are climbing 50 metres (about 170 feet for those who still think that way). Contour lines also give an indication of the steepness of the ground — the closer together the lines are, the steeper the ground is. Vertical ground is shown by brown or black symbols indicating earthy banks or crags — generally places for the inexeperienced to keep away from!

As an alternative to a circular walk you might like to reach a place of particular interest — a castle perhaps, or a zoo — by a linear walk. I find it can help to give children an objective to a walk — to say, "We're going to Doune Castle today, but instead of using the car we're going to walk there." Reaching the castle will keep them going, and the walk itself will be remembered as being both pleasant and purposeful.

HELP IS TO HAND

I may have suggested up to now that you are on your own in finding local walks. This does not have to be the case, although it is still always worth seeking out your own walks — it will help when you come to plan walks in more distant regions with which you are not familiar.

In recent years there has been an explosion of local footpath guides, covering almost every part of Britain. Checking with bookshops or your public library should establish if there is a guide for your area. If there is, buying it and following some of the walks it describes will both help you to get to know the area better and give you confidence in your ability to complete a walk of a decent length without mishap.

Even when using a guide I would always advise you to take the OS map with you. It can be great fun especially for children to relate the places mentioned in the guide book to the map, and spot them on the ground. A further point is that, although guide book writers always take great care to make their route descriptions as clear as possible, ambiguities can occur. The countryside is also changing all the time — fences, gates and stiles can be moved, unsurfaced lanes become tarred, woods

are planted or felled. If you have the OS map with you it will give you some clue as to where the next definite point is, should you be in doubt as to your location or route.

It will help at such times to have a compass with you as well as a map. Many people seem either to be scared of a compass or to regard it as some kind of magic instrument that will save them from whatever disaster threatens. In fact it is a precision-built navigational aid that is simple to use and, in conjunction with the map, enables you to locate your position and your correct direction of travel in virtually any situation.

The only compass worth considering for the walker is the light prismatic type developed in Sweden in the 1930s by the Kjellstrom brothers. They were looking for a compass that would serve the young sport of orienteering: it had to be light, hold its bearing while the user was running, and settle quickly on to the bearing at all times.

The compass they produced, after much experiment, is still in use with few changes today. It has a plastic baseplate with measuring scales round the edges, and a capsule which is rotated when taking bearings. The compass needle is liquid-damped, which effectively solves the 'spinning needle' problem found on earlier models.

Compasses of this type are used all over the world for orienteering (now a well-established sport in many countries, including Britain), by the armed forces, and by walkers. Useful features for the walker include a magnifying lens for reading fine detail and, on the more expensive models, fluorescent dots to indicate the major compass points at night.

The Silva model developed by the Kjellstroms is still one of the most popular.

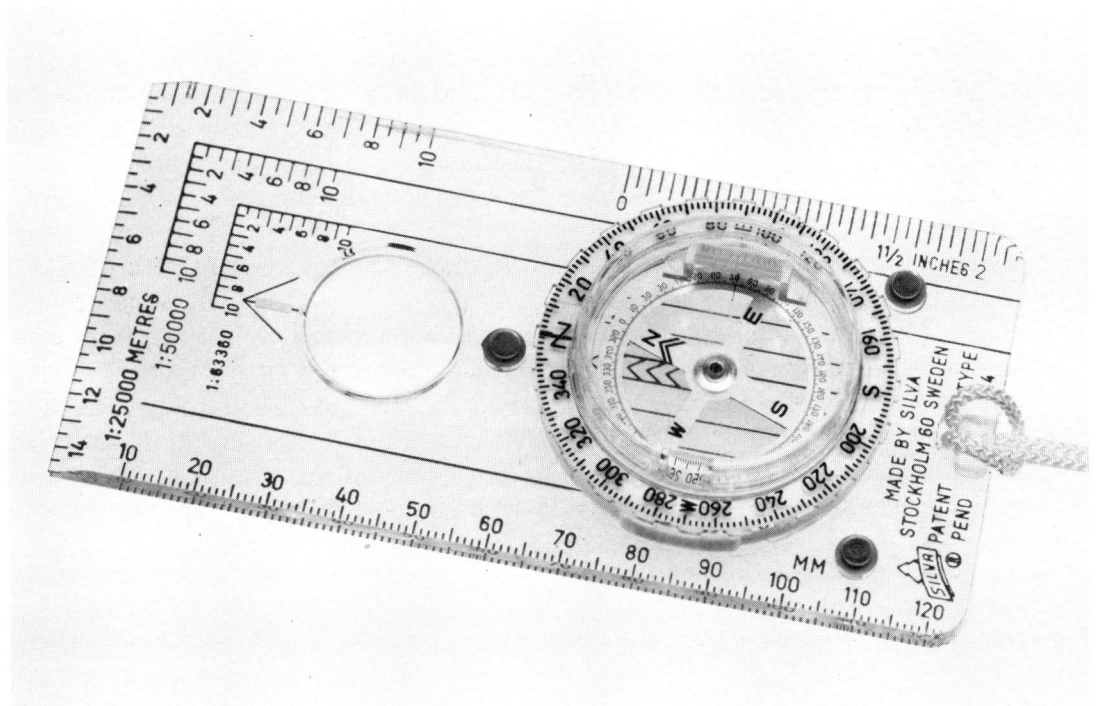

Silva-type compass.

The range goes from a basic compass for beginners up to larger models with sighting mirrors used for surveying. They even have a braille compass which blind people can use! I would suggest that for the modest outlay involved (five to ten pounds), investment in one of these compasses will pay handsome dividends.

The system used for obtaining and following bearings with these compasses is both simple and clever. The baseplate is equipped with 'direction of travel lines' and the dial with 'north lines'. By placing the long edge of the compass along your desired line of travel, and turning the dial until the north lines line up with north on the map, you can establish your desired direction. All you have to do after that is to turn the compass until the red end of the magnetic needle (which always points north) is aligned to the north lines on the dial. The direction of travel arrow on the baseplate is now showing you your way ahead.

This 1-2-3 procedure is well explained in the leaflet which accompanies the compass. It may sound a little complicated, but after some practice you will find that in fact it is very easy. Once you have established your line of travel, all you have to do (in open country) is to 'sight' on an object ahead of you and walk towards it. If the object is on your line of travel, you need not look at the compass again until you reach it.

A quick check with the compass can help to reassure you that you are taking the right path at a complicated junction. On a 280-mile walk across Scotland in May 1983 I used my compass 'in anger' just twice — once to check our line off the summit of a mist-enshrouded mountain, and once at a very confusing five-way junction of tracks in a forest. Five seconds' work in each case reassured me that we were heading in the right direction.

If you do walk your local paths, map in hand, you may well meet groups of other walkers, particularly at weekends. There are walking or rambling clubs in most areas, and virtually all of them have a planned programme of walks. Would you enjoy meeting other walkers regularly, and walking with them? If you would, then why not consider joining a club? You can find the addresses of clubs in your area by asking at the public library or by writing to the Ramblers' Association (address at end of chapter). The RA is a national organisation with about forty thousand members which does a great deal of work keeping rights of way open — even going to court if necessary — and encouraging people to take up and enjoy country walking.

The RA has about four hundred and fifty affiliated clubs throughout the country, so it is quite likely that there will be one near you. You need not worry that the walks they plan will be too strenuous — there are different grades and lengths of walks for people of different abilities and fitness.

Joining a club could be your introduction to walking in areas further afield. Many clubs organise weekends or whole weeks away in places like the Lake District, Yorkshire Dales, or Wales. If you are unused to walking in hilly country you may find the company of others, and the presence of an experienced leader, helpful in taking your first steps in the hills.

There are also a number of organisations and firms arranging walking holidays in Britain. Most of them will take children, though some have a lower age limit of 10 or 12. Some operate from a fixed base,

using transport to reach the start of the walk each day; some follow a route through a particular area of country, with most of your luggage taken on ahead so that all you need carry is a small rucksack with waterproofs, food, and camera.

SCENIC AREAS

It is impossible here to do more than outline some of the many beautiful walking areas available to us in Britain. Scotland deserves separate consideration, and will get it later, but for now let us take a look at England and Wales.

NATIONAL PARKS

As most people will know, we have ten National Parks — established in that heady period after the Second World War when the move to open up the countryside for public enjoyment was so strong. They are all great places for walking, and I will attempt a brief portrait of each of them below.

Peak District: The first park to be established, in 1951. Contrasting areas of wild moorland around the 2000-foot contour and gritstone escarpments or 'edges' much used by climbers. The White Peak, further south, is limestone country with many beautiful valleys, of which Dovedale is the most famous.

Lake District: The classic combination of lakes and mountains, immortalised in prose and verse by writers from Wordsworth onwards. Contains England's highest mountain, Scafell Pike (3210 feet), three other 3000-foot peaks, and dozens of other fine

A stop between Capel Curig and Idwal Cottage.

hills. Very popular and very well served by footpaths.

Yorkshire Dales: Less dramatic than the Lakes, perhaps, but no less beautiful. River valleys such as Swaledale, Wensleydale, and Wharfedale offer the contrast of waterside walking or climbing to the rolling hills above. Some parts have interesting mining remains.

North York Moors: High heathery uplands with wide views dominate the park; some of the small incut valleys, such as Great Fryup Dale, are gems. Farndale is renowned for its daffodils in spring. The peaty soil is unfortunately prone to erosion and the going can be very soggy at times.

Northumberland: A less-frequented area where the solitary walker can revel in the space and freedom. Cheviot Hills rise to well over 2000 feet and look north towards Scotland. Superb river valleys reach into them, and small upland villages add to the attraction.

Snowdonia: Dominated by Snowdon itself, the North Wales massif contains many other very fine hills, including the Carneddau and Glyder ranges. The park reaches to the coast and there is good low-level walking on forestry tracks. Snowdon has a mountain railway to the summit.

Brecon Beacons: A rich combination of highland — the Beacons escarpment itself is rightly renowned — and fine valley scenery. The ridge walking compares with any in Britain and the views, in the right conditions, are magnificent.

Pembrokeshire Coast: A quite splendid coastline, deeply indented and studded with little bays and headlands. Geologically a fascinating area, with rock strata clearly shown on the cliffs and many areas of fossil remains.

Exmoor: A small park displaying perfection in miniature with river valleys and rolling upland. *Lorna Doone* country with beautiful small villages tucked into the hills. A fine coastline, too.

Dartmoor: Our most southerly park, but wild enough for all that. The highest point, High Willhays, just attains 2000 feet but the notorious Dartmoor mist makes this an area where the walking can be as adventurous as anywhere.

There are many more fine walking areas in England and Wales. Even close to cities one can find such areas as the Chilterns, the Surrey Hills, and Lickey and Clent near Birmingham. I would prefer however to leave you to discover these areas for yourself. It adds greatly to the enjoyment that way!

LONG DISTANCE PATHS

Another post-war phenomenon has been the development of long distance paths. These fall into three broad categories. The Countryside Commission (address at end of chapter) has helped to set up, and maintain through grant-aid, 13 such paths in England and Wales. They cover hills, moors, and much fine coastline. They are all way-marked with an 'acorn' sign, and many of them can be confidently tackled by families.

Among those which you might consider are the *Ridgeway* (85 miles, Ivinghoe to near Marlborough); the *South Downs Way* (80 miles, Eastbourne to Petersfield); the *North Downs Way* (140 miles, Farnham to Dover); and the *Pembrokeshire Coast Path* (170 miles, Poppit Sands to Amroth). All of these can be broken down into easy days; if you are not camping, accommodation is only a problem on the Ridgeway. There are excellent guides to all these paths, and addresses for further information are given at the end of the chapter.

RECREATIONAL PATHS

The second category of paths is the recreational path. These are usually shorter than LDPs, are often established by local authorities with help from the Countryside Commission, and many of them are circular. A list is available from the Commission. The Leeds Countryway is a good example of such a path. It winds round the city, passing through some very pleasant countryside, and is readily accessible by public transport.

The initiative for many of the paths mentioned above came from individuals or clubs. This initiative has shown no sign of slowing down in recent years, so that we have in Britain something like two hundred 'named' walking routes, the great majority of which have been developed by enthusiasts. These unofficial paths are not usually waymarked but will have a guide book describing them — often a true labour of love by the route's originator. You can find them in bookshops and outdoor shops.

WALKING IN SCOTLAND

Scotland is different in many ways, as I can vouch, having been fortunate enough to live there since 1977.

There is a generally accepted — and practised — freedom of access in Scotland that is not found further south. It exists through a relationship of mutual trust and respect between landowner and walker, a relationship based on common sense and the recognition by both sides of the other's needs and desires.

Although there are rights of way in Scotland, and indeed many legal battles have been fought over them, they are not marked separately as such on Ordnance Survey maps. They are none the less important. The Scottish Rights of Way Society has been protecting them for well over one hundred years, and you will see their distinctive metal signposts in many places in Scotland. Whereas in England and Wales local authorities are obliged by law to signpost footpaths and bridleways where they leave public roads, no such obligation exists in Scotland, and so the SRoWS does the job wherever it can.

Some of these signposts are marvellously laconic, one of my favourites being the one in the Rothiemurchus Forest near Aviemore which says 'Braemar via Lairig Ghru 26 miles. Not suitable for cycles'. This is one of the toughest through walks in Britain!

Even where no proven rights of way exist, access to open country is generally permitted, and I am glad my children are growing up in a land where such a sensible attitude prevails. The exceptions to the 'freedom to roam' policy come in the autumn, when shooting and stalking parties are on the hill. The income from such activities is vital to the economy of many Scottish estates, and the restrictions imposed at such times are sensible and should be observed by all walkers.

The period of most restriction is from mid-August to late October. During this time, if you wish to walk on the hills and not just keep to the valley paths, you should endeavour to find out beforehand if shooting or stalking is taking place. Local enquiry to police stations or post offices will usually lead you, if not to a direct answer, at least to the name of the person who will know (the estate factor, in many cases). If you happen to be out and meet a shooting party, greet them politely and ask if it is all right to continue. I have had some very interesting encounters with such parties, being treated on one occasion to a fascinating description of the way grouse were raised, before I was allowed to go on my way unhindered.

I do not wish to dwell too long on these restrictions, but I know they are a puzzle to many people outside Scotland. Let us now concentrate on the times when you *can* walk freely. For those with school-age children there are two main possibilities — the Easter and summer holidays. The chief problem is that the weather can still swing to extremes at these times. At Easter I have known it to be really warm with cloudless skies and just a bit of snow on the tops — absolute magic for walking — or to be cold and miserable, as 1983 was. The summer, likewise, can be gloriously warm and sunny, or very wet. In general, the islands off the west coast, and the eastern part of Scotland, are drier than the western and central Highlands, which tend to be hit, weather-wise, by anything that is coming.

For family walking the glens offer great possibilities. The scenery is superb and there are often good tracks. There are also plenty of forest walks available. Smaller hills, or those nearer to a road, can be tackled with confidence in good conditions. As I have said, our children scaled their first 3000-foot mountain at the ages of five and three. I was quite happy to take them up it as it was only 1000 feet of climb from the road, and conditions were good. They have also been up Dumyat, an 1800-foot hill near where we live, lured there by the promise of a trig pillar and an extensive view, which we were lucky enough to enjoy to the full.

So, particularly as your children get older, don't leave Scotland out of your planning when you're thinking about a walking holiday. There are plenty of diversions in the shape of castles, museums, beaches, and so on, for those days when the weather or circumstances are against you.

KITTING THEM OUT

I have only one maxim to offer on the question of equipment for young walkers. It is simply this — buy the very best you can afford. I do realise that children grow out of things, but if you have more than one child, clothing — yes, even boots — can be passed on, and quite a number of shops operate a 'buy-back' policy on children's boots these days. It simply isn't worth the saving to get them cheap gear that does not protect them adequately. They just get fed up if they get soaked, and it puts them off walking. With good equipment, even the bad days can be enjoyed.

Let's start with footwear. Feet are the most important things in any walker's life, and they should be cared for accordingly. Should children wear walking boots at all? I firmly believe they should, from about the age of four on. Wellingtons, though ideal for many purposes, do not give sufficient grip for hill walking, nor do they fit closely enough.

You take care with your children's everyday shoes — do the same with their walking boots. Make sure there is enough room in the boot for the foot to 'breathe' a little by asking the child to push his foot forward until the toes touch the front of the boot. There should be enough room at the back to get a finger down behind the heel. Always get the child to wear the correct socks when getting boots — preferably two pairs for extra comfort.

Children's walking boots should be light in weight, but with good ankle support and proper lacing with hooks and eyes. Our kids love having the same kit as we have ourselves, and this extends to the same way of lacing their boots. Socks should be wool, and kept in good condition. Don't try to darn them on the sole or heel — it could lead to discomfort and perhaps a blister. And remember too that tight socks can be as uncomfortable and damaging as tight boots.

Waterproofs are the other very important item of gear for children. It's not difficult to ensure that they are warm — they will already have clothing which is adequate for that and which can be used for walking. Waterproofs, however, should be bought for the job. I don't believe that enough attention has been paid to children's

Cooking a tasty meal on the trail requires skill and concentration.

waterproofs by manufacturers; there are too many cheap models which are too simple in design (e.g. no pockets) and not strong enough to keep our roughest weather at bay.

You *can* find good waterproofs for children if you shop around — try a decent outdoor shop if you have one near you. Look for a good strong fabric, coated nylon or similar, and check that the stitching is strongly done. It can be a weak point. It may be worth giving the seams an extra coating with a waterproofing spray — these too are available at outdoor shops. Buy both jacket and leggings, to give the fullest protection. It is easier if the jacket has a full zip — kids find the 'over the head' type difficult to deal with, in my experience.

There is no need to give much in the way of specific advice for the rest of the gear you will use. If you do get into specialist areas such as rucksacks and sleeping bags, children very much enjoy having equipment 'just like Mummy and Daddy's' and smaller verions of your kit are available. As for yourself, much the same advice applies — keeping yourself well protected and comfortable is more easily achieved with better equipment.

BROADENING THE UNDERSTANDING

Walking is a marvellous way of seeing the countryside, and thereby of understanding it better. In four particular categories you can waken a child's imagination and keep his interest while out on walking trips.

The first is *history*. So much of our history is written on the landscape and is still clearly visible in terms of archaeological remains, castles, churches, ancient tracks and boundaries, for example. How much more impressive it is to approach one of our major archaeological sites on foot than by car! This is the way the people of the time would have come; the Ridgeway footpath in Wiltshire and Oxfordshire is especially exciting with this aspect, with such places as Barbury Castle on or near the path. A short day's walking can encompass Avebury, a truly magic place despite the village that has grown up round it, Silbury Hill, a mysterious mound whose real purpose is still not known, and West Kennet long barrow.

Wayland's Smithy, a prehistoric long barrow beside the Ridgeway.

There are similar though perhaps less impressive sites in many parts of the country. Study the OS map and look for signs marking tumuli and standing stones, then go out and try to find them. It will be a rewarding exercise.

Your children can become Roman soldiers for the day, too. Hadrian's Wall is particularly good for this; in some places you can actually walk on the Wall itself, and there are wonderfully well excavated forts and camps to explore. There are lots of Roman remains so there should be some near you, and the OS publish a special map showing these sites.

Later remains such as fortified towers, castles, and old churches abound in our countryside; nor should you neglect our marvellous industrial heritage of bridges, canals and mills. There is never a shortage of things to seek out on your walks. Encourage the children to draw what they see, or when they are older to take photographs and write a short account.

The second category is *geology*. The rocks, and in some places the fossils they contain, have a wonderful story to tell — a story that is still being unravelled and translated as more discoveries are made.

Good basic guidebooks are available which will tell you what to look for wherever you are walking — the limestone of the Yorkshire Dales or the Cotswolds, the gritstone of the Peak District, the chalk of the Sussex and Kent cliffs, and the incredibly ancient rocks of the Scottish Highlands. To touch a piece of gneiss and realise just how many millions of years have passed since it was first laid down is, to me, a profoundly humbling experience. We play our small part in the never-ending pageantry of the earth's history and then move on; the rocks remain. But even rocks are volatile, and understanding how they are formed and how they can move and change is a great thing for a child.

The third category is *wildlife*. Children are fascinated by living things and love to touch them and learn about them. We have many thousands of species of insects, for example. Our birdlife too is rich and complex, but if I am honest I must confess a shameful ignorance of it. Of course I know the commoner species such as the garden birds and the distinctive curlews, grouse, and lapwings that I see so often on my walks, but there are dozens of small woodland birds I cannot tell apart. Don't pass on your ignorance. Encourage children to investigate subjects of which you know little. It can be very rewarding to them to be able to teach *you* something.

Mammals too are a broad group. I have lived in Scotland for six years but have yet to see a wildcat or a pine marten. If you have woodlands near you I would be surprised if they did not harbour foxes and badgers, but have you seen them? Late evening or night-time walks with older children to try to spot these and other species are well worth trying.

The fourth category is to my mind the most important of all. It is *conservation*. I believe that we must teach our children that this beautiful earth is not ours to plunder, scar or despoil. We are merely the guardians of it and future generations will judge us by the way we care for it.

Take your children into the countryside and show them how marvellous the natural world is: the slow unfurling of a bracken frond, the tiny spring bubbling from its mossy bed that becomes a great river, the silent passage of an owl through a wood, the magic of frost patterns on dead grass. Every day the countryside is changing as it lives, in the same way as we ourselves are changing day by day and year by year. Teach your children to love nature and to respect and care for living things and you will have given them a great gift which they in turn can pass on to their children.

I hope you have many hours of happy walking and that this chapter will help and encourage you to share this simple and most rewarding of pastimes with your family.

USEFUL ADDRESSES

ENGLAND AND WALES

Camping Club of Great Britain and Ireland, 11 Lower Grosvenor Place, London SW1W 0EY. The Camping Club have about 50 sites of their own and publish a handbook listing over two thousand others. Monthly magazine *Camping and Caravanning*.

Council for the Protection of Rural England, 4 Hobart Place, London SW1W 0HY. The CPRE aims to protect all that is worthwhile in the English countryside; it has branches in most areas.

Council for the Protection of Rural Wales (Cymdeithas Diogelu Harddwch Cymru), 14 Broad Street, Welshpool, Powys.

Countryside Commission, John Dower House, Crescent Place, Cheltenham, Glos. GL50 2RA. Statutory body with responsibility for National Parks, long-distance footpaths, Areas of Outstanding Natural Beauty, country parks, ranger services, etc. The Commission publish very helpful leaflets on long-distance paths, National Parks, the Country Code, and many other topics.

Forestry Commission, 231 Corstorphine Road, Edinburgh EH12 7AT. The Forestry Commission operate a number of camp sites and have chalets for hire in some areas. Very useful maps called *See Your Forests* list forest walks, picnic sites, and other amenities. Publications list on request.

NATIONAL PARKS. All ten National Parks publish information including advice on walking and camping. The addresses are as follows.

Brecon Beacons National Park, 6 Glamorgan Street, Brecon, Powys.

Dartmoor National Park, Parke, Haytor Road, Bovey Tracey, Newton Abbot, Devon.

Exmoor National Park, Exmoor House, Dulverton, Somerset.

Lake District National Park, Information Centre, Brockhole, Windermere, Cumbria.

North York Moors National Park, The Old Vicarage, Bondgate, Helmsley, North Yorkshire YO6 5BP.

Northumberland National Park, Countryside Department, Northumberland County Council, Bede House, All Saints Centre, Newcastle upon Tyne NE1 2DH.

Peak District National Park, Aldern House, Baslow Road, Bakewell, Derbyshire DE4 1AE.

Pembrokeshire Coast National Park, County Offices, Haverfordwest, Dyfed.

Snowdonia National Park, Yr Hen Ysgol, Maentwrog, Blaenau Ffestiniog, Gwynedd.

Yorkshire Dales National Park, Colvend, Hebden Road, Grassington, Skipton, North Yorkshire.

The National Trust, 42 Queen Anne's Gate, London SW1. Founded in 1895, the NT now owns and cares for many large tracts of open country as well as historic houses, castles, etc.

Open Spaces Society, 25A Bell Street, Henley on Thames, Oxon. OSS — formerly the Commons, Footpaths and Open Spaces Preservation Society — has been fighting to protect our legal rights in the countryside for 120 years. It has a particular interest in common land.

Ordnance Survey, Romsey Road, Maybush, Southampton SO9 4DH. Great Britain's mapping agency. A catalogue of publications is available on request and visitors can be shown round the small museum and display unit at Maybush by prior arrangement.

Ramblers' Association, 1/5 Wandsworth Road, London SW8 2LJ. The RA has about forty thousand members and 450 affiliated clubs. Its magazine, *Rucksack*, is published quarterly. The RA, too, campaigns on the walker's behalf in protecting rights of way. Its clubs organise regular rambles, social events, and footpath clearance and maintenance work. It also publishes the *Ramblers' and Cyclists' Bed and Breakfast Guide* annually.

Youth Hostels Association, Trevelyan House, St. Stephen's Hill, St. Albans, Herts. AL1 2DY. The YHA runs a national network of over two hundred and fifty hotels, many of them on or near long-distance paths. Family membership is open to parents and children over five.

SCOTLAND

Association for the Preservation of Rural Scotland, 1 Thistle Court, Edinburgh EH2 1DE. APRS aims to protect rural scenery and amenities from unsightly or unnecessary development.

Countryside Commission for Scotland, Battleby House, Redgorton, Perth PH1 3TT. Similar aims to the English body. Publications relate to long-distance paths, country parks, and other matters.

Forestry Commission (address above). Information on forests in Scotland is available from the Edinburgh address.

National Trust for Scotland, 5 Charlotte Square, Edinburgh EH2 4DU. NTS was founded in 1931. It owns or protects many fine buildings and also mountain areas including Glencoe, Torridon, and Kintail. Publications list on request.

Scottish Rights of Way Society, 28 Rutland Square, Edinburgh EH1 2BW. The SRoWS defends the public's right of way over routes in all parts of Scotland, and maintains maps showing these routes. It has a modest publications list including some useful walkers' maps.

Scottish Tourist Board, 23 Ravelston Terrace, Edinburgh EH4 3EU. Many very useful publications including a good booklet *Hillwalking in Scotland.*

Scottish Youth Hostels Association, 7 Glebe Crescent, Stirling FK8 2JA. The SYHA maintains a network of 80 hostels all over Scotland, including some in remote areas which are accessible only by foot.

NORTHERN IRELAND

Forest Service of Northern Ireland, Dundonald House, Belfast 4. Has a number of useful guides available on forest walks, picnic sites, etc.

Northern Ireland Tourist Board, River House, 48 High Street, Belfast BT1 2DS. Publications list on request, including some information useful to walkers.

Ordnance Survey of Northern Ireland, Ladas Drive, Belfast BT6 9FJ. For information on maps of Ulster.

Sports Council for Northern Ireland, 49 Malone Road, Belfast BT9 6RZ. The Council has assisted with the setting up of the Ulster Way long-distance path which encircles the province, and it has very useful publications.

PUBLICATIONS

BOOKS

There are very many books on walking, and it would be quite impossible to list them all here! Your public library or nearest good outdoor shop should have a selection. For general advice, the following can be safely recommended.

The Walker's Handbook by H.D. Westacott (Penguin Books).

Tackle Rambling by Alan Mattingly (Stanley Paul).

Walking in the Countryside by David Sharp (David & Charles).

Walking in Scotland edited by Roger Smith (Spurbooks).

MAGAZINES

The Great Outdoors, Ravenseft House, 302–304 St Vincent Street, Glasgow G2 5NL. One of the best monthly magazines for all walkers, with articles on particular areas, advice on equipment, reviews of footpath guides, etc.

Climber and Rambler (same address as TGO). More for the mountaineer but has some very interesting articles on hard walking and backpacking.

Footloose, The Birches, Kincraig, Kingussie, Inverness-shire. Bi-monthly journal with wide coverage of countryside matters.

Camping, Link House, Dingwall Avenue, Croydon CR9 2TA. More for the family camper but often has articles of interest to walkers and backpackers.

Practical Camper, 38–42 Hampton Road, Teddington, Middlesex TW11 0JE. Camping, backpacking and some walking articles. Monthly.

Strider, Foxhollow, Coxhill, Chobham, Woking, Surrey GU24 8AZ. The magazine of the Long Distance Walkers Association, published three times a year.

and absorb the beauty of your surroundings. The worries and problems of civilisation are soon left behind. Together, as a family, you decide where to ford a stream or what to do if the weather deteriorates; children can help to make these decisions and usually have very sensible ideas. Don't worry about mud or midges — there is so much to enjoy!'

The National Organising Secretary of the Backpackers Club, Eric R. Gurney F.R.G.S., describes Christine Roche as 'a backpacker/ walker/camper of fine experience'. Her introduction to backpacking is full of practical advice based on her own expeditions with her family and she never allows us to forget for a moment the sheer enjoyment of it all!

Christine Roche lives in Sandbach in Cheshire. She backpacks with her husband Jack and three children, Maurice, Paula and Trevor — not forgetting Rusty, their collie. Favourite backpacking expeditions have included the West Highland Way, the Pembrokeshire Coast Path, Offa's Dyke Path and the Cleveland Way.

Christine is a contributor to *Backpack*, the magazine of the Backpackers' Club. She writes, 'In describing family backpacking I hope to share my pleasure with you so that you will try it for yourselves. It is so satisfying to set out, knowing you have all you need — or where you will be able to obtain further supplies on the way — and that all you have to do is follow your chosen route

Backpacking

CHRISTINE ROCHE

It is just beginning to get light and I am awake to enjoy this special time of day. I can hear a sheep munching the turf near the tent; the stream a few yards away is rushing over the stones, a sound I heard as I fell asleep last night. The light increases and I unzip the tent to see the sky, the brightness in the east, the shapes of the surrounding hills, the mist in the valley. I hear a lapwing call, and farther off, the 'go-back, go-back' of a grouse. Now the first rays of the sun appear, illuminating the full beauty of my surroundings. A new day begins.

I put the kettle on for early morning tea for anyone who wants it ... then the sound of the boys' tent zip and a voice saying, "Can I have my breakfast now?" Eventually we have all had breakfast, washed up, packed everything and checked that nothing is left where the tents were pitched. Another look at the map and we are on our way again. High above us a lark is singing: his song expresses the exhilaration I feel.

Jack and I, and our three children, have backpacked over 1225 miles in the last four years. We started backpacking with the family in 1979 when Trevor was seven, Paula 10, and Maurice 12 years old. They were all used to walking, having been introduced to the hills in a 'Papoose' carrier as babies, then gradually increasing the distances they could cover. Trevor had walked 10 miles at the age of three years and 10 months, on a sponsored walk for Christian Aid. At the end he had only complained of being hungry, not tired. The leaders of the group had not thought it worthwhile to stop for lunch! Maurice had managed 11 miles at four years old while we were on a caravan holiday at Harlech. The walk should have been only about seven miles, but a path shown on the map was not visible on the ground so we had to go further than we intended. By the time we decided to backpack with them, the children had walked up to 14 miles in a day (and were experienced campers) but we did not know how far they would be able to walk carrying packs.

We were tempted to try backpacking when we read about the Offa's Dyke Path not far from where we live. We divided the

The Roche family follow a riverside path with Paula and Maurice leading, Christine with Rusty, and Jack bringing up the rear.

walk into three stages to suit the time we had available and access by railway. Our first three days, in May 1979, took us from Chepstow to Knighton and it rained the whole time! But we had better weather for our second stage in July, from Knighton to Chirk, and for the final stage, three days at the beginning of September, when we walked from Chirk to Prestatyn. We found that we averaged 12½ miles a day over the whole distance. Split in this way the children had no difficulty in coping and Maurice particularly enjoyed the train journeys.

"Can we do that?" asked a boy who was with his family on a boat on the Llangollen canal. "You won't get me staggering along under loads like theirs," was his mother's reply. We did not feel we were staggering although it was our first expedition — the nearest we have been to staggering was up Win Hill in Derbyshire one very hot August day. So how heavy are our loads? When we all go together, Jack and I carry about 30 lbs each and the children considerably less, but of course the weight decreases as we use up our food and fuel. When Paula and I go on our own I start with up to 32 lbs and Paula 26–28 lbs (at age 13–14 years).

RUCKSACKS

Jack and I each have a Karrimor Annapurna 2. We find them just the right size to hold our requirements. Paula, 14, carries a Karrimor Jaguar 1 although if she has to carry extra she borrows Jack's Annapurna 2. Maurice has a Karrimor Lynx 11 in which, at 15, he carries about 26 lbs comfortably. Trevor, 11, takes about 17 lbs in Maurice's old rucksack, a Karibou, which has no frame but a padded back. He now wants a rucksack with a frame. (When he began backpacking at the age of seven, he carried about 11 lbs in a small day sack containing sleeping bag, tent inner and pegs, spare clothing, waterproofs, dish, mug, cutlery and some food.)

TENTS

The boys' tent is a Saunders Fellpine weighing 4½ lbs. They carry that between them. Jack, Paula and I take the Romany, a transverse ridge type made by Ultimate Equipment for Scout shops, and weighing 6½ lbs. Although Ultimate Equipment no longer make the Romany there are many similar tents which are ideal for families. This kind of tent has two large bell ends which give plenty of room. One side can be used for boots, wet waterproofs, etc., and the other for cooking, while there is sufficient space inside for the family to sit down for a meal together if it is wet, and to play games in the evening. Also, children going in or out do not have to use the entrance where cooking is in progress. The only disadvantage of this

tent is that it cannot be pitched fly-sheet first in wet weather but as two people can pitch it in only a few minutes this has not proved too inconvenient in practice. The groundsheets are protected and kept clean by a sheet of strong polythene under each one, with Karrimats (closed cell foam insulated mats) placed between polythene sheet and groundsheet for each sleeper.

Top: A good backpacker's tent, light and easily erected.

An excellent tent for high level camping.

SLEEPING BAGS

The warmest, but most expensive bags are down filled. Bags with synthetic fillings are cheaper and dry out more quickly when wet but are heavy and bulky to pack. We compromise with bags filled with a mixture of feather and down, which are cheaper than all-down and less heavy and bulky to carry than those filled with synthetic fibres, weighing only 2 lbs 14 ozs. If you buy ones marked '2—3 season' they will be comfortable in all but winter conditions. Although it is a lengthy process, both all-down and feather and down bags can be washed, using special cleaners like 'Soppy' available from good outdoor shops. At first we used sheet liners in our sleeping bags, but then I made machine-knitted liners in three-ply thermal-knit which are warm and weigh only 12 ozs.

STOVES

We already had a Calor Primus stove and lamp when we began backpacking and as they were suitable we continued to use them. One self-sealing cartridge of butane fuel lasts us about five days on the stove. Any small amount left in after that is used up on the lamp. We use the stove outside or under the unzipped fly-sheet and we make sure there is some ventilation for it and the lamp. This stove is not very stable on uneven ground so we have bought another, a Vango ALP 7000, which the children can use safely and enables the boys to cook their own breakfast at their tent.

WATER CARRIER

We are very pleased with the Field and Trek waterbag, capacity 2 gallons, which is very light (4 ozs) but strong, and replaces a roll-up water carrier which developed leaks and was twice as heavy.

OTHER ITEMS

Paula usually carries the kettle which holds 1½ pints. Jack takes the large saucepan, Maurice the frying pan, and I take a small set which includes my plate. Trevor takes a disposable, but washable, tea towel and sponge/scourer. I also take a small Tupperware bowl for washing, etc., and a milk flask. We take eggs in polythene bottles with screw tops as containers with snap-on lids can get squashed and the lids forced off.

This leaves the smaller things such as the first-aid set with two needles — a fine one for pricking blisters and a stronger one for mending — and a box of matches well wrapped in cling film. (You can put matches in something waterproof such as a film cassette container but we have always found the cling film satisfactory.) A spare polythene bag for rubbish is useful. Then there are toothbrushes. You can buy a travelling one which fits into its own handle. (No toothpaste — salt or just water will do for a few days!) And we also pack, in polythene bags, very small pieces of soap, toilet paper, a small towel, folding brush and comb, camera, notebook or diary and pen, string or cord, spare bootlaces, emergency food such as Kendal Mint Cake, maps, map case, books, compass, and water purifying tablets. We also find a corner for a small trowel.

PACKING A RUCKSACK

Packing your rucksack is a compromise. The aim is to keep the things you need during the day easily accessible — including,

INSIDE A RUCKSACK

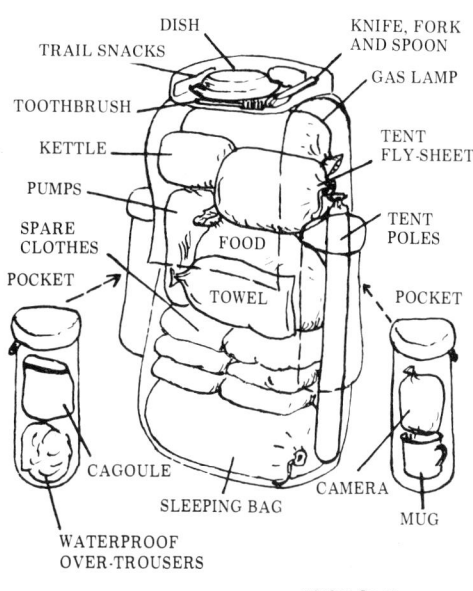

DISH
TRAIL SNACKS
KNIFE, FORK AND SPOON
GAS LAMP
TOOTHBRUSH
TENT FLY-SHEET
KETTLE
PUMPS
SPARE CLOTHES
TENT POLES
POCKET
FOOD
TOWEL
POCKET
CAGOULE
SLEEPING BAG
CAMERA
MUG
WATERPROOF OVER-TROUSERS

MAURICE ROCHE

of course, the tent — while trying to place the heaviest items high up and close to your back and shoulders so that the weight is comfortable to carry. If you have carried a baby in a papoose you may have found that the most difficult times were when the baby was leaning backwards or sideways and that you were most comfortable when the baby was leaning forward with the weight over your shoulders.

Try putting spare clothing and nightwear at the bottom of your pack, then your sleeping bag, then any food that will not be needed during the day close to your back. Then pack spare shoes or training shoes, hat and gloves (unless you think you may need them that day), towel, torch and water carrier, then tent and waterproofs. You can push the tent poles down one corner of your pack or strap them to the outside. You can also strap your Karrimat to either the top or bottom of the rucksack.

In the top pocket we find it convenient to keep first-aid and toilet requirements, camera, diary or notebook, pen, tissues, trail snacks and water purifying tablets. One side pocket may take the stove and perhaps a polythene bottle of eggs and the other a mug containing matches, tea bags in a polythene bag secured with a rubber band, and perhaps some dried fruit for instant energy. The milk flask fits neatly next to it, also knife, fork, spoon, and anything we want handy for lunch such as an apple or cake.

To keep your belongings dry you can put everything in a dustbin liner inside the pack. We prefer to put specific items in individual polythene bags. For further protection from the rain you can place a waterproof or showerproof cover over the pack. At first it is wise to make sure children remember to put their sleeping bags back in their polythene covers and that they keep their waterproofs easily accessible. As they become more experienced they will need less supervision. Show them how to fold and roll their clothes so that they take up less room but do not become creased, then place the clothing in a polythene bag with a strong rubber band round it.

CLOTHING

"What is the minimum amount of clothing you can take?" I have been asked. Obviously with a family you will want to take as little as possible to keep the weight down, yet not be without warm clothing should the weather turn wintry. A cotton or thermal T-shirt with possibly a warm shirt over it for chilly times, then a lightweight woollen zip-up cardigan and a windproof jacket, trousers but not jeans (they take a long time to dry and are cold to wear wet) should be ideal. Thermal T-shirts and long pants make good nightwear, with a spare jumper and socks if it is cold. You may manage without spare trousers to save weight but it may be better for young children to have a pair — shorts will do — as they are quite likely to slip while looking at something and sit down in wet and muddy places! You will also need reliable waterproof cagoules and over-trousers. Gaiters are useful in muddy, boggy or snowy conditions. Even in August try to find a corner for a woolly hat and gloves.

BOOTS

Now for your most vital piece of equipment — your boots. Go to a good outdoor shop for these and take their advice. Good, strong but lightweight boots can now be bought with tough Vibram soles and comfortable padding round the ankles. When you try them on wear the thick socks you intend to walk in — if you haven't yet bought any the shop will usually lend you some to try. Make sure the children can wriggle their toes freely inside the boot. We each wear two pairs of socks, one thick pair and one finer pair underneath, wool mixture. You will need spare pairs of socks depending on the length of time you will be away and the chances of drying them when they are washed. If you are not used to boots, wear them in round the garden and on short walks before setting off on longer hikes. Cover any hint of a blister with plaster immediately.

FOOD AND COOKING

"I'm hungry," is a statement often heard from growing children. Out in the fresh air all day burning up the calories, they certainly do get hungry and, depending on age, will eat as much or even more than adults. Since a lot of food is needed to feed a family it must be well planned in advance. It is useful to keep a box stocked up with dehydrated foods and other items so that there is not too much to buy just before you go. If you are going backpacking for the weekend it is easy to carry all you need but if you will be away for a week or more you may find it easier to take four or five days' supply and buy the rest. (Find out whether there is a village with a shop on or near your route. Don't forget early closing!)

I asked my family for their favourite backpacking meals and what they told me will give you a good idea of what we take with us.

Maurice:

> *Breakfast* — Jordan's Crunchy, Eggy Breadcrumbs (a sort of bread omelette) and bacon, bread and honey.
> *Lunch* — Fish and chips if available!
> *Main meal* — Burgamix with mash and dried carrots, bread and butter and honey, cake, tea.

Paula:

> *Breakfast* — Porridge, fried egg and Sosmix.
> *Lunch* — Cheese rolls, Yoghurt Whirl or Angel Delight, drink of Apeel.
> *Main meal* — Oxtail soup with macaroni and mixed dried vegetables.

Trevor:

> *Breakfast* — Muesli, egg and potato cakes and soft cod roes.
> *Lunch* — Sardine rolls, dried apricots and instant chocolate custard, Apeel or Rise and Shine.
> *Main meal* — Tomato soup with spaghetti and peas or Snackpots or Pot Rice, bread and cheese spread (from a tube), cake, tea.

My husband's preferences are similar but his favourite breakfast is bacon and mushroom omelette and he likes tomato in his cheese rolls. If the evening meal is late the children may not want anything else before they go to bed, but if it is early we have a drink and biscuits later. We carry a few biscuits each, tightly wrapped in cling film.

Snacks during the day are important as with children it is best to walk for an hour or so, then stop for a few minutes' refreshment. These foods provide plenty of energy: chocolate, glucose tablets, raisins, salted peanuts, chocolate biscuits, muesli

Everyone can take part in organising and cooking the family meals. Children find domestic chores fun in camp.

bars and shortbread. We generally take an apple or two each for the first two days then try to buy fruit to eat straight away as it is heavy to carry. Always keep something back for emergencies, perhaps Kendal Mint Cake or chocolate. If not used it will keep until next time or there will be no shortage of volunteers to eat it going home!

We take home-made wholemeal bread, which we slice and put in bags fastened with wire ties. It travels well like this but if the last few slices break up they are used for Maurice's favourite 'eggy breadcrumbs'. We use salt or honey on porridge and never take sugar with us (none of us take it in tea anyway). The honey is put in a plastic squeeze tube. These tubes are useful for any squeezable food such as peanut butter or soft margarine. The latter can be hard to squeeze in cold weather so you may have to remove the clip from the end of the tube to get it out with a knife. We also take Ryvita, tea bags — as many as we expect to use plus two or three extra — Pint Size or other milk powder, and de-caffeinated coffee, which you can get in individual sachets in some health food shops.

There are accelerated freeze-dried foods, obtainable from outdoor shops, which only need the addition of boiling water and then leaving to stand for a few minutes, saving time and fuel. But their cost makes them rather expensive for feeding a family so we tend to use things which cook quickly, such as a 1½-pint packet of soup with some quick cooking macaroni and dried vegetables. Just bring it to the boil and simmer for a few minutes. Burgamix and Sosmix both have to be soaked in water for a few minutes then shaped and fried. If you use the amount of water required for your mashed potato to cook your peas, beans or other vegetables, you can add the potato powder to the cooking liquid and mix the potato with your vege-tables (the children's suggestion). Cover to keep hot while frying the Burgamix. You can shorten the cooking time for dired carrots by soaking them for an hour before cooking.

We do not need to carry a tin opener as we never take tinned food other than sardines or soft cod roes which open with a key or ring pull, and the empties are small and flat to pack away easily until they can be disposed of. The cod roes are usually carried as an emergency in case we are unable to get eggs, hence Trevor's favourite breakfast which uses just one egg. The egg and potato cakes he mentions are mashed potato mixed with an egg and fried. Other convenient breakfast dishes are scrambled eggs and omelettes, with dried mushrooms, onions or red and green peppers to give variety. Muesli can either be packed as the amount required for everyone in a separate polythene bag for each day, or each member of the family can take a bag with sufficient for the number of days you are out. The former is probably better for younger children. A good breakfast will get the family going and once on the move you will be eating smaller amounts frequently.

At lunch time we usually drink Apeel or Rise and Shine, which take away the taste of the Puritabs if you get your water from a stream. If you are unlikely to be near a suitable source of water you will have to take some with you to make a drink. The family also appreciate fish and chip shops and cafés in the right place at the right time and it is nice to buy a meal to cele-brate someone's birthday or the completion of your walk!

Other foods we use are dried bananas, prunes, apricots, dried fruit salad, pear halves, and apple rings from our local wholefood shop. Packets of apple sauce mix or apple flakes can be varied with raisins or dates or, at the appropriate time of the year, with bilberries or blackberries if you find any. Chickweed and young dandelion leaves go well with cheese rolls. We have also tried some delicious fish and shellfish soups which you simmer for five minutes and then add nearly half a pint of milk and bring to the boil again. Protoveg soya protein food in various flavours is preferable in the minced form which cooks in two to three minutes; the chunky type takes much longer. Instant soups make a welcome snack, particularly in cold wet weather.

Here are the recipes for the cakes we take with us — each carrying our own!

Grasmere Gingerbread

6 ozs self-raising flour, 2 ozs wholemeal flour, 1 dessertsp. ground ginger, a pinch of salt, ½ teasp. bicarbonate of soda, 4 ozs soft brown sugar, 4 ozs butter or margarine, 1 tbsp. golden syrup.

Sieve flour, ginger, salt, bicarbonate of soda together. Cream sugar, butter and syrup, add to the dry ingredients, mix well. Press into a greased tin and bake at 310°F, gas mark 2, for about forty minutes, but it is quite satisfactory if you are using a hotter oven to put it on a lower shelf. Cut into squares while hot — it will be hard to cut when cold. Makes about fifteen squares.

Devonshire Block Cake

8 ozs self-raising flour, 4 ozs butter or margarine, 4 ozs caster sugar, 3 ozs black treacle, 2 eggs, 6 ozs sultanas, 4 ozs currants, 2–3 ozs mixed peel, 2 fl ozs lukewarm milk.

Grease and line a 9 × 5 in loaf tin. Sieve flour, cream butter and sugar together and beat in treacle. Add eggs, ½ at a time, beating well, then add lukewarm milk. Stir in fruit and flour. Turn into prepared tin and bake at

310°F, gas mark 2, for one and a half to two hours. This cake is also delicious made with 4 ozs self-raising flour and 4 ozs wholemeal flour.

You may be able to buy eggs and milk from farms. Some farmers will sell milk if you have your own container so a milk flask is useful to have with you. You can reconstitute powdered milk also in the flask and it is handy too if you buy a carton of fruit juice to drink straight away and have some left over.

We make out a menu, usually a week or so before we go, listing the meals for each day and the food required so that we are sure we have everything and it is clear what food will have to be bought later on if our expedition is to last longer than four days. While backpacking we keep the menu inside the map case for easy reference.

If we are travelling some distance to our starting point we take sandwiches and perhaps a fruit pie on a foil plate, prepared in advance. These are convenient to eat in car or train.

Sometimes the weather is fit to cook outside, but more often in camp you will find that you are cooking in a bell end of the tent under the fly-sheet, which is unzipped for ventilation. Make sure the stove is on level ground and a sensible distance from the tent inner or fly-sheet. The children will enjoy helping with the cooking but should be encouraged to help wash-up too, even if they just wash and dry their own things and pack them away.

CHOOSING WHERE TO CAMP

Good camp site directories, such as the one published by the Camping Club of Great Britain, are easily available and there are more specialised lists of campsites for

specific areas such as the accommodation booklet and camping list published by the Offa's Dyke Association. With these, you can choose sites to suit your daily mileage. It may be, however, that your chosen area lacks information as yet, so use your map to find likely farms or wild pitches. You may be able to book a farm pitch in advance or it may be a case of 'We'll ask at the next farm'. We are rarely refused permission to camp, even with a dog, and often we are made very welcome. Return their hospitality by making certain the family observe the Country Code, being particularly careful to fasten all gates and to ensure that no litter is left on the pitch.

The best pitches of all are in the wild,

The Roche family setting up camp in the Peak District.

perhaps high up in the hills. Here you may find a clear stream to camp beside, far from the noise of traffic and the bustle of crowds.

YOUR FIRST TIME OUT WITH THE FAMILY

Assuming that the family are used to walking, you may, as I did, know how far your children can walk but wonder how far they will manage carrying packs. So one or two trial weekends are a good idea before trying longer distances. Adjust the size and weight of your packs to suit the age of the child and try perhaps about eight miles the first day, allowing an average of two miles an hour including stops. Aim to walk for about an hour and then stop for ten minutes. Have a snack — perhaps some dried fruit or chocolate — and make sure everyone's feet are comfortable. The children may like to choose where to stop for lunch; even a three-year-old can find a sheltered hollow out of the wind. On a hot day you may find a stream where they can paddle and refresh their feet.

You have probably decided where you intend to camp that night so make sure, at first, that you arrive while there is plenty of daylight left. Later on you will find that you can pitch tent in a few minutes even in the dark in wind and rain, but your first backpacking trip should be at a time of year when you can at least rely on light evenings.

Children vary in their moods after a meal in camp. Some fall asleep almost instantly. Others find renewed energy, and, having changed into training shoes or other light footwear, want to play games, explore the campsite or walk into a nearby village. Remember it is wise to allow yourselves plenty of time in the morning so try to get them to sleep reasonably early.

In the morning an early start means you can get on well in cooler walking conditions and you will then have less distance to cover in the heat of the afternoon. If possible, while you cook breakfast and wash up, put sleeping bags and liners to air, inside-out, over a wall perhaps. Before you leave let the children check with you that nothing has been left behind and that the only sign you have been there is perhaps some slightly flattened grass!

As you return home, planning your next trip, you will have learned a good deal. You will have found out how fast the family walk on average, suiting the pace to the youngest. (We often have trouble now keeping up with the youngest, especially uphill!) You will know what you took and found unnecessary and what you wish you had taken — the sun cream maybe, as we discovered one very hot Easter. You may have visited interesting places, you will have seen all sorts of fascinating plants and wildlife (or had this pointed out to you by the children if you did not see it first), and you will all have shared the satisfaction of coping with the weather and finding your way.

You will soon be getting the maps out to plan your route for next time. There is much to be said for trying some of the Long Distance Paths. One we have enjoyed particularly is the Pembrokeshire Coast Path. We travelled by train to Aberystwyth and caught the bus to Cardigan. We walked from there to the beginning of the path at Dogmaels and after finishing at Amroth a fortnight later we walked to Kilgetty Station. It was Easter and there were wild flowers all the way — violets, primroses, bluebells, thrift — and birds and seals, and always the sea not far away. When you plan your own route you have to be prepared to find some paths overgrown and others, marked on the map, may no longer exist so you may have to change your plans. However, planning your own route is satisfying. You can include the hills, valleys, villages or stretches of moorland that appeal to you, and you can start and finish wherever is convenient. You will all share the sense of achievement at finding your way along little-used paths, probably with the aid of your compass, and arriving safely at your destination.

DOGS

A note about dogs before I describe three family expeditions, as we took our own dog, Rusty, on two of them. He is a Collie cross with some Alsatian in him. It may be wise if you have any doubts about your dog's obedience to leave him with friends or in kennels if you plan to backpack at lambing time, or if a great deal of car or train travel is involved and he is not a good traveller. Check if you might be visiting sites where dogs are not permitted. (These are usually the larger, commercial sites like those in the New Forest which you may wish to avoid anyway, but you can look in the Sites Directory.) But Rusty adds so much to our enjoyment that we take him whenever we can. As dogs now have to be kept on the lead more, especially when passing through fields of livestock, a long lead is useful. The usual length is too short when climbing over stiles. I have made an adjustable one from a length of terylene webbing with a sliding buckle attached to one end. The other end passes through a spring clip (perhaps off an old lead or bought from a pet shop), and is then threaded through the buckle and a loop sewn over at the end. The shortened lead is used along roads or in towns and villages and the longer version when using stepping stones or climbing stiles. It also gives plenty of length to tie him up when necessary — to a pack frame if nothing else is available — outside a shop or some place of interest, or to a fence or tree while we are pitching the tents. Use a quick release knot so that if he pulls it tight you can still pull the end to undo it. It is an advantage to be able to leave him guarding our packs while we visit a museum, cathedral or castle.

We carry Frolic or Omega dried dog food, weighed out into bags holding a day's supply. We each take a few dog biscuits and we take a small plastic dish for his food and water. On longer backpacks when we have not been able to get dried dog food we have bought scraps and bones to help out. Rusty is supposed to sleep at the bottom of the tent by our feet, where he usually settles down as soon as the tent is pitched, but sometimes he comes up between the sleeping bags during the night. As soon as someone wakes he is up, wagging his tail, eager for another lovely long walk!

THREE FAMILY EXPEDITIONS
Welsh Steam Railway Backpack
August 1980 (all the family and Rusty)

Maps used: OS Landranger 1:50 000 sheet 135 Aberystwyth, 124 Dolgellau. OS Outdoor Leisure Map 1:25 000 Snowdonia National Park, Cader Idris/Dovey Forest.

Timetables of The Great Little Trains of Wales can be obtained from the Tourist Board of Wales, Brunel House, Cardiff. Tel: (0222) 27281.

———————

We planned this expedition to include as many steam railways as would fit conveniently into a week's tour. And apart from trains which delighted the boys we wanted to climb Cader Idris. We had set out to climb this mountain years before with Maurice in the papoose but had had to turn back because of rain.

We started by catching the train to Aberystwyth. Here, without leaving the station, we were able to catch the train to the Vale of Rheidol. A journey through pleasant scenery above the Afon Rheidol took us to Devil's Bridge. We left the train here and, instead of following the crowds to see the waterfalls (the cost would have been three pounds for all of us), we made our way northwards to Ponterwyd, a village which has a post office/shop, and from there along the A44 to the Llywernog Silver-Lead Mine. We left our packs in Rusty's care to follow the miners' trail with the aid of an interesting facts sheet. We visited an exhibition of old photographs and miners' tools and afterwards enjoyed a short film show in one of the old buildings.

We returned to Ponterwyd and followed a lane to a nearby farm where the farmer kindly allowed us to pitch for the night by a stream in a field full of sheep!

Next morning we woke to find ourselves surrounded by mist so we abandoned our route over Plynlimon and, when rain was added to the mist, had an early lunch at Blaen Peithnant before taking the lane to Nant-y-moch Reservoir. The mist was so thick that we could not see the water although we were very near to it. We crossed Nant y Llyn but missed a footbridge over Afon Hengwm and so continued along a track by the river until we heard the roar of a waterfall. Then we saw it, silver, grey and white in the mist, and we realised that we had come the wrong way. We decided to stop early and to go back to where we had crossed the Nant y Llyn the next day in — we hoped — better visibility. We went up Cwm Gwarin until we were above the waterfall, paddled across, and found a level spot beside some rocks near the top of the falls. I wondered if the noise of the rushing water would keep us awake, but we could hardly hear it for the sound of the wind which got up in the night. By morning the wind had blown the mist away, the sun shone from a clear sky and we could see the full beauty of the waterfall and rocks. We remember this as one of the loveliest wild pitches we have ever found.

We went back along the Afon Hengwm to the footbridge, clear enough now the mist had vanished, and had a day on hill and forest tracks, then lanes, via Glaspwll, to Machynlleth from where we could see a small camp site below us as we came down the lane.

Next morning after shopping in Machynlleth we went by train to Tywyn for the Tal-y-Llyn Railway to Abergynolwyn. We found that the Slate Museum marked on the OS Outdoor Leisure Map was no longer open so followed the path over the hillside to Llanfihangel-y-Pennant. About half a mile along the lane from here was a farm, Tyn-y-fach, with a sign 'Camping' at the gate. We were told to go to the bridge and turn right, and that water could be obtained from the old farm buildings further on. Just over the bridge, as shown on the map, is the site of Mary Jones' cottage, with a memorial inside, inscribed in Welsh and in English: 'In memory of Mary Jones, who in the year 1800, at the age of 16, walked from here to Bala to procure from the Revd. Thomas Charles B.A. a copy of the Welsh Bible. This incident was the occasion of the formation of the British and Foreign Bible Society.' She walked barefoot carrying her boots to save wearing them out; it is 25 miles to Bala.

Perhaps Mary's walk would be worth following — we shall have to look at the maps and the book which tells her story to see. Anyway we went, as she did, up Cader Idris (2928 ft.) and had our lunch at the top. Then, after taking in the view on all sides and scrambling round the rocks, we went down, down, down the north side and followed the paths via Kings' Youth Hostel and the Llynnau Cregennan to Garth-y-fog Farm near Arthog.

Next morning we went on our third

little railway, the Fairbourne, to catch the ferry to Barmouth. It was a hot day and we appreciated the coolness of the Lifeboat museum. We were also pleased to find a pet shop which sold dried meat for Rusty. We spent the afternoon on the beach. We camped again at a farm that night and as darkness fell we heard strange deep breathing noises outside the tent. I wondered whether it could be the cattle in the next field, but the sounds appeared to be coming from above our heads in the trees. In the morning we discovered it was barn owls which apparently do snore in that strange way!

The next day we walked to Tal-y-Bont Station and caught a train to Talsarnau, the station after Harlech, shortening our planned route because Jack was not feeling well. We went by lane and track past Llyn Tecwyn Uchaf to Maentwrog and on up the road to Tan-y-Bwlch Station on the Festiniog line.

From here, next morning, we caught our last little train to Tanygrisiau where, after looking round the shops and market at Blaenau Ffestiniog, we caught the train home. (The Llechwedd Slate Quarries are worth a visit but we had already been there on a previous occasion.)

Colne—Hardcastle Crags—Withins—Lothersdale—Pinhaw Beacon

May 1980 (four of us and Rusty — Paula was at Guide Camp)

Maps used: OS Outdoor Leisure Map 1:25 000 South Pennines, OS 1:50 000 sheet 103 (we used our old sheet 95 1-in. map Blackburn and Burnley).

This expedition lasted three days and two nights and we walked 35 miles. We started and finished at Colne Station.

From the station we walked up through the town centre to Carry Lane, down to Carry Bridge and up the flagged footpath which goes over the hill to come out further along the lane to Trawden. From here we had a choice of paths to join the track at the foot of Boulsworth Hill, where we turned right to Thursden. We went via Coldwell Reservoirs to the road. Here there are various routes to High Greenwood Farm (grid ref. 969307), a small camp site where we camped that night, but that hot, dry May much of the moorland was either burnt or smouldering so we had to use the road for some of the way.

Next morning we took the path from the farm, signposted 'Hardcastle Crags', went through the woods with their masses of bluebells, crossed the bridge, and went up the other side of Hebden Water to Walshaw. We intended to go via Dean Gate to Walshaw Dene Reservoirs, but a sign on the gate told us it was closed due to fire. So we went along the track over New Laithe Moor to join the Pennine Way at Walshaw Dene, to Withins (Wuthering Heights) and Ponden Hall (camping, if required, and refreshments), then Oakworth Moor and Ickornshaw Moor, down to Lumb and across the A6068 at Cowling. We continued along the Pennine Way to Wood Head Farm, Lothersdale (grid ref. 960455) (milk and eggs available), where we spent our second night.

We had walked 16 miles that day and Trevor, who was eight years old at the time, fell asleep when we had had a meal. When we woke him up at about nine o'clock to have a drink and biscuit and get ready for bed, he asked, "Is it morning?"

When the morning came we went down into Lothersdale and up to Pinhaw Beacon (1273 ft.), from which we could see for miles as it was a clear day. On reaching the road, we turned left and followed it to Hainslack, just before Black Lane Ends. We crossed the fields to Copy House — I wanted to show the boys Copy House Farm where I used to ride and help with the haymaking in my school holidays. We went along the track, turned left at the 'crossroads' to Noyna Bottom, and turned right along the lane and over the stile leading to Noyna Rocks, where we had our lunch. Afterwards we went by lanes and footpaths down to the A6068 (at grid ref. 902404), down Cotton Tree Lane to the bridge where a footpath to the right took us back to Carry Bridge again, and up into the town for tea and scones before catching the train home.

The route can be varied in many ways; this is all lovely walking country.

Forden–Corndon Hill–Stiperstones– Long Mynd–All Stretton–Wilstone Hill– Little Stretton–Cardingmill Valley
May 1981 (the children and myself with Trevor's friend, Martin)

Maps used: OS 1:50 000 sheet 126 Shrewsbury (we found the HMSO publication on Offa's Dyke Path clearer for this section). OS 1:50 000 sheet 137 Ludlow and Wenlock Edge.

———

This memorable backpack took four days.

Jack took us by car to Forden to join Offa's Dyke Path (you can join it nearer Welshpool at Buttington or Lower Lieghton). We walked southwards down Offa's Dyke for a little over five miles to Ditches Farm (grid ref. 248939) where we camped the first night.

There is a footpath shown on the map to Rockley and Rhiston, to the north-east of Ditches, but the farmer told us it was fenced off and no longer walkable and we should return up the dyke to the lane, turn right and continue to the main road, the A490. So we did. We crossed the road and went down a wet track to a bridge, from which it was not far to Corndon Hill. During this time we had several showers — the last about a mile from the top was of hail — but the sun shone between them. We had our lunch at the top of Corndon Hill (1683 ft.), then packed up hurriedly as another dark cloud approached. Fortunately this was blown northwards and missed us.

After regaining the track we thought it might be interesting to see Mitchell's Fold Stone Circle, about a mile to the north. However, seeing 'Giant's Cave' marked on the map we changed our plan and made our way towards it. However, the intriguing name is just a farm today, the cave evidently fallen in long ago, although there is still a pile of stones on the hillside where it is supposed to have been.

We were now heading for Stiperstones and intending to use the bridleway which leaves the A488 at grid ref. 321981. Sure enough there was a signpost, 'Bridleway', at the roadside, but the poor wearer of the bridle would have to jump over several barbed-wire fences to follow it! Somewhere along it we camped near a stream and woke to the sound of heavy rain next morning. It was less heavy by the time we had finished our breakfast, but still falling steadily as we used the compass to follow the invisible 'bridleway' over stiles to the farm track at grid ref. 348981. Then followed a lovely walk along the Stiperstones Ridge, stopping to scramble up rocks now and then. We ate our lunch in the rain (which had started once more) with some shelter from overhanging rocks.

We went down the hill and along the lane to Bridges, where we again sheltered from the rain for a while, and along the track to Coates, Medlicott and Pole Bank, turning left before reaching the road. Martin's feet were very wet by this time as he had no boots, so we stopped early when we found a suitable water supply and he felt better as soon as he had dry socks on and a hot meal inside him.

'Morning has broken, like the first morning', and what a sunrise and what a morning it was after the rain the day before! Larks were singing and soon the sun was really warm as we went over the hill, down the track to the lane and down to All Stretton. After visiting the shop there we crossed over the A49. The first footpath we tried proved too wet for Martin's footwear so we turned back to the road for a short distance, left it at a lane which runs parallel to it, and turned left along the track which goes between Caer Caradoc and Helmeth Hill. By now it felt far too hot to climb Caer Caradoc so we went over Wilstone Hill and Hope Bowdler Hill, then via Hope Bowdler, Dryhill and a path to the south of Ragleth Hill to Little Stretton where there is a camp site at Small Batch.

After a meal of Burgamix, mash, green beans, bread, honey, cake, and tea, the children still had the energy, although they had walked 12 miles on a hot day, to join some other children in a game of football, so I took Rusty for a walk up Ashes Hollow. I came back to find them sliding down a steep, grassy bank in plastic fertilizer sacks!

On the last morning we took the path from Little Stretton over the Round Hill earthwork to the Port Way. By now it was raining again so we made our way, mostly along the road, to Cardingmill Valley where we enjoyed a hot meal and shelter in the National Trust café. We walked on to Church Stretton station to start the journey home.

That was some years ago. Recently, when I saw Martin, I asked if he remembered it, thinking he would probably mention the rain. But no. "That was great!" was his reply. Thank you, Martin, it was.

SPECIAL POINTS FOR FAMILIES

Here are a few points which will make backpacking with the family easier and more enjoyable.

Family Railcard: One of these soon pays for itself as children under 16 travel for £1 each and adults for half fare. Children love trains and it means that you can get to the nearest station for the beginning of your walk and return from somewhere else at the end without the worry of leaving a car in a strange place and having to get back to it.

Locating the food: We used to find that the children said, "I haven't got the peas" (or macaroni or whatever was required), and time was wasted while everyone searched for it. So now I put the initial of the person taking each item against it on the menu when we are packing the food so that I know who has whatever is needed each mealtime.

Drying the washing: In winter when drying may be difficult you will have to carry several pairs of socks if you are away for longer than a weekend. But during the rest of the year you can wash them and tuck them under your rucksack straps to dry in the sun and wind as you walk. Check they don't get caught in bushes and trees in overgrown places! Other garments dried in this way may cause amused smiles but your pack will be lighter. I have sewn tape loops inside the ridge of our tent so that damp socks can be hung there overnight, and also tea towels and hand towels, if they are not too heavy. Weather permitting, they can be hung outside in the morning. Otherwise put the damp things in a polythene bag until you pitch for the night.

Walking at the front or back: Some members of the family will prefer walking at the front, others at the back. We have a rule: whoever walks in front takes the map, whoever walks at the back shuts the gates!

Camp games for the family: Have a store of games to play in the evenings or on exceptionally wet days. You need spoken games which are useful in poor light and written ones when odd scraps of paper are available. Our written games include dot-to-dot squares, consequences, drawing animals (head, fold over, body, fold over, legs, and see the strange result!), and Connect 4 played in the same way on paper as noughts and crosses. The spoken games include going through the alphabet naming various things (birds, animals, or whatever you have seen that day), and an old favourite 'Mrs Brown went to town', where each player adds to her shopping list after repeating the items previously said. Mrs Brown's last purchases included a metal detector (we were on Hadrian's Wall), a picture of Sandbach Crosses, a car sponge with an eagle on it, and an ice axe!

Notebooks: On longer expeditions the children have notebooks which are used for games, as log-books of the walk, as account books, for writing down recipes and for drawing in. Trevor has given permission to quote from the notes which he wrote at

nine years of age on the Pembrokeshire Coast Path: 'Sunday (5th April 1981). Found yellowy coloured rock. Took photo of an old blowhole called Pwll y wrach (Witch's Pool). Saw some seals. Rusty chased a rabbit.' Later the book reads like this: 'Friday (17th April 1981). Get up 6.00. Breakfast 6.30. Wash up, pack up 7.30. Leave 8.07. Stop for chocolate 9.00. Stop for raisins 10.00. Giltar Point stop for glucose tablets 11.45. Tenby 1.00 for steak and kidney pie, chips and ice-cream ... Wiseman's Bridge 6.30. Stile No. 1 6.45. Finish path 7.30.'

Weather and the time of the year: Get used to backpacking in spring, summer and autumn before trying winter. But once you become experienced you will find you can backpack all the year round. It is quite easy to keep warm on a cold night but beware of really windy weather. It can be difficult to sleep on a windy night when the fly-sheet is catching each gust and you wonder if the tent pegs will hold. Make sure you have left nothing under the fly-sheet which could blow away if a peg does come out — we once had to chase a frying pan down a hillside at seven o'clock on a February morning in the Lake District!

Unless it is very heavy indeed, rain should not bother you. Good waterproofs will keep it out. But a lot of rain over a long period will make streams and rivers rise, a point to bear in mind if you intend to cross them or camp beside them. If you listen to the weather forecast for the area you are going to walk in for a week or two up to your departure, you will know whether the going may be wet or boggy or mainly dry.

Mist, particularly in the hills, can be dangerous. Make sure the children know how to use a compass as soon as they are old enough and never walk without one. If mist descends on you unexpectedly, especially if you feel you may have gone the wrong way, find your position on the map and perhaps, depending on the time of day and the sort of country you are in, pitch where you are and hope it has cleared by morning. Avoid high ground if the cloud is low on the hills — plan an alternative route.

The sun is lovely in spring, autumn and winter but can prove a problem in summer. Protect everyone from sunburn and try to start early in the day before the sun gets too hot. Children often find the heat more tiring than any other weather and may need longer stops during the day. You can make up the miles in the evening when it is cooler.

Get used to other conditions first before venturing into snow and read *The Spur Master Guide to Snow Camping* by Cameron McNeish. We have had some good times in snow, but I do not recommend it for young children.

Books: There are books to read before you go; others may be more interesting when

High camp in winter below Snowdon.

you get back, but first let's consider books to take with you. If you are following one of the Long Distance Footpaths an obvious choice is the appropriate HMSO guide which, besides maps and route descriptions, includes chapters on the plants, birds, geology, and history of the area. A browse round a bookshop will reveal many other guides to specific areas. Some may list information such as early closing days, especially useful for young families. The guide-book can be carried in your map case for easy reference.

When considering books to take with you, obviously size and weight are important. But I find it is pleasant to have something to read in the evening or the early morning before anyone else is awake, or if we have had to stop early or set off late because of heavy rain. I take my smallest book, a French *Nouveau Testament*, which is about two-and-a-half inches by three-and-a-half inches and less than half an inch thick! Young children may like to take a comic with them, older ones something concerning their interests — our boys often take train spotting books. Also, you may buy a book about the area in which you are backpacking, such as a booklet on Well Dressing in Derbyshire or Birds of Devon which will be light to carry and can be packed in a polythene bag. Before you go, read as much as you can about backpacking.

MAPS

Maps are essential reading! You need to study them not only for route finding, but also for planning your route in advance, finding farms where you might pitch for the night, noting streams to provide water for a wild pitch, calculating distances to villages and railway stations — all the basic information you need for a successful trip. They will tell you in advance whether your route involves steep hills, whether there are precipices or bogs to avoid so that you can form a picture in your mind of the kind of country you will encounter. The Ordnance Survey Landranger Series, Scale 1:50000, are satisfactory but more detail is given on the 1:25000 scale maps which can be a great help to the backpacker. Of course the larger scale maps cover smaller areas so you may have the inconvenience of having to carry more than one. The Outdoor Leisure Series are good, but only cover certain areas as yet.

However carefully you plan, there will always be times when you have to change your route. There is much a map cannot tell you. Areas of trees may have been planted after the map was printed, footbridges washed away, little-used paths become blocked or fenced off or footpaths diverted. Small streams shown on the map dry up in summer, especially in limestone regions, so your expected water supply may be further away than you expected. One hot day we were approaching a large area of Forestry Commission land and looking forward to the shade of the trees, only to find they were about two feet high! If you read books by people who have backpacked long distances, such as John Merrill, John Hillaby, and Hamish Brown, you will be able to learn a great deal from their experience.

A FINAL NOTE

When you have climbed your mountain you not only feel a sense of achievement at doing what you set out to do; you look back at the way you have come and see its beauty from a different angle. You see the hills you crossed yesterday, the forest which gave you shade, a bridge, a river you followed, and you are thankful for it all. Then you look ahead, to the immediate way down, the stream which will refresh you, the next hill or mountain and those in the distance, and look forward to what is to come.

So it is with backpacking. We have had some wonderful times backpacking as a family and we know there are many more places waiting for us to enjoy in the future. It is my hope that, through reading this, you will experience the joys of backpacking for yourself and share my pleasure.

PUBLICATIONS

BOOKS

Backpacking in Britain Derrick Booth (Oxford Illustrated Press 1974).

The Backpacker's Handbook Derrick Booth (Robert Hale).

The Spur Book of Map and Compass Brown and Hunter (Spurbooks).

Also, read books on the weather and any book you can find about the area in which you intend to backpack so that you can include interesting places that might be just off your chosen route and worth a short detour. Read books written by people who have captured the special atmosphere of the district; for example the novels of Thomas Hardy if you visit 'Wessex'; those of the Brontë sisters for the Yorkshire moors and *Kilvert's Diary* for the Hay-on-Wye region. We have always treasured our copy of *The Concise British Flora* by W. Keble Martin. We read the story of his life spent collecting flowers and drawing them so it was a real delight to see the ruins of the small stone church on Dartmoor built by himself and his friends, just off the Two Moors Way.

MAGAZINES

If you are a member of the Backpackers' Club you will receive a quarterly magazine, *Backpacker*, written by members for members, full of useful and interesting information. The address of the Backpackers' Club is: The National Organiser, 20 St. Michael's Road, Tilehurst, Reading, Berks. RG3 4RP.

The Great Outdoors published monthly contains a great deal to interest the backpacker.

Footloose published bi-monthly covers a wide range of activities including backpacking.

Stiles come in many varieties.
This is one that has to be climbed.

Peter Knottley, bicycle tourist and author, lives in Surrey. He has led many tours at home and abroad and is involved in a great deal of voluntary work to promote cycling in organisations which include the Youth Hostels Association, the Cyclists' Touring Club, and the Duke of Edinburgh's Award Scheme.

Recently Peter topped over three hundred thousand miles — all for pleasure! he writes, "The cycle must be reckoned one of the most inspired inventions ever. Simple and practical, capable of years of good service with minimal upkeep, convenient, non-polluting and versatile, it is a power for good. Had it been a recent invention (instead of one which pre-dated motor transport) it would be hailed as the perfect answer to a lot of our environmental, economic and health problems.

It can still be the answer, but to my way of thinking all these advantages are incidental. The real reason for cycling is that it is enjoyable and a way of life which, once found, has a continuing appeal."

Peter Knottley's books include: *Cycle Touring in Britain and the Rest of Europe* (Constable and Co. 2nd ed.). A complete introduction to touring by cycle at home and on the Continent. Family cycling is included with maps and suggested tours. *The Spur Book of Cycling* (Fredk. Warne and Co.). *Half Way Round*, a short story of a ride by Colin Martin on a Moulton bicycle from England to Australia in 1970. Edited letters from the rider with added narrative by Peter Knottley. Obtainable only from the British Cycling Federation or Cyclists' Touring Club at £2 post paid (see address at end of this chapter).

Peter Knottley is Touring Adviser and a regular contributor to *Cycling* weekly magazine and also to *Cyclist Monthly* (both published by Business Press International, Specialist and Professional Press Division, Sutton, Surrey).

Cycling and Cycle Touring

PETER KNOTTLEY

Kids and bikes belong together! Today, with modern lightweight machines fitted with the correct gears, cycle touring is easy and enjoyable for every member of the family. And in Britain there is still a vast network of quiet minor roads and byways waiting to be explored.

The independence and freedom enjoyed by the cyclist are unequalled and the interesting experiences that come his way innumerable. He really gets to know people and places and becomes part of the world about him. For families it is the ideal form of recreation, travel and holidaymaking.

The most important point to remember if you intend to cycle as a family is that cycling should be easy for every member of your group. There should be no stress or strain. The art of riding a bike well is easily mastered and then the rest is simple and great fun. A great deal of the fun comes from finding your own routes and learning from experience. With the family, it is wise to seek quiet roads and here in Britain we are particularly fortunate in having a vast network of minor roads and byways which see very little traffic. Join the other cycle tourists on these roads and you will discover that another, more tranquil world exists.

There is no need to be afraid of hills. Given a suitable cycle fitted with an appropriate range of gears and using the correct riding position and style, you will be able to cope with almost any terrain. With practice the actual propulsion of the cycle becomes as natural as walking. In fact it is less fatiguing and has been aptly described as 'geared walking' for you get further on a bike than on foot for the same expenditure of energy. Like the walker, the cyclist has the freedom to look about him and appreciate his surroundings. Unlike the walker, he probably won't have to return to the point at which he started, maybe where the car is parked or to keep an appointment with a public transport vehicle. These are advantages you will quickly discover. Perhaps at first, if you have not cycled as a family before, you may not wish to invest much money in something new. The chances are that there are cycles in the family already that you can use for some short preliminary runs.

Equally, the clothing you wear for jogging or tennis will do fine for the first cycling forays. But once you discover the enjoyment of cycling — it won't take long — and that the journey itself is more important than the arrival, an enlightening reversal of usual attitudes, you will want to complete your satisfaction by using the right equipment.

Then, with the right approach and a little forethought, you will find cycling a simple, easy and wholly pleasurable activity bringing you its own special feeling of well-being, the perfect antidote for everyday hassle. But above all, you will have fun.

Cycling along quiet leafy lanes is the perfect antidote for stresses and strains.

CHOOSING A CYCLE

Almost anyone can get on almost any bike and ride it. But it isn't much fun. The cycle should be carefully chosen with regard to the characteristics of the rider, and although the main considerations are few they are very important. Cycling and cycles are essentially simple things, but too often they are made to sound complex and technical in a way that is discouraging. That's a pity!

First of all, correct cycle frame size is essential. An error here will make cycling hard work and uncomfortable as well as having an adverse effect on control of the machine. A good rule-of-thumb method of deciding your own probable optimum frame size is to take your inside leg measurement and deduct nine inches. Frame size is traditionally stated as 'the length of the seat (or vertical) tube of the frame from its top centreline on the top tube to the bottom axle centreline'. The commonest sizes are between 21 and 23 inches, though they can come in all sizes from 19½ to 25½ inches. For young or small-built people there are smaller frames but they take smaller wheels — 24 inches or 20 inches in diameter instead of the usual 27 inches.

Frame size is right if you can place the ball of one foot on the ground whilst sitting comfortably on the saddle and if, when pedalling, the knee joint is slightly bent when the pedal is at its lowest position, i.e. the leg should not be quite fully extended.

Saddle and handlebar height can be adjusted to give maximum comfort. This is usually achieved when the bars are level with — or slightly higher than — the saddle, and so the rider's weight is more or less evenly distributed between handlebars, saddle and pedals.

*Peter Knottley with Ancient and Modern —
a 56-inch and a 17-inch wheel.*

Gearing is also important. Cycle gears are expressed in inches too, the figure denoting the diameter of an imaginary wheel which would be turned once for one turn of the pedals — a sort of 'historical accident' from the days of Ordinary (or 'penny farthing') cycles on which that is just what did happen.

The touring cycle has derailleur gears, with which you can fit the gear ratios you like. Production machines usually have five or ten gears but they are often higher than they really should be for their purpose.

You can have the gears changed to suit your wishes; the dealer will tell you what ranges are possible with the various models of gear mechanism.

You can indeed have a one-for-one or 'direct drive' like a penny-farthing which will be a gear of 27 inches with a 27-inch diameter wheel — and this is low enough to enable most folk to tackle steep hills of some length without undue effort. Low gears are also advantageous when carrying a touring weight on the cycle, or when meeting a headwind.

Top gears can be up to 100 inches or even higher and that sort will set you sailing along at 20 mph on a good road in good conditions — exhilarating, but much too fast to appreciate the passing scene!

Gears make a vital contribution to the whole idea of cycling, which is that it should be easy and enjoyable going. A range of gears from the low 30s up to the mid-70s will be just right for most tourists.

The saddle also can make or break your feelings. It should be broad enough to support the bones yet not so broad as to chafe the inside legs. Natural leather is still favourite though plastic saddles are also popular.

A note about handlebars. It is popularly thought that a cycle with dropped handlebars is a 'racer', but this is not necessarily so. Dropped handlebars are a useful feature of a lightweight machine whatever its purpose and are very suitable for touring.

Dropped bars give three different gripping positions for the hands — down on the 'drops', round the curve with the hands resting on the brake fittings and levers, or on the straight central part of the bars. A change of position from time to time whilst riding avoids possible fatigue from getting 'set' in one position for too long.

In practice, most tourists reserve the 'drops' for getting down to it in a headwind — you are more streamlined in that position. If, nevertheless, you favour flat handlebars they can be fitted to a lightweight machine to your special order. They give a comfortable if rather stately riding position but they are suitable rather for the short-distance rider as continuous riding in such a position becomes very tiring.

THE RIGHT BIKE FOR YOUR CHILD

Parents who appreciate the pleasures and benefits of cycling will want their children to share them. They must not be disappointed if the youngsters are not keen to take it up, for you cannot and should not try to force an interest where none exists. But, as has been the case ever since the cycle was invented, the great majority of children rate the possession of a bike highly, and if a suitable one can be provided the natural appeal of easy riding will do more than anything else to encourage liking for the pastime and to develop a responsible attitude.

It follows that the choice of a cycle for a child is an important decision. The producers of bicycles in quantity tend to direct their appeal to the competitive and daredevil spirit in their endeavours to obtain a mass market, hence the current ubiquity of the 'BMX' or 'bicycle moto-cross' bikes. They can certainly claim to be sturdily built — they have to be — but they are machines which are very basic and do not pretend to be good for much more than the hard treatment which BMX inflicts.

Yet it must be said that these cycles are reasonably priced, do not *have* to be thrown around BMX-fashion, and are perfectly all right for learning to ride and for short local outings.

But if it becomes clear that a youngster is beginning to see just how much potential for exploration and enjoyment a bicycle has, a more conventional machine is essential for that potential to be realised.

Here is where a visit to a knowledgeable dealer will pay handsome dividends. There are a few 'diamond-framed' cycles made in junior sizes but the majority of cycles are now the small-wheel variety — that is to say, with 14-inch to 18-inch diameter wheels and a main frame relying on a heavy, large-diameter steel tube, as against the 20-inch and upwards wheels of the traditional lightweight steel frame.

The models in production are changed from time to time and it is therefore not useful to quote specific types of cycle, but there is always a wide range of 'off the peg' machines on offer. It is even less possible to quote prices as they so soon get out of date, but the cost of cycles has not risen any more than prices generally and good ones for children are not too expensive considering their durability and usefulness.

If a young person has the cycling 'bug' it will be pursued whatever the bike available. But there is much to be said for discreet encouragement of such a beneficial activity and a good machine will do most in this direction. For the not-so-sure youngster, on the other hand, the quality and suitability of the bicycle may well be the deciding factor.

WHERE TO BUY YOUR CYCLE

The choice of dealer is important when buying a bicycle. Find one who will make sure the machine is properly adjusted and roadworthy before you leave the shop, and who can offer after-sales service. A member of the Association of Cycle Traders has an interest in upholding the reputation of the trade for good service. It is worth finding a dealer who is a member even if it means shopping a little further afield.

Mail order companies cannot give you

A picnic in the forest, easily reached by bike.

the attention you need and shops for whom the sale of cycles is a sideline are unlikely to have the facilities to do so. A specialist dealer may well be a practising rider himself; at any rate he will have a knowledgeable and wide clientele to keep him on his toes and up-to-date. He will thus be able to advise you on all aspects of the machine suitable for you.

CHECKING OVER YOUR NEW MACHINE

Here is a list of checks which should be made on a new cycle. Any failures to comply should be rectified before the purchase is completed.

Brakes: Front — wheel the cycle a few steps at walking pace and apply the brake smartly. The stop should be immediate, and the back wheel may tend to jump from the ground — it won't happen when you're riding! Rear — same procedure. The rear wheel should lock. Both — levers should move only about ¼ inch when making these tests. Both brake blocks in each pair should reach the rim simultaneously.

Wheels: Check for truth. Lift the wheels clear of the ground one at a time and spin them by hand. The rim should remain at exactly the same distance from the brake blocks throughout the revolution, and there should be no up-and-down movement of the rim in relation to the brake blocks.

Tyres: Inspect for blemishes or distortion.

Bottom bracket: It's not really at the bottom, and it's not really a bracket, but this is the name given to the cylindrical housing where the seat and down tubes of the cycle frame meet. In it and protrud-ing from each side is the heavy axle which runs on internal bearings and to which, on the outside, the cranks and pedals are fitted. There should be no play in the cranks. Grip both at once and make sure there is no movement from side to side. Cranks should spin backwards freely.

Headset: The assembly of bolts in the short front tube of the cycle which carries the handlebar stem and which receives the front fork tube at its lower end. There should be no looseness. With the cycle stationary, apply the front brake hard and push the machine to and fro against the brake. Any play in the headset will cause the frame to judder. This means that the headset requires tightening.

Pedals: Should spin freely, but there should be no side play.

Frame: Check that it is not distorted. Get someone to hold the cycle straight and upright while you walk back a few feet from it to make sure the front and rear wheels are dead in line. The only other quick test is to ride the cycle, releasing your hold on the handlebars until you are only just touching them with the tips of your fingers. If the bars tend to turn one way or the other, the frame is out of truth. There is not always an opportunity to make this test, but do so if you can. The only remedy for a faulty frame is another, good, frame!

Gears: The gear cannot be changed unless the pedals are turned. The only way to check it on a stationary cycle is to suspend the machine (the dealer should have a suit-able stand or suspension) and, whilst turning the pedals with one hand, run through the gears with the other. They should engage smoothly, rapidly and without undue noise.

Chain: Tension should be such that the up-and-down play, both top and bottom, with the cycle at rest, should be between ½ inch and one inch.

General: Check that mudguards are fitted symmetrically and do not foul the tyres at any point. Check lamps if they are included. Check that the wheel locknuts are tight. Grip the cycle at the centre of the handlebars and saddle and 'bounce' it gently. Any loose nuts or fittings will make themselves heard.

Second-hand cycles: There is a booming market in these, and while many are offered in good faith a word of caution is necessary. It is wise to ask the vendor why the cycle is being disposed of, and to make sure that it bears a genuine maker's name, and that it is stamped with a frame number. The high incidence of cycle theft makes such precautions necessary. Do not buy unless you are satisfied that all is well.

In addition to the checks for a new cycle, pay special attention to the frame of a used one. Inspect it for dents. Be suspicious if the frame has been repainted, perhaps to cover rust, cracks or twists. Cracking or peeling paint is a sign of these things also. Make sure the forks are not damaged.

Remember that you have no legal consumer's rights protection in a *private* deal of this kind, as you have with a trader.

The AM7 Moulton cycle with seven gears and dropped handlebars.

THE MOULTON CYCLE

Almost all that has been said applies to all kinds of cycle. For 'serious' riding (as opposed to simply local or occasional riding) the conventional diamond frame remains the popular choice, because the small-wheel cycles (with one exception) are of heavier and somewhat clumsy construction so that although they are much used for shopping and short trips, they are not suitable for longer recreational rides and touring.

The one exception to this is the Moulton cycle, which was the original small-wheel machine and which is based upon a sound engineering design. The distinguished engineer and inventor, Dr Alex Moulton CBE, introduced the machine as a result of his own design and development work in the 1960s. Several models of the cycle bearing his name were manufactured, with progressively improved features. Common to all of them were front and rear suspension systems which gave a smooth, steady and pleasant ride.

Dr Moulton's initiative had the effect of stimulating cycle manufacturers in general to enter the small-wheel market, but with basic cycles of heavy construction and lacking refinement. However, as down-to-earth, down-to-a-price bikes for general local use they were and are practical and reliable.

In 1983 Dr Moulton launched his 'Advanced Engineering Bicycle', which like the earlier models is the result of his extensive personal research and development work. (Dr Moulton is himself a keen cyclist of many years' experience.) This latest advance in bicycle technology is produced in Dr Moulton's own workshop. It is a machine for the connoisseur, which has refined suspension front and rear and can be quickly split into two parts for carriage by rail, car boot, air, etc.

The entirely new concept of a lightweight but immensely strong multi-tubular frame with excellent luggage-carrying provision and comfort and ease of propulsion make the new Moulton a most welcome progression in bicycle engineering which had been virtually static until the arrival on the scene of these Moulton machines. There are two standard modern Moultons, the AM2, a two-speed flat handlebar version primarily for town riding, and the AM7, which has seven gears and dropped handlebars — ideal for the longer distance rider and tourist.

GETTING THE FAMILY STARTED

The art of riding a bicycle is rapidly learned by almost all children; a few 'rides' with an adult holding on to the saddle, or with stabilisers for the very young, will quickly result in mastery of balance and steering. And, like so many things we learn in childhood, riding a bicycle is never forgotten.

First rides should be on private ground or on quiet roads and under a parent's eyes. It is best of course if parents ride with their children. The age at which children are allowed to ride will depend upon the parent's assessment of their ability but there is much to be said for an early start so that the idea of being a moving item in traffic is more easily acquired. This will stand them in good stead in later years.

At nine years old young riders can enter for the national cycling proficiency test, which is run and supervised by the Royal Society for the Prevention of Accidents and operated by many schools and local authorities. Most of the participants enjoy the training and succeed in passing the test and receiving a certificate of cycling proficiency.

RoSPA has recently been instrumental in launching the 'National Bike Club' in association with the British Cycling Federation. It is hoped that many recruits to the NBC will come from Proficiency Test entrants, as well as from young cyclists in general, as the club has been primarily formed with the object of enabling them to get together to share the fun of cycling.

The Cyclists Touring Club has local sections in many areas of the country and many of these have family groups who arrange rides, holidays and other activities specially for parents cycling with children. If you join one of these groups you will quickly be initiated into cycle touring, as you will be able to share the experience of families with a great deal of acquired knowledge of holiday tours and weekending. You will soon learn what you need to take with you and how to pack it in your cycle bags, how to avoid the traffic and what roads and places are specially enjoyable.

You'll find that it is quite possible to cater for the individual fancies of your children, to carry those little bits and pieces without which they perhaps cannot imagine leaving home, and to provide whatever refreshment they will need. One of the special advantages of cycling is that you can stop at will — just to stare maybe, have a quick snack or take a breather.

Most children will enjoy cycling for its own sake but there is an added pleasure if you can devise an objective for the ride. Older children may like to visit an old castle perhaps but younger ones will probably be quite happy to follow a riverside or find a particularly good tree to climb or hillside to roll down! Start with short rides and you will soon discover how far the children (and you) like to go. Don't overdo it — that can be most off-putting. Stop while everyone wishes there were more to come.

Some parents take their children cycling at a very early age — sometimes at just a few weeks old! Pre-walking age children can be safely carried in 'kiddie-seats' which usually fit over the rear wheel so that the baby is close behind the parent on the cycle (or parents on the tandem, to which machine a kiddie-seat attaches equally well). The child seat which fits over the cycle top tube (conventional cycle

A tandem tricycle with touring and camping kit, an unusual but effective family outfit.

only) nesting the child between the arms of the rider is really only good for very short rides. A particularly popular method of conveying children is by means of a 'Rann' trailer — rather like a lightweight sidecar but towed behind the cycle/tandem to which it is attached by a bar and ball joint under the saddle. These are not made at present so there is a brisk market in second-hand models. The CTC can provide members with detailed information about methods of carrying small children by cycle as one of its many services.

When travelling as a family remember to keep any young children between the parents, and to ride in single file. Also, don't stick too close together; it is safer, and better for other traffic, if you are spaced out.

A family outing with child carriers and front wheel panniers.

LOADING YOUR BIKE

Even for a day outing it is wise to carry some spare clothing and perhaps some food and drink. It is good to have that feeling of complete independence, to know that if food is not available along the road there is no need to worry. And there is always the camera and other small personal items to be taken along.

When you get to the stage of weekends away, or full-length holidays awheel, more carrying capacity will be needed. Packing cycle bags is an art but one that is quickly learned and it is amazing how much can be stowed in them. The solo rider is not overburdened and can carry all his needs quite well, and if you are going with family or friends the heavier items like tools and spares can be shared out.

For general use the saddlebag is favourite. Saddlebags come in various sizes but they are all light in weight so it pays to get a fairly large one which can be used for varying circumstances. Pannier bags for front or rear (mounted by means of specially fitted racks on the bike) are commonly used for longer trips, usually in addition to the saddlebag.

Handlebar bags, again using a special attachment to the bars for support, are small but extremely useful for carrying the oddments almost certain to be required on the road — maps, camera, chocolate, sunglasses, and so on.

But you should never need to use all kinds of bag at once — it is very easy to pack too much, and after a few rides you will find out just how much and how little is needed. It will be far less than you imagined! Think very hard about taking again any article which is carried a couple of times but not used.

And remember that it is a cardinal rule that nothing, but nothing, should ever be carried by a cyclist on his or her back. It is not only uncomfortable and annoying to do so: it also interferes with control of the machine.

WHAT TO WEAR

In this country we do not have a climate, just weather, and we soon learn to dress according to the temperature and not the calendar. Extremes of temperature do not affect the cyclist quite so much as others; when it is cold the exercise soon gets the circulation going, and creates a warm glow, and when it is warm the movement creates a gentle breeze which prevents overheating (it is warmer when you stop).

The general rule for cycling clothing is to wear loose layers, the number of garments depending on the temperature and one's own susceptibility to cold or heat. In summer a single upper garment will often suffice; at other times up to four may be required. They should fit loosely over one another to allow layers of air in between, on the eiderdown principle.

In cold or windy conditions the top layer is ideally a lightweight windproof jacket. Wear gloves when you need them. Always carry a spare pullover or jersey in case it turns colder than you expect. Stop and don it if you feel cold — and stop and remove a layer if, as you may well find, you get warmer than you thought you would.

Most leisure wear is suitable for cycling in, but special cycling clothing (for the development of which the racing fraternity are to be thanked) takes the form of tight-fitting track suit bottoms and shorts, track tops, vests and shirts with rear pockets if required, and specially designed light, flexible shoes.

The tight trousers ensure that they won't get caught up in the chain, and they are also warm and comfortable; the shorts usually have a chamois leather seat insert which thoughtfully aids comfort where one comes into close and constant contact with the saddle.

Pockets at the back of vests or shirts are very practical as there aren't many pockets anywhere else in cycling gear. There may be a small one in track suit bottoms; another in the top or a breast pocket in the conventional sports shirt is about the limit.

Anything carried in the pockets of touring or sports shorts is uncomfortable and chafes the leg; racing cycling shorts are close-fitting and without pockets and are the best for touring too. Note that cycling clothing is unobtainable at ordinary sports shops. It can be obtained only from specialist cycle dealers who have a clothing section or through mail order (see the column of the cycling periodicals).

Don't ever worry about 'what people think'. Dress for your own comfort and for the activity you follow, and if people think anything at all they will be envious thoughts!

The ideal rainwear for cycling has yet to be invented, but the traditional cape is a very effective garment. It should be of ample size so that it covers the hands on the handlebars and drapes a little below knee level at the sides, and below the saddle at the back. It will give some protection to the saddlebag but occasionally when it is wet *and* windy you can sit on the tail of the cape to anchor it down!

With the continual improvement of lightweight waterproof materials and design the increasingly popular alternative is a jacket and overtrousers, which are less cumbersome and hot to wear. There may be a little dampness inside from condensation, depending upon the amount of body heat being generated, but the latest materials reduce this risk to a minimum.

Jackets with hoods attached are rarely suitable for cycling as the hood does not turn with the head and vision is very restricted — all that can be seen is the inside of the hood and not the state of the road or the countryside.

Also specially for cyclists there are waterproof 'spattees' or abbreviated leggings which cover the front of the legs and shoes (useful for keeping the feet warm in cold weather as well as when it is wet),

peaked cloth caps, woollen bobble hats and even fur-lined cycling shoes. But rain looks much worse through the window than it does when you're out in it! It will be no deterrent once you're hooked on cycling.

GOING ON TOUR

All sorts of accommodation are used by cycle tourists. Youth hostels are the least formal kind and are as much 'do-as-you-please' as 'do-it-yourself' places now that most of the rules which were applicable for many years have been relaxed. You can arrive up to 11 p.m., there is no set time for turning in and no 'rising bell' in the morning. The programme of change includes the transformation of large dormitories into more and smaller ones, and there is video and other entertainment in many hostels.

There are a number of hostels with special accommodation for families, where you may stay for a week at a time and come and go during the day as you wish. There is an all-inclusive charge for the use of this special facility, which includes the under-fives. Where dormitory arrangements permit, those who look after hostels will often arrange for at least semi-private rooms for family groups.

The Cyclists' Touring Club, in conjunction with the Ramblers' Association, publishes an annual handbook which contains a large number of overnight accommodation addresses which have been recommended by members. They vary from simple bed-and-breakfast houses and farmhouses to hotels. The regional tourist boards publish accommodation lists for their respective areas which embrace all grades.

With the perfection of lightweight kit, cycle camping has become extremely popular, giving the ultimate in freedom of movement and — in some districts remotely populated — the possibility of touring where it otherwise might not be practicable.

I find that I can pack my tent, which has a combined groundsheet, the fly-sheet, a filled sleeping bag and a pair of trainers into a single large saddlebag and still leave room for some odds and ends. This leaves the pannier bags for clothing, cooking equipment and food. On a long tour the addition of a small handlebar bag completes the carrying capacity which is in fact a little more than it need be simply because it is so convenient to have a bit of space to spare for the occasional purchase. It also takes the hassle out of packing.

And that's for a lone camper. Things are even easier for the family camping, when things can be shared among the group.

All that has been said applies equally to continental cycle touring. There are youth hostels in some fifty other countries affiliated to the International Youth Hostel Federation, in which our own membership cards are valid without further formality. An international handbook can be purchased giving full details of youth hostels abroad.

Among the lanes and byways of Wales.

FINDING YOUR WAY

Many cycle tourists favour the National Map Series published by Bartholomew's and widely available in bookshops and stores. The scale is 1:100,000 (one centimetre = one kilometre, or about 1½ miles to an inch). Coloured contour lines show at a glance when the going will get hilly, up or down! Most minor roads and byways are shown, together with some bridleways, unsurfaced tracks which cyclists share (legally) with walkers and horse-riders.

The whole of England, Scotland and Wales is covered by 62 sheets of these maps, so a maximum of say 10 sheets will cover ambitious tours and fewer will suffice for most outings — you can get immense fun and pleasure out of simply exploring the district covered by your own local map sheet.

The most comprehensive maps are those of the Ordnance Survey which are very professional productions of high quality and great utility. The popular series is on a 1:50,000 scale meaning that four times as many sheets are needed to cover the area of one Bartholomew's map.

Unfortunately this means that sheer numbers of maps — let alone their cost — precludes their use for complete tours and most tourists have to limit themselves to OS sheets for the districts in which they are particularly interested or which for some reason they wish to explore very fully. But the amount of detail on these maps is tremendous, and makes real sense of the term 'reading' a map.

Another tip — don't take too much notice of signposts. They are almost always accurate and reliable in the lanes, but wherever there might be heavy traffic they are situated and marked to direct that traffic to the places named by the quickest, most convenient route. Perhaps this will be along a bypass and so you might miss the interesting village you planned to visit. Whenever you are in doubt, check the map. The quiet cyclist does not want to join the throng!

You can also tell roughly how far it is between places with a map — it is surprising how few signposts carry this information. Continental signposts are generally more informative in this respect. Very similar map series are published in most countries of Europe which — both the maps and the countries — are ideal for cycle tourists.

A WORD ON SAFETY

It is a great pity that some people are deterred from cycling because of a notion that it is dangerous. The bicycle is an inherently safe and inoffensive machine, offering little or no danger to its rider or to others — in fact its greater use should be actively promoted.

Based on the traditional insurers' method of assessing risk (i.e. the time exposed to it), the cyclist's chance of being involved in an accident is much the same as that of a motorist, and it is significant that so slight is the risk of third-party claims against cyclists, and hence so low the cost of such insurance cover, that the national cycling organisations include third-party insurance cover as a benefit of membership at no extra cost.

Most accidents occur where there is a lot of traffic and the cycle tourist quickly becomes adept at finding the quiet ways which are there in profusion and which are so much more pleasant than busy ones. The cyclist has the great advantage that his vision and hearing are completely un-

hampered and cycling clothing is often brightly coloured to make the wearer conspicuous on the road. And there are various garments, belts and reflective attachments on the market aimed at enhancing the visibility of cyclists. It is a wise rule never to wear anything which restricts movement or feels uncomfortable, or which induces an unjustified sense of security.

Another matter for personal judgement is the wearing of a helmet. The Royal Society for the Prevention of Accidents feels that the wearing of helmets results in certain disadvantages: restrictions on head movement and hearing, and over-heating. They do not promote the use of helmets, nor does the Department of

Touring abroad, looking at the Great Canyon of the Verdon river, Provence, southern France.

Transport. They judge the number of accidents to cyclists in which a helmet would save life or prevent serious injury as too small to justify their adoption.

TRANSPORTING YOUR CYCLE

Of course, it isn't always feasible to cycle all the way to and from the area in which you are going to have a cycling holiday. Taking the cycles on a car roof-rack and the family inside is a popular way of solving the problem but it has one drawback: the tour has to end where it began, back at the car. A circular tour is sometimes appropriate but not always the ideal plan.

Cycles are still taken free of charge (accompanied) by British Rail on most of its services even though there are a number of exceptions: cycles are not carried at certain times on some routes and on others there is a charge at certain times or a need to pre-book the space on the train. There is a leaflet obtainable from British Rail which gives all the details; it is not as complicated as it sounds and rail is a fast and usually efficient way of getting around.

A nominal charge is made for accompanied cycles on inland air services. The cycle is part of the passenger's 44-lb free baggage allowance on scheduled European flights and, as a saddlebag forms the free hand luggage element of one's kit, it may be possible to keep within the limit and incur no excess charge for overweight luggage.

It is as well to notify the wish to take cycles by air especially if there is more than one cycle involved and there may be space problems in the baggage hold. You may well be asked to turn the handlebars parallel with the frame, to turn the pedals inwards and to wrap the chain, in deference to other baggage being carried.

A FEW LAST TIPS

There are two major cycling organisations in Britain. The Cyclists' Touring Club is concerned solely with recreational and leisure cycling, while the British Cycling Federation, although it has a private members' section, is essentially a federation of clubs who are mainly interested in competitive cycling.

Both offer similar benefits to members.

The CTC has many local sections up and down the country, each with social and riding programmes throughout the year which have been tailored for the various kinds of tourist — typical section names are 'Loiterers', 'Hardriders', 'Saturday Afternoon', and 'Family Section'. Members receive a handsome illustrated magazine by post every two months. There is a touring bureau from which information about cycling all over the world may be obtained as well as useful papers on cycle purchase, maintenance and spares, and on the results of trials of various pieces of equipment.

Each summer there is a wide selection of group holiday tours to choose from. These are organised to many areas in this country and abroad by members acting under the auspices of the CTC or by the club office itself.

There is also a legal aid service for members who may be involved in a mishap — with another road user, through a bad road surface or for any other reason.

Both the CTC and the BCF include world-wide third-party insurance up to £500,000 in the membership fee, and both of them have retail departments from which maps, cycling books, etc., may be bought.

The BCF touring service is similar to that of the CTC, but the tours take the form of a large number of standard routes which can be easily followed at any time.

The CTC handbook includes full information about the club, its services and local officials, together with a lot of useful touring information and a long list of accommodation addresses. The BCF annual handbook also includes accommodation addresses and other touring information, but it is mainly concerned with the annual programme of track and road racing for which sports it is the governing body in this country.

Members of both organisations will be very glad to see you and there will be a warm welcome whenever you make contact with them. Especially, there will be a readiness to help and advise in any way and to assist newcomers to cycle touring or those returning to it after a spell away.

You see, cycling is not only a thoroughly good and enjoyable thing to do; it also brings many and lasting friendships. Do come in.

USEFUL ADDRESSES

National Bike Club and British Cycling Federation, 16 Upper Woburn Place, London WC1H 0QP.

Cyclists' Touring Club, 69 Meadrow, Godalming, Surrey GU7 3HS.

English Schools Cycling Association, 31 Trafford Road, Norwich, Norfolk.

English Tourist Board, 4 Grosvenor Gardens, London SW1.

Association of Cycle Traders, 31A High Street, Tunbridge Wells, Kent TN1 1XN.

YHA Adventure Shop (equipment, books, bikes, etc.), 14 Southampton Street, London WC2E 7HY (branches in Manchester, Birmingham, and Cardiff).

PUBLICATIONS

BOOKS

As well as Peter Knottley's *Cycle Touring in Britain and the Rest of Europe*, the editors recommend:

Bicycle Touring in Europe Karen and Gary Hawkins (Sidgwick and Jackson).

England by Bicycle Frederick Alderson (David and Charles).

Skilful Cycling (Royal Society for the Prevention of Accidents, Royal Oak Centre, Brighton Road, Purley, Surrey CR2 2UR). Especially for children.

Richard's Bicycle Book Richard Ballantyne (Richard Clay).

All About Bikes and Bicycling Max Alth (Bailey Brothers and Swinfern).

Ramblers' and Cyclists' Bed and Breakfast Guide (Cyclists' Touring Club).

MAGAZINES

Cycletouring Journal of the Cyclists' Touring Club published every two months. Sent free to members and available to non-members on annual postal subscription.

Cycling published every Wednesday from newsagents or on postal subscription from I.P.C. Specialist and Professional Press Ltd., Surrey House, Sutton, Surrey SM1 4QQ.

Relaxing outside the family annexe at Hindhead Youth Hostel, Surrey.

Youth Hostelling

PETER KNOTTLEY

Forget any ideas that youth hostels are spartan places where you wash in cold water and light your way to bed with an oil lamp! There are now grades of hostels to suit everyone and special facilities for families. Hostels provide so much more than accommodation. You will enjoy their bright informal atmosphere and the companionship they continue to offer to all travellers.

Youth hostels are ideal whether you want a leisurely family holiday, overnight stops on a tour or accommodation from which your family can pursue hobbies and interests. There are no age limits to membership of the Youth Hostels Association. Children under nine must be accompanied by a parent/guardian/responsible person of the same sex, and under-12s by adults, but from then on they may go 'hostelling' alone or with friends, leaving parents in the knowledge that at night they are in a homely and secure environment.

The YHA makes a special effort to attract families with children under five years old by providing annexes or other self-contained family accommodation at an increasing number of hostels. These can be booked for a week at a time and occupants can come and go as they please during the day. The inclusive charge is very moderate, like all the others which the YHA makes for its services.

In addition to those hostels with rooms specially for families, there are many others which can occasionally accommodate families in small dormitories when they are not required for general use.

GRADES OF HOSTEL

Most hostels these days are very sophisticated and are graded according to the standard of facilities they provide. Those with central heating and all mod. cons., which can include a laundry room for members' use, are 'superior' grade. The charges at these hostels are naturally higher than those at the 'standard' grade where fewer facilities are provided. The lowest charges are at the 'simple' grade hostels which are generally in the heart of the countryside and are of the basic type that flourished in the early days of the youth hostelling movement over half a century ago. However, simplicity does not mean primitiveness. Like many dwellings in quiet places they remain untouched by some of the elaborations of modern living. These hostels sometimes make it possible to visit regions where no other accommodation is available and are a good choice if you feel like a real break from routine and stress.

Historic cities and towns, and places on the tourist routes generally have 'standard' or 'superior' grade hostels. A few very popular centres, such as London, and Ambleside in the Lake District, have 'special' grade hostels which means you can gain access during the day to leave luggage and book beds. Generally, hostels are closed between 10 a.m. and 5 p.m.

BECOMING A MEMBER

Membership fees are modest. The lowest fees are for the under-16s. Between 16 and 20 you pay a little more, and more still if you are over 20. The membership year ends on 31 December, but if you join or renew your membership on or after 1 October you receive a card which is valid until 31 December of the following year. You can try hostelling without becoming a full member by simply asking for a 'guest pass' on arrival at a hostel. The pass can be used for two nights and costs about one-third of the membership fee (hostel charges have to be paid as usual of course). There is no limit to the number of these passes you may have and since they can be put towards the cost of membership it makes sense to obtain a full membership card in this way.

The best bargain is reserved for families. Children between five and 15 are enrolled free when both parents enrol (or the parent in the case of one-parent families). Where children under five can be accommodated no membership formalities are required for them.

Members receive a copy of the annual handbook listing all the hostels in England and Wales and giving a great deal of other information about the YHA. They also receive a quarterly copy of *Hostelling News* through the post.

AT THE HOSTEL

One of the major charms of hostelling is the variety of buildings you will find used as hostels. I have stayed in a rectory, an oast house, a Norman castle, several manor houses, school houses in villages, shops, and a variety of mansions and town houses — all converted to give the basic services common to all hostels whatever their grading.

Routine in all hostels is friendly and soon becomes familiar. You sign the housebook on arrival and surrender your Youth Hosteller's card to the warden until you depart. You will be allocated a bed and it is a good idea to make it up as soon as you can. Then the hostel is your home. Depending on usage and the area served by the hostel, there will be entertainment (games, TV, perhaps video games — this sort of thing is the subject of a development programme). There will also be a hostel shop where you can buy packet food and drinks, and often handbooks, guides, stationery, and those items which one always seems somehow to forget, like soap or a pen.

Pen y Pass Youth Hostel, ideally situated for walking and climbing in the Snowdon group.

At many hostels full evening meals and breakfast are served for those who have ordered them in advance and as the cafeteria arrangement is gaining popularity you may find light meals available during quite long periods.

At almost all hostels there is a kitchen, fully equipped for those who like to cater for themselves, which does give more flexibility over mealtimes and perhaps a wider choice of food.

Gone are the days when lights out was at 10.30 p.m. The time now is nearer 11.30 and there is no longer a rising bell to wake you in the morning. But as most hostels do close during the day, it is necessary to plan to leave by 10 a.m.

Time was when youth hostels in this country were only for those going under

Setting out to walk up Snowdon by the Pig Track which begins at Pen y Pass.

their own steam, but this rule has long since been abandoned and all comers are now welcome. Cyclists have no parking problems — secure covered accommodation for cycles is the norm — and whenever possible the hostels provide free parking for cars. When this is not possible hostel users must be responsible for their own vehicles.

However, the YHA still firmly believes in fostering outdoor activities. In areas where walking, climbing and similar pursuits are popular, hostels have local information about routes, a weather service, and helpful leaflets and hints to help hostellers to enjoy these pursuits in safety.

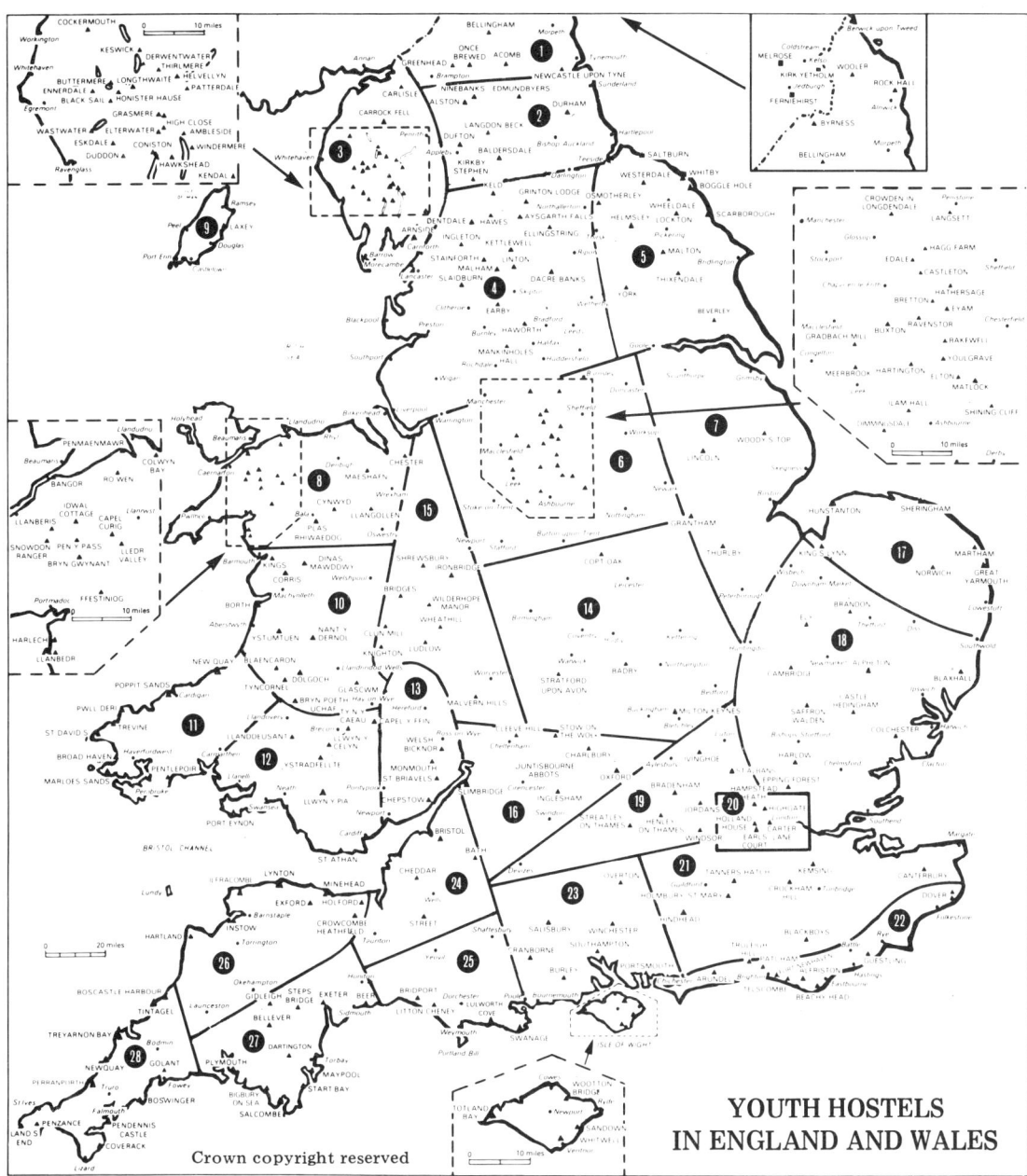

Crown copyright reserved

**YOUTH HOSTELS
IN ENGLAND AND WALES**

KEY

1 Northumbria and Roman Wall, 2 North Pennines, 3 Lake District, 4 Yorkshire Dales, 5 Yorkshire Coast, Moors and Wolds, 6 Peak District, 7 Lincolnshire, 8 North Wales, 9 Isle of Man, 10 Mid Wales, 11 West Wales, 12 Brecon Beacons and South Wales, 13 Wye Valley and Forest of Dean, 14 Central England, 15 Shropshire Hills and Malvern Hills, 16 Cotswolds, 17 Norfolk Coast and Broads, 18 East Anglia, 19 Chiltern Hills and Thames, 20 London, 21 North Downs Way and Weald, 22 South Coast, 23 New Forest and Isle of Wight, 24 Avon and Mendips, 25 Dorset Coast, 26 North Devon, Exmoor and Quantocks, 27 South Devon and Dartmoor, 28 Cornwall.

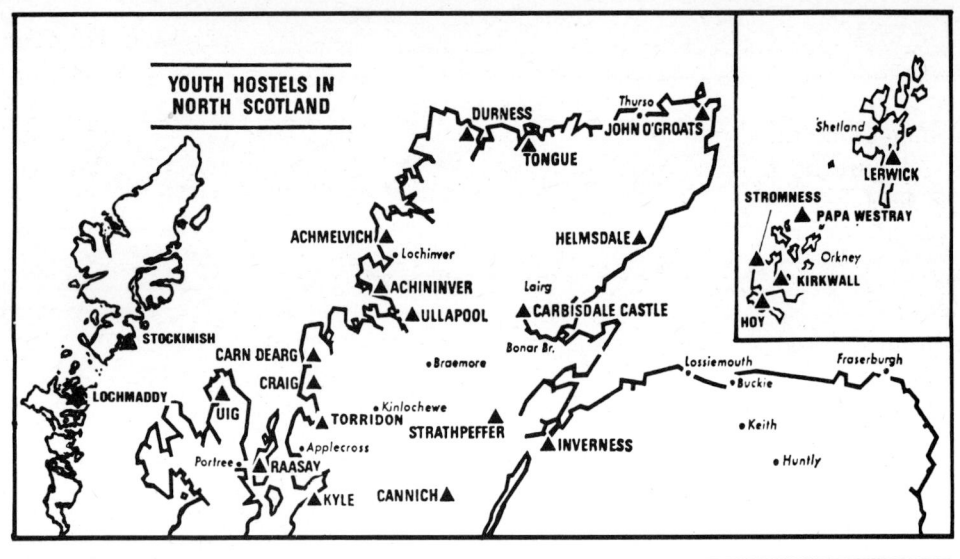

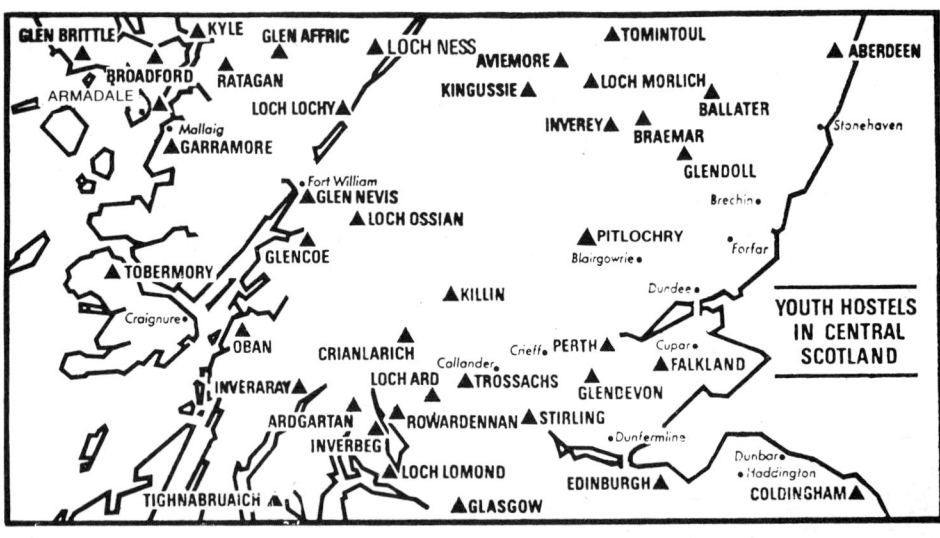

An increasing number of hostels offer cycles for hire at a modest daily charge and the hostel will usually be able to give you details of interesting quiet routes nearby, perhaps between that hostel and the next, although normally a cycle has to be returned to the hostel from which it was hired.

'YHA ready routes' are all-in package weeks with overnight bookings made. Full details about the places visited on each route are supplied. Tours available include walking weeks in Yorkshire, Lakeland, Devon, the area crossed by the Roman Wall in Northumbria, a car tour of National Trust properties in Devon, guided pony

Relaxing in the sitting room, Pen y Pass.

trekking in Lakeland, and cycling in the Cotswolds, East Anglia, the South Downs, and Snowdonia in North Wales. There is a brochure published annually covering all these, obtainable from YHA offices and shops.

OTHER FACETS OF THE YHA

Although the main aim of the YHA is to help everyone to enjoy and care for the countryside while travelling through it, and the hostels are obviously the prime way in which it achieves that aim, it has other associated activities directed towards the same objective.

The YHA operates retail stores in London, Manchester, Birmingham, and Cardiff at which an extensive range of equipment for all outdoor activities can be purchased, including walking, cycling, climbing, skiing, and canoeing, and help on selection given by practising experts. There is a comprehensive travel agency. Every year a programme of package holidays is offered, each with an experienced leader. The holidays cover a very wide range of activities, not all energetic. For example, they include photography, brass rubbing, and bird watching. Some holidays are carefully planned to suit the needs of particular age groups. All are inexpensive and thoroughly good value.

Leaflets about all YHA activities are obtainable from the National Office at St. Albans. Members of the Association receive all the latest news in their quarterly copy of *Hostelling News*.

YHA members meet socially in many centres up and down the country, having formed local groups. Meetings are usually weekly and apart from entertainment hostellers can discuss their plans for weekends and holidays. Local groups are spontaneous affairs which have sprung up on a do-it-yourself basis and are run by members for members. So, indeed, is the Association itself, for it is governed by national and regional councils and committees to which every member is eligible for election.

The hostelling movement is world-wide. In this chapter I have described the facilities offered by the YHA of England and Wales. There are separate associations for Scotland, Northern Ireland, and the Republic of Ireland, where routine is very much the same.

There are some fifty countries overseas (in all continents) which have Youth Hostels Associations affiliated to the International Youth Hostels Federation. In all these hostels your home membership card is valid provided you insert a passport-type photograph of yourself. So membership of the YHA is not only the key to immense pleasure and fun in this country, but also the means of unlocking treasures abroad. Everywhere you will find the main characteristics of hostelling: informality and friendliness coupled with a lack of pressure and a general air of good humour. There cannot be many places where such a splendid combination can be found.

FAMILY ACCOMMODATION

ENGLAND AND WALES

Many hostels can offer dormitory accommodation on occasion to families, but the following hostels provide separate annexes for families with children under five:

Ninebanks, Osmotherley, Buttermere, Kirkby Stephen, Earby, Ellingstring, Malton, Stainforth, Langsett, Ravenstor, Bryn gwy Nant, Cynwyd, Broad

Haven, Corris, Knighton, New Quay, Poppit Sands, St. Davids, Welshbicknor, Bradenham, Hindhead, Boswinger.

SCOTLAND

Family rooms are available in the following hostels:

Ardgartan, Aberdeen, Aviemore, Ayr, Carbisdale, Cannich, Garramore, Glendoll, Kirkwall, Kirk Yetholm, Loch Ness, Lochranza, Perth, Rowardennan, Stirling, Torridon, Uig.

At all other hostels family rooms may be available during quieter periods at the discretion of the warden. They are not available to families with children under five. Family accommodation for families with at least one child under five is now available at Cannich, Kirkwall, and Loch Ness Youth Hostels.

USEFUL ADDRESSES

YHA (England & Wales), Trevelyan House, St. Stephen's Hill, St. Albans, Herts. AL1 2DY.

Scottish YHA, 7 Glebe Crescent, Stirling FK8 2JA.

YHA of Northern Ireland, 56 Bradbury Place, Belfast.

An Oige (YHA of Irish Republic), 39 Mountjoy Square, Dublin 1.

YHA Shop and Travel Agency, 14 Southampton Street, London WC2E 7HY.
Branches: 166 Deansgate, Manchester M3 3FE, 90-98 Corporation Street, Birmingham B4 6XS, 131 Woodville Road, Cardiff CF2 4DZ.

trade and as a climbing instructor in Britain and the Alps, he is now concentrating on mountain writing and photography. He wrote *Scrambles in Snowdonia* (Cicerone Press) and is currently working on two other mountaineering guidebooks. He contributes a regular column to *Climber and Rambler* magazine and provides the climbing press with a photographic service.

Steve Ashton is married with two children. For the last 10 years he has lived in the Ogwen Valley in the heart of Snowdonia. He holds a degree in Mathematics and Oceanography. He began rock climbing 14 years ago after an apprenticeship of hill walking in the Lake District. He has climbed on rock and ice in most areas of Britain in addition to five seasons in the Alps.

Although he has pioneered a few first ascents in Britain and the Dolomites, and is able to lead the averagely difficult *Extremes* (the most advanced grade of climb) on a good day, he feels he is best classified as an all-rounder as he enjoys hill walking in summer and winter, scrambling, snow and ice climbing, rock climbing on outcrops and mountain crags, solo climbing, and bouldering.

Having worked in the climbing retail

Mountaineering

STEVE ASHTON

This is a very personal and exciting introduction to one of the most thrilling of all activities — mountain climbing. It is written for older members of the family, experienced perhaps in hill walking and scrambling. As they enter their teens they will demand greater challenges and mountaineering is possibly the answer. Here you will find the practical information needed and also something unique — a young climber's definition of his own response to the challenge.

YOU DON'T HAVE TO LIKE MOUNTAINS

Hill walking is generally thought to be the best apprenticeship for mountaineering. Developing an affinity for mountains is a slow process, something which can be obscured by the drama of more demanding ascents. Walking in the hills helps clarify your motives for being there. But many people, young people especially, find themselves impatient with hill walking and wish to tackle rock climbing straight away. This is understandable. Besides, rock climbing — as well as being central to mountaineering — also exists as an end in itself. In fact many of today's most accomplished climbers have no interest in big mountains at all. They can thrive solely on the powerful gymnastic and psychological challenges of outcrop walls.

Nevertheless, a love of climbing which has no foundation beyond a simple lust for steep rock is perhaps nothing more than infatuation. So what . . . when the novelty wears off simply switch to something else. But that is a shallow existence and it would be a pity to miss the more subtle aspects of the mountains. Those who are already hill walkers will be able to appreciate this sentiment; those who are not might simply accept its sincerity.

CLIMBING IS EASY

You don't need anyone to tell you how to climb. Like swimming it comes naturally: get yourself in the right medium, the right frame of mind, on the right day, and let it happen. If you have any doubts about this then take a walk in the park and watch those three-year-olds on the climbing frame. The trouble is, a large part of our youth is spend being taught *not* to climb — whether it be trees, scaffolding, furniture, or whatever. The fun of it was there all the time; it's just that, like school history, it's been bashed out of us. The fun is still there. It just needs liberating.

FALLING IS EASIER

There is always a snag. The snag with climbing is *falling*. So although no one can teach you how to climb, they *can* show you how to climb efficiently and safely. Both are prerequisites to longevity and enjoyment. Even within the anarchy of climbing there is a place for formal instruction.

It *is* possible to learn technique by yourself. It is a long and painful process. I shudder now when I remember the appalling misconceptions I held about rope method. And yet I value those formative years far more than any recent experiences. Nowadays I can climb harder routes and appear to take greater risks than during those early years. But I've learnt a lot since then. And what of any lingering misconceptions about safety? Well, I have to admit that I must still hold them to be true. No one said climbing was safe.

COMMITMENT

When you commit yourself to a climb (there must always be *some* commitment), then the climb in turn commits you to some unpleasant possible consequences; in their worst form, that you and your companions will all be killed. It happens. This aspect of the commitment is not easily assimilated. Most climbers hide the

sickly knowledge in some corner of the mind where it will do no harm. Otherwise the perpetual reminder of consequence can be totally disabling. It grips you, freezes you to immobility, makes you beyond help. It makes you scared out of your mind. I've witnessed this in others a few times and sensed it rising within myself on more than one occasion. How you deal with it is your own problem — just one more psychological barrier to surmount. But one thing is certain: you may be able to hide it, but you'll never destroy it.

There is another side to this: if you don't let yourself be overwhelmed by the fear then it can be used to advantage. It fuels action. Some of the best moments on a climb — yes, even at the time of happening — are when all is lost and you cross the fear threshold into the realm of animal instinct. Nothing to lose and everything to gain. The exhilaration can be tremendous as you fight a way out of the predicament. Of course this might not work, which is why you normally back up your commitment with a rope, a companion, an armoury of safety equipment and, hopefully, the ability to handle all three. Climbing is about risk, but it makes sense to know which risk you are about to take.

ELEMENTS OF MOUNTAINEERING

WINTER WALKING

The transition from summer to winter hill walking is gradual, insidious. Most seasoned walkers will have experienced that gut feeling when suddenly the weather and ground conditions deteriorate. Gentle

A youngster tackles 'Eliminate C', graded as 'very severe', on Dow Crag.

slopes, under ice, become treacherous slides; deep powder snow saps strength and enthusiasm; paths and landmarks are obscured; daylight fades. Life becomes a struggle. But if that transition is made knowingly — equipped, prepared, and during good snow conditions — then the rewards are immense.

Winter is not the time to introduce groups of young people or adults to the hills. Not only must the leader be extremely competent in *all* aspects of winter mountaineering, but also the party must be properly equipped and prepared for the unexpected. Young people are particularly at risk to exhaustion, especially as their equipment is almost invariably substandard.

For those with experience of summer walking and scrambling, the progression on to winter terrain is a natural one and without need of formal introduction. Nevertheless, special attention will need to be given to navigation, ice-axe braking, use of crampons, elementary ropework, judging snow and ice conditions, special equipment, and weather. If you feel uncertain about tackling any one of these subjects by yourself then find someone who is able to show you: an experienced friend or a professional guide. A formal course in winter hill craft is useful if you

Winter walking on Snowdon.

think you may later progress to more serious winter climbing, and essential if you are determined to take inexperienced people — perhaps family and friends or a youth group — into the hills during late autumn, winter or spring.

Whether joining a course or planning your own trip, preparation is crucial. Make allowances for having become unfit over the autumn; check equipment carefully, paying special attention to head-torch, compass, boots, mitts, axe, and crampons; monitor weather reports in the week leading up to your visit and obtain a local forecast the night, or preferably morning, before the walk; ask locally about ground conditions at altitude and start early to make best use of daylight and good snow.

Favourite summer walking areas (Scotland, Lake District, North Wales) also give magnificent winter walking. On the other hand, areas which in summer are less immediately dramatic (Peak District, mid-Wales, North-East, Ireland) can be totally transformed in winter and then become even more serious and demanding than their more popular counterparts. It is usually best to visit areas with which you are already familiar in summer, the winter conditions providing a new dimension and impetus. Remember though that a favourite walk could well become a much more difficult proposition, and a simple scramble perhaps turn into a fully-fledged winter climb.

Beyond those first ventures into the winter hills lies the fascinating world of winter mountaineering. Sooner or later the steeper slopes, ridge crests and gullies will exert their pull. Or perhaps the urge to extend the endurance aspect will lead towards long distance winter walking. It is within these realms that our modest hills pose challenges equal to some alpine climbs. The scope in either direction, and despite fickle British weather, is tremendous.

Mountains in winter are unforgiving. And yet under snow and ice they are incomparably beautiful and inspiring. The finest memories are of winter days: why deny them?

SCRAMBLING

Just as walking in winter adds another dimension to familiar hills, then so can rock scrambling in summer. Even in its simplest form it can open up some wild and dramatic scenery hitherto denied the walker. A traditional definition of scrambling is that hands are also needed for the ascent, but in practice the division between walking and scrambling is slight and variable. My own working definition is that a dangerous fall when walking is unlikely, whereas when scrambling it is a certainty unless prevented. Scrambling is always a serious proposition. It is also extremely satisfying and exhilarating.

Most walkers will have encountered a section of scrambling at some time or other. Many of the classic 'walks' such as Striding Edge, the Aonach Eagach Ridge, and the Snowdon Horseshoe involve some exposed scrambling where a slip has serious consequences. The ability to enjoy these situations is as much to do with mental approach as with physical agility or any inherent quality of the scramble. Some people will always feel nervous and uneasy about tackling these routes. There is no sure way of finding this out beforehand, although practice scrambling on pathside boulders can help develop an affinity for rock, which is half the battle.

Children are the most agile scramblers. Naturally more athletic, they are also less inhibited by caution. Watch them like a hawk! And it is no use shouting advice from the path while they scramble over some direct rocky alternative. You need to be up there with them, one step ahead, and — if there is the remotest chance of a slip — using a rope. If elementary rope technique is beyond your experience then hire a guide for a day and ask specifically to be shown how to use a rope to protect a scramble. The guide will also be able to advise on the best type and length of rope for your needs. Children love scrambling and it is unfair to prevent them from doing it; but no matter how adept they become, the ultimate responsibility for their safety is yours. A sobering thought.

Many people will see scrambling as a stepping stone towards the classic ridge

Scrambling, crossing the Knife Edge on Crib Goch, the most famous scramble in Britain.

walks or towards rock climbing. But scrambling can also be an end in itself, a kind of subsport within mountaineering as a whole. In its most advanced form this involves trying to move safely over potentially very dangerous and perhaps previously unclimbed terrain. Though very serious in this form it comes closer to pioneering than the more refined art of rock climbing. To participate you need only a love of rock and remote places, and an urge to see what lies around the next corner.

ROCK CLIMBING

Rock climbing is central to the art of mountaineering. It is a natural and perhaps instinctive thing to do. Anyone can rock climb and age is also less restrictive than might be supposed. Some rock climbers are leading routes of extreme difficulty by the age of 13 or 14. Others are still leading *Extremes* in their fifties. Just recently a member of the Rucksack Club climbed Grooved Arete — a classic rock climb on Tryfan in North Wales — to celebrate his eightieth birthday. There is simply no blueprint for a rock climber beyond that affinity with steep places.

Unlike scrambling and winter walking, rock climbing needs to be demonstrated to the beginner. Moving over rock is natural enough, but rope technique — even at a basic level — is very involved. To simply buy the equipment and go out to teach yourself is suicidal. Ask a friend who already climbs to take you out; failing that, join a climbing club that encourages beginners. Personally I would not advise a formal course of instruction as your initiation to rock climbing. There are two reasons for this. First, it is worth finding out beforehand if you like it before committing yourself to a possibly expensive and perhaps miserable holiday (all climbing courses make considerable mental and physical demands on their participants). Second, although courses are useful for obtaining technique which can then be applied to your own climbing, the environment and atmosphere both on and off the climbs is contrived and so cannot be compared with that generated by a group of friends.

Rock climbing is geographically much more available than other facets of mountaineering. Besides the main centres, outcrops of thirty or forty feet are found in most areas of the country and can offer equally absorbing climbing. Many climbers

Hard rock climbing at The Roaches, a gritstone outcrop in North Staffordshire.

keep fit during winter by training on anything vaguely rock-like they can find: stone buildings, bridge supports, house walls, are all used to develop and retain finger strength and balance. More recently, purpose-made climbing walls in sports centres have supplanted these makeshift gymnasiums. Though useful as a training aid it would be a mistake to begin climbing on an artificial wall. Not only are they designed to represent quite difficult climbs, but also the *feel* is so divorced from real outcrops and mountain rock that they will leave an entirely false impression of the sport.

Once you have acquired the basic techniques and equipment through the combined help of friends, clubs, and perhaps professional instructors, the scope for developing your experience is unlimited. Gaining experience is a slow (and infinite) process, and one not to be rushed. Some people will find a slot within a climbing club (there being great advantages in shared transport and a large pool of potential climbing partners); others will form a lasting climbing partnership with one person. A mastery of rock climbing is thoroughly rewarding in itself. It is also a prerequisite for advanced mountaineering. And in that realm lies the totality of mountain rock climbs, winter climbing, and alpinism.

ALLIED INTERESTS

Mountaineers are recruited from all sections of society, each bringing his own particular skill and outlook to enrich the group. A structure totally devoid of class division means that there has always been a free interchange of ideas within mountaineering. Owing to this ready assimilation of ideas

and philosophies, it is not unusual for mountaineers to develop an outside interest within the context of the sport. Geology, art, botany, geography, literature, photography, philosophy, ornithology, and history, are all obvious examples. There are numerous formal outlets for these interests, including club talks and slide shows, and publication in club journals and national magazines. Many people find that this allied interest gives added impetus to visit mountain areas which otherwise they might have missed. And if nothing else, a secondary interest gives you something other than climbing to talk about during those long, cold hours of sleepless bivouacs!

Above: This steep limestone outcrop in Clwyd offers opportunities for graphic photography.
Right: Rock climbing on Milestone Buttress, Snowdonia

ADVANCED MOUNTAINEERING

Without wishing to tie the connection too securely, those elements of mountaineering titled **Winter Walking** and **Scrambling** become, in their advanced form, **Winter Climbing** and **Alpinism**; whereas **Rock Climbing** simply becomes **Hard Rock Climbing**. The connections remain loose because, unlike say a golf handicap, there is no accepted progression in mountaineering achievement. The score does not matter.

WINTER CLIMBING

The difference between winter walking and climbing is that the slopes are steeper, ice is sought not shunned, and difficulties are relished rather than circumvented. Now, axe and crampons are not used merely to make an ascent safer; instead they become extensions to your hands and feet. Clumsy they may be, but without them your handicap is total.

In time a rhythm develops whereby your progress up an icefall or steep snow gully is secure and inevitable — axe picks biting deep at alternate strokes and feet scuttling behind on their crab claws. At first this is all very thrilling; in time it would become boring if it were not for the treacherous nature of cliffs in winter. Most gullies never quite fill up completely with drifting snow. There is always a rock barrier, or ice chute, or exit cornice which has to be tunnelled. Add to this the unlimited diversity of snow structure and winter weather conditions, and any suggestion of repetition evaporates.

I regret not having had a formal introduction to snow and ice climbing. My first experience was terrifying and for many years I avoided the stuff as much as possible.

Winter climbing on Ben Nevis. Note the two ice axes, rigid boots with crampons, and large selection of ice screws.

There are so many unknowns. With rock, you can *feel* that things are right. With ice you can never be sure. I think this is one area where courses of instruction are invaluable. It makes sense to enrol for one which takes place in Scotland, where conditions are more reliable than in Wales or the Lake District. Remember too that you will be expected to have previous mountaineering experience, including rock climbing up to about *Very Difficult* standard.

HARD ROCK CLIMBING

It is said that there are only two kinds of rock climb: those you can get up, and those you can't. The saying is not quite so flippant as it might first seem because hard climbing is all about attempting climbs of uncertain outcome. It is pioneering within your own psyche. Despite the system of grading rock climbs (see table), hard climbing is entirely subjective and takes place within all grades. Thus if

GRADING OF BRITISH CLIMBS

British rock climbs

Easy *Moderate*	Scrambles and easiest rock climbs
Difficult *Very Difficult*	Usual standard for beginners
Severe *Very Severe*	Standard that the majority will normally climb
Hard Very Severe *Extremely Severe*	Standard requiring the dedication of regular climbing

British snow and ice climbs

I II	Simple gullies and easy ridges
III IV	Technical climbs on steep snow and ice
V VI	As above with added seriousness of length etc.

normally you climb at *Severe* and attempt after due consideration a *Very Severe* then your commitment and daring are comparable to those of someone who attempts an *Extreme* when his normal standard is *Very Severe.*

Rock climbing need not develop simply in the direction of technical difficulty. Another direction is towards mountain rock climbs. Here, length and position are paramount, technical difficulty being of secondary importance. Although this aspect of climbing is likely to appeal more to traditionalists (whose background involves hill walking and scrambling) as opposed to rock technicians (who perhaps came to the mountains via outcrops and climbing walls), there are few climbers who would slot easily into one or other category. More typical is the all-rounder who chooses a climb according to the preference of the moment, time of year, and prevailing weather. Looking back over my own climbs I see that on one outing I covered more than five thousand feet of climbing in an afternoon, while on another I finally succeeded in solving a 20-foot boulder problem after attempts spread over eight years! Neither achievement was greater or less than the other because the experiences cannot be compared.

The scope for hard climbing is unrestricted. Every outcrop has its testpiece, every mountain its bastion. Although British climbs are in no way inferior (they have an international reputation), climbers are going abroad in increasing numbers, not — as was once the case — to traditional alpine centres, but to outcrops similar to our own. France is especially popular (high standard limestone climbing) and so is the United States (various rock types and settings including the 3000-foot walls of

Yosemite Valley). Rock climbing even has its own (impoverished) jet set who tour the world following the sun and hearsay of good climbing.

ALPINISM

The word **Alpinism** has evolved from a style of climbing practised in the European Alps since the early 19th century. Nowadays it can equally refer to high altitude mountaineering in Norway, North and South America, Africa, New Zealand, the Himalayas — in fact any place where snow accumulates to form permanent snow fields and glaciers. It is a style of mountaineering dictated by the environment, where speed over difficult ground and all round competence are at a premium.

Many climbers regard the Alps and alpinism as the coming together of all mountaineering skills and aspirations. Others have no inclination to climb these mountains at all. Such is the diversity of climbing ambition.

The Alps — over a hundred and fifty years ago — is where it all began. Oddly enough it was the British who spearheaded this modern, sporting approach to the mountains (perhaps it could only have been the British at that time). They hired local guides and porters to help them on their ascents, but there is no doubt who provided the motivation.

For a while it remained traditional to hire guides and climb mountains by their easiest ways (this tradition is manifest today as when tourists hire guides to take them up the Matterhorn or Mont Blanc). In time, mountaineers dispensed with both these traditions and alpinism proper was born. The new breed pioneered climbs on long and difficult faces, subjecting themselves to great hardship and danger, some-

times for many days at a time. The history of alpinism is punctuated by their great successes, failures, and tragedies. The names of these pioneers have entered legend; their written accounts inspire each new generation.

The sense of wonder and awe at being among these mountains cannot be conveyed in a few words. Perhaps the following account of one climb which I made with a friend will go a little way towards exploring the mind-game of alpine mountaineering, but in the end you have to find out for yourself; you have to *be there*; *you* have to climb.

A CLIMB IN THE FRENCH ALPS

The ice shifted a little; a rock suddenly tilted from precarious balance on the crevasse edge and slithered into its blue depth, smooth as a seal. "It's like the Somme," Tony said, as we picked up our rucksacks and continued threading a way through the glacier morain and its desolate scenery.

The sun burned down remorselessly. From time to time we could see a distant figure cresting a hump in the acres of rock debris, promising a better path. But there were so many suggestions of tracks, so many crevasses to negotiate ... We had been two hours on the glacier and the maze had lost its novelty.

The track ended quite suddenly at the glacier edge beneath a vertical wall of rock. Bolted to the wall, and snaking skyward for hundreds of feet, was an ancient metal ladder. A diffuse flash of lightning was followed almost instantly by its thunder. Afternoon storm. We waited. A figure came scuttling crablike down the ladder, lightly gripping the iron rungs slippery

with drainage water. Another lightning flash seemed to unhinge him from his steps and he tumbled the final few feet on to the ice. He saw our astonished faces but said nothing, disappearing into the morain fields at a run. We waited.

The storm passed and we began our ascent of the ladder. A hundred feet above the ice and still the angle had not lessened. Our pace was slow yet rhythmic. I looked down and felt the wash of sinister unease. Tony clambered up immediately behind; but it didn't matter to him or me that I would wipe him off the ladder if I fell: I would not fall.

After 500 feet the ladder ended at a rock ledge. We crossed a natural gangway and gained the snowfields of the upper plateau. The storm resumed; but now we could see the hut, only a mile away, perched improbably on an island of rock above the snow. It would be a race against the coming rain. Our rucksacks were heavy; the snow was soft. We lost.

We were ill-prepared for the crush of humanity at the hut, even though during August in the Mont Blanc region of the French Alps it was only to be expected. We matched stares with stares and retreated into a corner, jealous of our plans and privacy. Tony prepared food while I dried our clothes and divided up the climbing gear into equal weights for tomorrow. Sometime during the night it began to snow.

It was six a.m. Feet in boots, minds asleep. I uncoiled the rope, throwing stiff loops into the soft snow. Tony looked up at the wall and frowned — a morning mist obscured all but the first hundred feet or so. The rock was streaked black with running water, some of which had frozen in the crack where we must go. Little glints of ice. We said nothing. Brothers.

When I reached the first ledge, after perhaps a hundred feet of climbing, it was already eight a.m. Two hours for one pitch! The whole climb was about twenty pitches. We had calculated being up and down in 10 or 12 hours, and so carried no proper bivouac equipment or spare clothing so as to save weight and therefore time. Just a nylon bag big enough for two. Ten or 12 hours — two gone already! Two hours in the steep wet crack choked with ice. Frozen fingers . . . slipping feet . . . tired brain wanting to be asleep . . .

Tony's sudden arrival at the ledge jolted my thoughts back to the task ahead — a leering crack which curved steeply up from the ledge. A solitary piton protruded from the crack at about half way, its metal eye winking in the sun now risen above the mist.

Another two inches and I could grab the piton. But how? Already I was beginning to teeter out of balance. The fingers of my left hand were curled over a small flake of rock. They were strained white with effort. My left foot was stretched out on a slightly sloping edge about half an inch wide. The leg was shaking a little, though not badly enough to dislodge the foot. I ignored it and stretched another inch with my right hand, crawling it up the rock like a spider, the piton nearly grasped. I heard voices below — another climbing party heading for a different peak — but the mist was now a carpet so dense that they could not be seen. Perhaps I could fall on the carpet and be saved? Stretching. It looked so soft. Reaching. So inviting. Got it! I tested the piton with a quick tug before trusting my rope to it. It came out in my hand. For a moment I held on to it stupidly, staring; then I abandoned it to the mist where now I was sure to follow. Soft, blanket mist. Intellect collapsed in the face of these impossible odds, resigning me to fate. But something powerful was at work: an animal clawing at the rock, lurching upward on sudden strength. Unseemly instincts. No fear; none at all.

Intellect caught up on the balcony above the crack. I had climbed into and out of catastrophe. Now all was calm again. I glanced down at Tony who had been paying out the rope conscientiously throughout. He smiled but said nothing. He knew.

We were lost. The leering crack and its hard but honest struggles were 1000 feet below. Now we faced instead an insidious, lingering uncertainty. During an overwhelming feeling of frustration I had begun to traverse the wall rightwards, heading for a huge corner which curved upward into a barrier of overhangs. An unlikely escape; but there was nowhere else to go. At the end of the traverse, and just when Tony had no more rope remaining to pay out, I had reached a large spike of rock over which I could flick a tape loop in order to tie myself securely to the face. There was no ledge to stand on; but by bracing my feet I could find a position of relative comfort supported in my harness. The drop beneath of 1000 feet no longer held any meaning or fascination. I watched intently as Tony began climbing towards me.

He was about eighty feet away to my left when he stopped. I knew exactly the move that confronted him: it was like trying to step across on to a tray of ball-bearings — a sloping ledge covered in granite dust. He looked across at me for a moment, despairing. There was nothing I could do. The rope hung in a lazy arc between us; should he slip the fall would

be unsurvivable. The minutes passed. It began to hail; not much — just a few frozen drops skittering down the slabs around us. The sky was a deep and thunderous grey. He stepped across once more, his foot searching the ledge like a tentacle until it lodged. He hesitated a moment, glancing over towards me again — this time without expression — and then resolutely transferred his weight on to the ledge. Within a minute he had arrived at my precarious stance, the moment already forgotten. Above rose the great corner, its cold unyielding stone like the interior of a cathedral. And beyond that?

"It's no use," I shouted down to Tony, sinking back from the ridge, "everywhere's plastered with ice." So much for our great escape. The corner had become increasingly difficult; sunk in its depths we had succumbed to a sense of foreboding, convincing ourselves it was a trap. And now there was no way out. I climbed back across the wall to where Tony was belayed in the angle of the corner. "The corner then," he said, in a matter-of-fact tone, as if graciously accepting a second choice whisky.

The vaulted ceiling of granite was indeed elegant, but untenable. Its barrier to our progress was absolute. In 20 feet the corner would lose itself in this arching sculpture. I continued to climb what was left of the corner, there being nowhere else to go. Already it was late; we were high on the face and so retreat would be extremely hazardous.

My helmet bumped against the first overhang. That was it: finished, I looked around, hopefully but expecting nothing. Out left ran a thin ragged crack. There were no footholds beneath it. Perhaps. Before there was time to consider, my

hands had grabbed the opportunity and were lurching out across the crackline, feet scrabbling beneath as they could. Life in the fast lane.

It worked. The rock above lay at a more reasonable angle, the cathedral overhang completely flanked. I thought I saw the summit above me — briefly through a sudden parting of the cloud. It looked close. Don't be fooled, I told myself.

The snow had drifted to a depth of three feet or so. It was completely unstable, all of it the product of the previous night's snowfall. So this was the 'easy summit ridge' we had heard about. For the second time I fell out of the snow chimney to land gently in the drift at its base. It was already dusk, the sky beginning to clear itself for a cold night.

There was no way this chimney was going to beat us. We could smell the summit. I climbed back down the ridge to where Tony was crouched in a shallow cave. I caught him yawning:

"I haven't been *that* long!" I handed the ice axe to him. "Anyway, you're supposed to be the snow and ice man."

He suppressed a smile at this — it was I who was covered in snow from the drift — but took the axe and disappeared upward into the gloom.

The summit was an anti-climax. A black scavenging bird hopped around us while we ate our first food since leaving the hut 14 hours before. We were otherwise alone. The snow had melted on our clothing and so we were quite wet and cold despite the energy of our struggle to get here. The sky was lead, obscuring any view. We devoted our attention instead to the food, sharing everything between us meticulously and

trying to let the bird have as little as possible while at the same time appearing to feed it — as seemed only proper. There was no longer any rush. It was almost dark. We would not get down tonight.

Tony found the bivouac site. He guided my feet on to the ledge when I came down through the darkness to join him. Our home for the night was four feet long, three feet wide, and covered in snow. Big enough to sit down with our backs against the wall, but not to lie down. Not that there would be much sleep. As we levelled the snow and laid down the rope for insulation there was plenty of time to regret our lightweight tactics. At least we had the nylon bag. We tied ourselves to the rock and entered its clammy interior, our heads protruding from purpose-made holes — a mutant terrapin. Within an hour the clouds had cleared completely to reveal a sky of stars so vividly bright that its reality was in doubt. The familiar shapes of neighbouring mountains — the Grandes Jorasses, Mont Blanc, the Aiguilles — loomed around us like a school of whales, dark shapes in a sea of total black.

Within an hour our boots had frozen and the bag become rimed with ice. The night was ours.

We had fallen quiet. I was trying to remember the names of all the climbs I had ever done, but kept dozing off to sleep — which had been the intention — and so losing track of where I was with the count. I nudged Tony with my elbow: "What was that route called we did at Lad's Leap rocks, the one with the loose block at the top?" His head slowly rotated in the socket of the bag; his eyes open but staring, as if in a trance. He started to say something but stopped when he realised his speech was slurred. He started again: "Where's Lad's Leap?" His head swung back without waiting for an answer, eyes scanning the night. Or were they turned inward? I fell asleep wondering if a two-headed terrapin could hold a meaningful conversation with itself.

Against all expectations we slept for a couple of hours, missing a probably spectacular sunrise. The sun was full up when I woke. I felt hollow, drained of all feeling and emotion. It hadn't been a bad night as such nights go. Merely cold. I crawled out of the bag so the sun could get at the frozen part of my shirt. I tried to put on my boots but they remained frozen solid. Should have kept them on. I sat them in the sun also to warm up, tying them to the rock as a precaution.

The view was spectacular but I could take no pleasure in it: my eyes prickled from exhaustion and glare. And still we had to get down. No incentive to hurry. Tony woke with a frown. He looked no better.

The heat was debilitating. After two hours we were still making our way down laboriously, zig-zagging down a system of ledges and easy slabs. Normally we would climb unroped over this type of ground, but the night had left us feeble and unsteady. We kept the rope on.

"Dead end," Tony replied to my query. I went down to join him. We were perched on a rock promontory above gentle and inviting snowfields at the foot of the face. That snow meant safety and the end of our troubles. But it was 50 vertical, smooth feet away. The obvious answer was to abseil down the rope. That had been our intention. Except that now we had arrived there were no decent cracks in which to hammer a piton.

"There's only this," Tony said when I arrived, pointing to a knife blade piton he had placed in a hairline crack. I asked him what he thought about it. "Snow's soft anyway," he said, his eyes tracing out the parabola of a falling climber. The alternative to trusting that pathetic sliver of metal was to go back up for 300 feet and find another way down. We were tired; the sun had made our every movement sluggish. Only 50 feet.

"OK, if you're happy about it," I said, emerging a little from lethargy at this slightly dangerous prospect. I clipped on to the piton and surveyed the distant mountains while Tony passed the rope through a tape loop. He threw down the rope ends into the snow, clipped on his abseiling device, and stepped backwards until he was at the edge.

"You can unclip from that if you like," he said, indicating the very insubstantial-looking piton — our sole means of support — which even now bent alarmingly under his weight. I shrugged unconcernedly for his benefit and unclipped, secretly relieved, for mine. No point in us both being pulled off. He grinned and stepped over the edge, knowing all along the piton was good.

We stopped at the hut only long enough to collect the bits of gear we had left there, before continuing our descent to the valley. Our exhaustion had stabilised into a zombie-like trance: useful for dealing with the many hours of tedious hard work ahead, but not much use for the aesthetic appraisal of the mountain setting. We cursed the snow, the mountains, the burning sun.

I had forgotten about descending the ladder. Dredging up a few odd scraps of caution, we clunked our way down hand over hand. I jumped the last few feet to the glacier, my legs crumpling unexpectedly under the strain. A pair of fresh-looking climbers stood politely to one side, waiting their turn to climb up to the hut. I picked myself up and absorbed their stare of astonishment into my own blank expression. I turned and, without a word, ran out on to the delicious flatness of the glacier.

WHAT IT'S ALL ABOUT

MOUNTAINS

Our climb was not extraordinary. The mountain summoned no unnatural forces to hinder us. It was we who labelled the features on the face of that inert mass of granite and snow, called it beautiful, ugly, benign, sinister. In a geological timespan the mountain is an unstable protuberance which, like a wave breaking on a sea-shore in our own timespan, is in the process of disintegrating into the surface from which it rose. Unable to synchronise with its wavelike pulse, our presence on the mountain was fleeting and insignificant. Like beetles on an elephant's back we fought nothing but our own shortcomings.

MOUNTAINEERS

Mountaineers do not live to see any real change in their mountains. The fascination lies instead within the continuing change wrought in themselves. It is as if climbers are lost souls haunting steep places in search of completeness. Towards this end they upturn stones and explore summits. But they are never satisfied and always they must go on looking, dragging their weary bodies behind them.

MOUNTAINEERING

When, after all the talking is over, you finally put mountains and mountaineers together, a strange thing happens: all the talk, the promises, the boasts, are put aside. Ambition falters. And so it would end, except that mountains have a way of gripping climbers by the throat. Why else would they continually submit themselves to discomfort, fear, and danger? Mountain literature and philosophy feeds on such riddles but there are no binding answers. Most climbers operate in ignorance (or defiance) of the questions and maintain that climbing is its own justification.

Good health, comradeship, and unsurpassed views are traditionally put forward as the motives and rewards of this sport. Maybe. I would rather say that *danger* is the raw material of mountaineering; and *escaping danger*, the art form.

EQUIPMENT

When buying equipment at first you will be relying heavily on the advice of friends and the retailer. They may have great ambitions for you (". . . this one will work a treat on the Eiger . . .") and so a touch of scepticism on your part will help steer a sensible line between compromise and performance.

By careful choice and a little forethought it is possible to build up your equipment with a minimum of redundancy and a maximum of versatility.

A brief survey on the following page of some of the more important items will help in choosing for versatility, and to indicate the costs involved.

Equipment for scrambling	Equipment for summer walking	Plus	Medium weight boots, 9 mm rope, small selection slings and karabiners
Equipment for winter walking	Equipment for summer walking Plus scrambling	Plus	Crampons, gaiters, breeches/salopettes, quilted jacket, thick mitts and balaclava, ice axe
Equipment for rock climbing	Equipment for summer walking Plus scrambling	Plus	Rock boots, safety helmet, harness, belay plate, extended selection slings and karabiners etc., second 9mm rope
Equipment for winter climbing	Equipment for summer walking Plus scrambling Plus winter walking Plus rock climbing	Plus	Stiff boots, short hammer, axe, alpine rucksack, small selection pitons and ice screws etc.
Equipment for alpine climbing	Equipment for summer walking Plus scrambling Plus winter walking Plus rock climbing Plus winter climbing	Plus	Extended selection pitons and ice screws etc., improved emergency bivouac equipment

BOOTS

The most important item of your equipment and also the most difficult to choose correctly. Never buy them mail order, and go to a shop where you can try on at least two or three pairs within the range you are considering. Unless buying highly specialised footwear — where the quality brands are well known — you are very much at the mercy of the sales assistant and the integrity of the buyers and manufacturers. However, reputations within the climbing equipment trade are hard won and jealously guarded so you are likely to be given a fair deal. Be wary, though, of second-hand or special offer boots. There *are* bargains to be had but the risk is too great for something as important as footwear. The table below identifies the main classes of boots and their uses (Table 1).

ROPE

It is best not to buy rope until you are competent in its use. By that time you will also have a better idea which type you need. However, it is useful to be aware of the various kinds and their uses (Table 2).

RUCKSACKS

This is a long-term investment so needs careful forethought. It is tempting to buy one that is big enough to cover all needs, or alternatively one that compromises all likely requirements. Instead, consider buying two — a daysack and a larger sack for winter/alps. As for the quality aspect of choosing a sack — you get what you pay for (Table 3).

AXES AND CRAMPONS

The choice within this range of winter hardware is considerable. Again, they are long-term investments so it is worth trying to spend some time making the right choice in the first instance. You will be forced to rely heavily on the advice of others so get a number of opinions on what you need (Table 4).

TABLE 1: MAIN BOOT TYPES AND THEIR USES

Boot type	Cost	Summer walking	Winter walking	Scrambling	Rock climbing	Alpine walking/ scrambling	Hard rock climbing	Winter climbing	Alpine climbing
Traditional lightweight	£18—£35	●	○	○	○	○	×	×	×
New style lightweight	£30—£50	●	○	●	○	○	×	×	×
Medium weight	£40—£55	●	●	●	●	●	○	○	○
Alpine/high mountain	£50—£100+	○	●	○	●	●	○	●	●
Rock boot	£25—£45	×	×	×	●	×	●	×	×
Running shoes/ trainers	—	○	×	○	○	×	×	×	×

Key: ● = ideal, ○ = serviceable, × = unsuitable

TABLE 2: CLIMBING ROPES AND THEIR USES

Rope type	Cost	Summer walking	Winter walking	Scrambling	Rock climbing	Alpine walking/ scrambling	Hard rock climbing	Winter climbing	Alpine climbing
8 mm × 18 m	£10—£12	●	○	○†	×	●	×	×	×
9 mm × 45 m	£30—£40	○	●	●†	×	○	×	○†	×
11 mm × 45 m	£40—£55	×	○	○	●	×	○	●	○
9 mm × 45 m × 2 of	£60—£80	×	×	×	○	×	●	●	●

Key: ● = ideal, ○ = serviceable, × = unsuitable, † = used double when necessary

TABLE 3: RUCKSACKS AND THEIR SUITABILITY

Rucksack type (capacity in litres)	Cost	Summer walking	Winter walking	Scrambling	Rock climbing	Alpine walking/ scrambling	Hard rock climbing	Winter climbing	Alpine climbing
Bum-bag (3–15)	£4–£8	○	×	○	○	○	×	×	×
Daysack (15–30)	£6–£30	●	●	●	●	●	×	○	○
All-round (30–45)	£12–£35	●	●	○	○	●	×	○	×
Alpine daysack (30–50)	£20–£35	○	●	○	○	●	×	●	●
Large frameless (50–75)	£25–£60	×	○	×	×	○	×	●	●
Pack frame sack (30–90)	£15–£45	○	×	×	×	×	×	×	×

Key: ● = ideal, ○ = serviceable, × = unsuitable

TABLE 4: ICE AXES AND CRAMPONS, AND THEIR USES

Item (length in cms)	Cost	Summer walking	Winter walking	Scrambling	Rock climbing	Alpine walking/ scrambling	Hard rock climbing	Winter climbing	Alpine climbing
Medium/long axe (65–85)	£17–£35	n.a.	●	n.a.	n.a.	●	n.a.	○	○
Short/medium axe (50–65)	£25–£35	n.a.	○	n.a.	n.a.	○	n.a.	●	●
Ice hammer	£8–£35	n.a.	×	n.a.	n.a.	×	n.a.	●	●
Matched set of short axe and hammer	£50–£70	n.a.	×	n.a.	n.a.	×	n.a.	●	○/×
Instep crampons	£5–£10	n.a.	○	n.a.	n.a.	○	n.a.	×	×
12-point crampons	£20–£35	n.a.	●	n.a.	n.a.	●	n.a.	●	●

Key: ● = ideal, ○ = serviceable, × = unsuitable

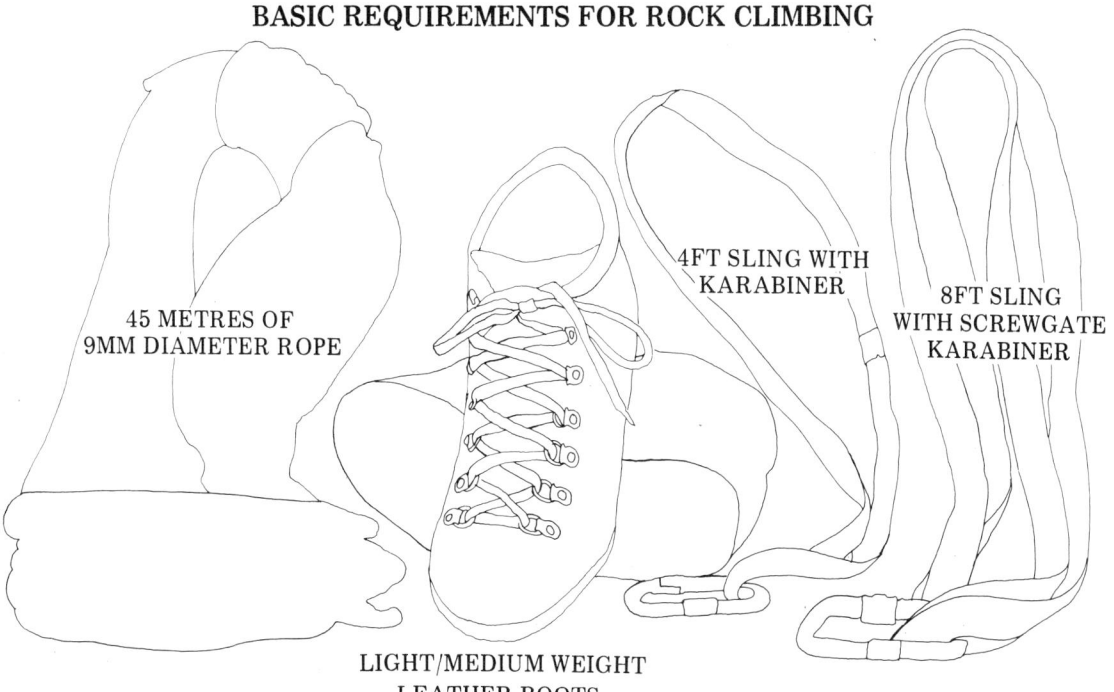

BASIC REQUIREMENTS FOR ROCK CLIMBING

45 METRES OF
9MM DIAMETER ROPE

LIGHT/MEDIUM WEIGHT
LEATHER BOOTS

4FT SLING WITH
KARABINER

8FT SLING
WITH SCREWGATE
KARABINER

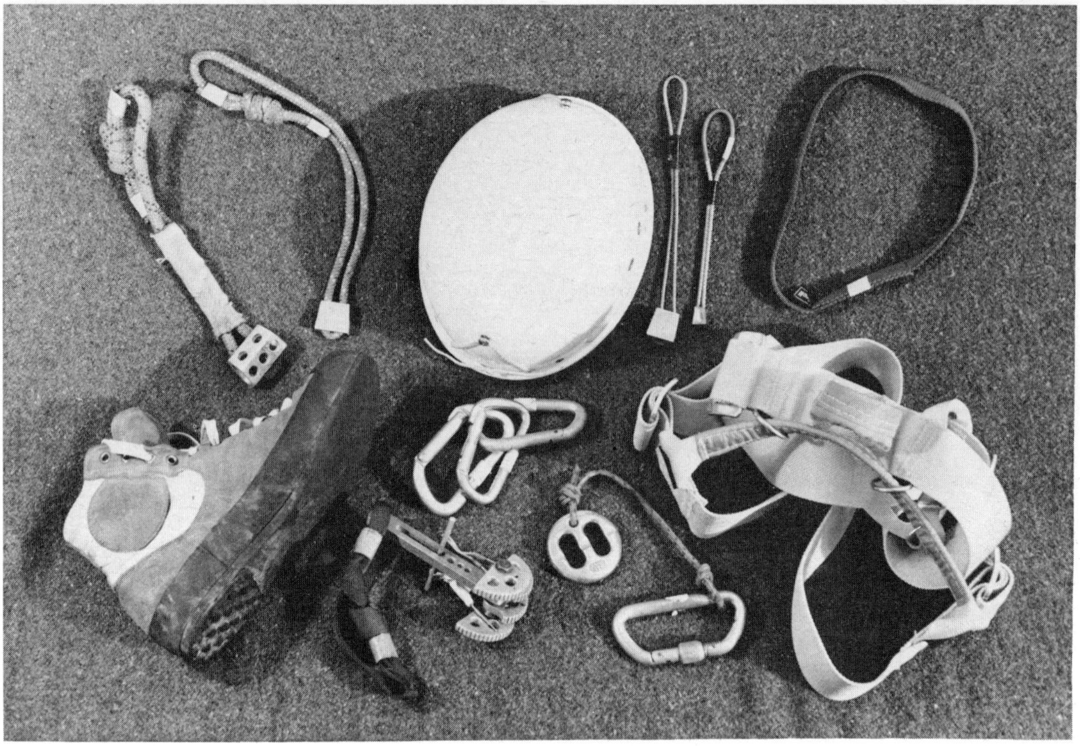

EXTRA ITEMS REQUIRED FOR ROCK CLIMBING

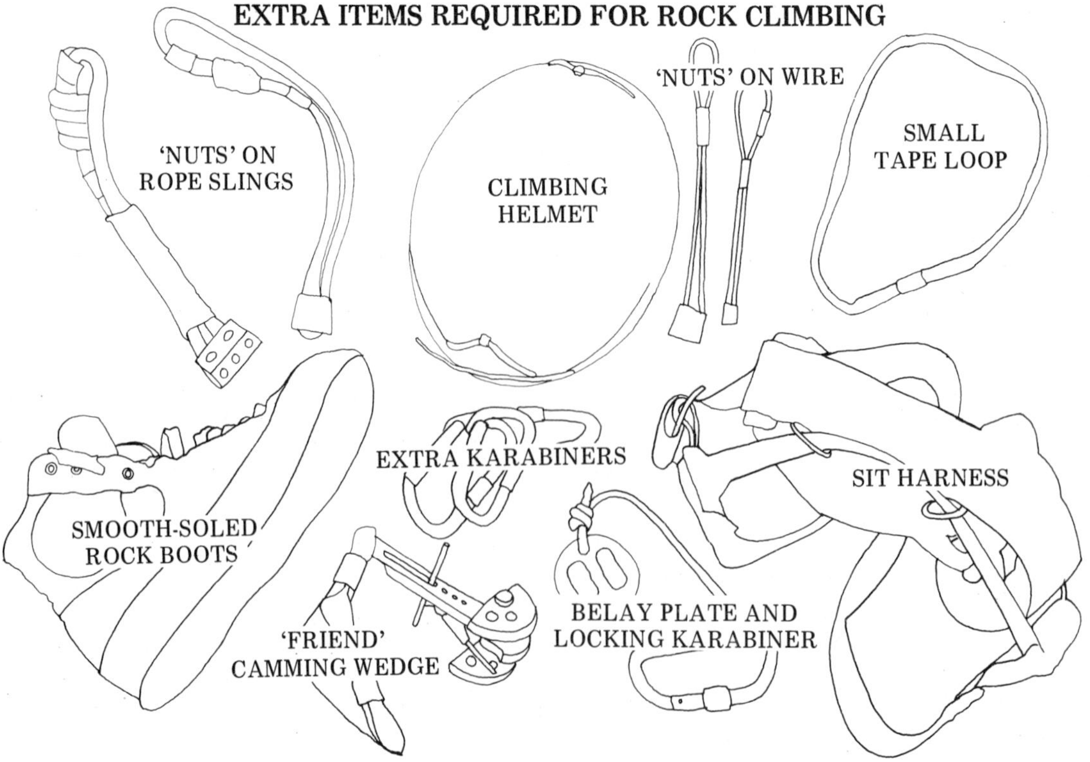

'NUTS' ON
ROPE SLINGS

'NUTS' ON WIRE

CLIMBING
HELMET

SMALL
TAPE LOOP

EXTRA KARABINERS

SMOOTH-SOLED
ROCK BOOTS

SIT HARNESS

'FRIEND'
CAMMING WEDGE

BELAY PLATE AND
LOCKING KARABINER

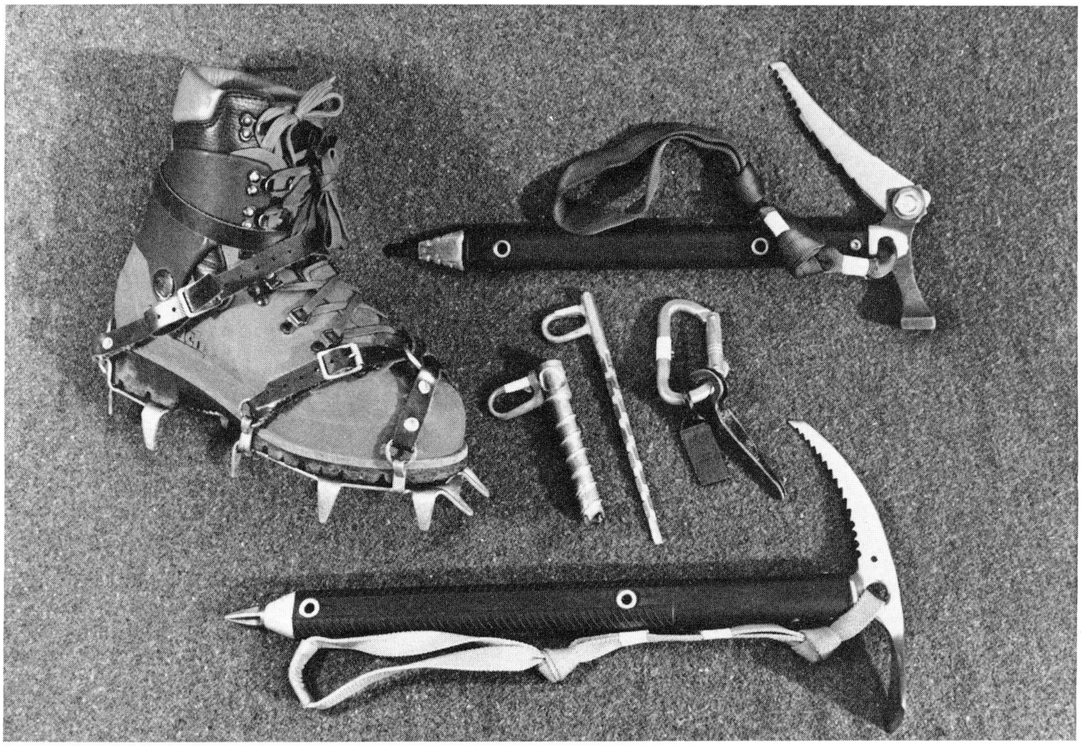

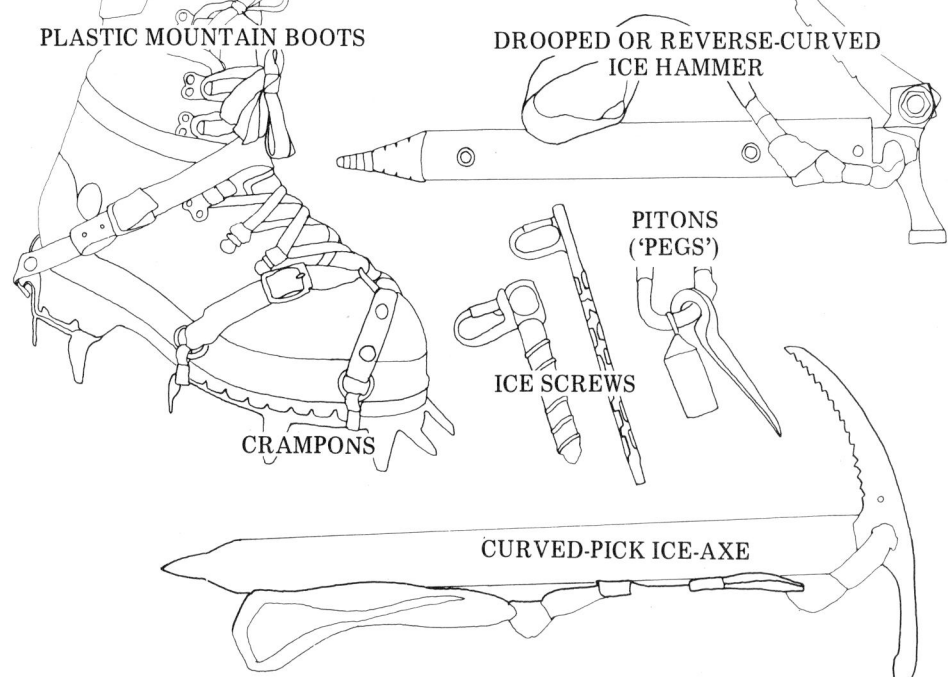

EXTRA ITEMS REQUIRED FOR WINTER CLIMBING

PLASTIC MOUNTAIN BOOTS

DROOPED OR REVERSE-CURVED
ICE HAMMER

PITONS
('PEGS')

ICE SCREWS

CRAMPONS

CURVED-PICK ICE-AXE

BUYING EQUIPMENT FOR CHILDREN

Serious mountaineering demands serious equipment; the mountains are no place for inadequately equipped children. The cost, particularly for those items which will be outgrown, is staggering. One answer is to buy second hand. Some shops will accept outgrown children's boots as trade-ins, but not clothing. Alternatively, use hire services if equipment will be used only occasionally. The situation is not quite so depressing as it might first appear because most children will participate via a youth group, school club, or residential course, where stocks of personal equipment are normally kept. In any case it makes sense to use discretion over buying equipment until you are sure the interest is likely to continue and develop.

FINAL NOTE

A principle among mountaineers is that climbing equipment should be bought only when necessary and used only of necessity. Equipment intrudes in the communication between you and the mountain. It also has to be carried!

CLUBS, COURSES, ORGANISATIONS

Clubs: Probably the best way to start and continue climbing is informally with friends met through a club. *Climber & Rambler* magazine lists many of the town clubs, while nearly all universities and colleges, and some schools, will have a climbing club. Joining a club is particularly worthwhile if you live in an area far removed from the hills, as transport costs will be less and the difficulty of finding partners reduced. Most, though not all, clubs are willing to accept beginners. This is usually indicated in the club notes in *Climber & Rambler*.

Courses: The classified advertisements section of the magazine contains dozens of entries detailing courses varying from basic climbing to alpine mountaineering. Many of these commercial concerns are small enterprises run by BMC (British Mountaineering Council) guides or ex-instructors from school climbing centres. Prices per person can be as little as £80 per week, all in, but are very variable according to location, accommodation, and staff/student ratio. In addition the Sports Council subsidises two main mountaineering centres at Plas y Brenin (North Wales) and Glenmore Lodge (Cairngorms). Though more expensive (up to £180 per week) they offer a comprehensive range of courses and usually superior accommodation. Their brochures can be obtained from the addresses below. An expensive but reliable way of learning the basics is to hire a guide for a day or two (variable rates in the region of £30/day). The personal attention and quality of instruction by this method is unparalleled.

Organisations: As well as providing its own range of economy courses (achieved through a self-catering system) in Britain and the Alps, the British Mountaineering Council provides a range of services in general to the mountaineering community. This includes special insurance, cheap foreign travel, and information on access and training facilities. Membership of the BMC has many short term financial advantages as well as being a worthwhile investment in the future of British climbing.

WHERE TO CLIMB IN BRITAIN

NORTHERN
HIGHLANDS

SKYE

•INVERNESS

BEN NEVIS
&
GLENCOE
AREA

CAIRNGORMS

ARROCHAR

EDINBURGH

GLASGOW

ARRAN

ANTRIM
COAST

NEWCASTLE

CARLISLE

N.YORKSHIRE
MOORS

DONEGAL

BELFAST

LAKE
DISTRICT

MOURNE

ISLE
OF
MAN

YORK

CONNEMARA

LANCASHIRE
QUARRIES

YORKSHIRE

LIMESTONE &
GRITSTONE

MANCHESTER

DUBLIN

GOGARTH
SEA CLIFFS

LIVERPOOL

SHEFFIELD

WICKLOW

BANGOR

SNOWDONIA

PEAK
DISTRICT

MT. BRANDON &
MACGILLICUDDY'S
REEKS

MID WALES

BIRMINGHAM

PEMBROKE & GOWER
SEA CLIFFS

LONDON

CARDIFF

SOUTH—EAST
SANDSTONE

BRISTOL
AVON &
CHEDDAR GORGES

CORNISH &
NORTH DEVON
SEA CLIFFS

DARTMOOR
OUTCROPS

SWANAGE
SEA CLIFFS

PLYMOUTH

KEY

 = Mountain Areas with Rock Climbing, Scrambling, Hill Walking and possibly Winter Climbing.

= Outcrop and Sea Cliff Areas giving normally only Rock Climbing.

USEFUL ADDRESSES

Sports Council Mountaineering Centres:

Plas y Brenin, Capel Curig, Gwynedd LL24 0ET (Tel: 06904 214).

Glenmore Lodge, Aviemore, Inverness-shire PH22 1QU (Tel: 047986 276).

BMC, Crawford House, Precinct Centre, Booth Street East, Manchester M13 9RZ (Tel: 061-273 5835).

PUBLICATIONS

GUIDEBOOKS

Apart from walking guides, each main mountain area has a four-tiered system of guidebooks covering all requirements. They are:

Definitive rock climbing guides: Produced on a non-profit-making basis by a national club or the BMC. Numerous volumes for each area.

Selected rock climbing guides: Produced commercially and including 200 or so of the best climbs. Useful for occasional visits to an area.

Winter climbs guides: Usually commercially produced (but included in the definitive guides in Scotland).

Scrambling guides: Commercially produced for most mountain areas.

Most large climbing shops carry a near complete range of these publications and will be able to advise on which book you need for any particular area you wish to visit. It is worth noting that whereas a walking guide is a luxury, a climbing guide — summer or winter — is essential.

INSTRUCTIONAL BOOKS

There are a large number of books in print which deal with basic climbing and rope technique and it is a major task to sort out the good from the bad and the indifferent. To simplify matters I will recommend just two for purchase (both are relatively inexpensive paperbacks) and a third (unfortunately out of print and somewhat dated in certain respects) which should be available from most libraries:

Modern Rope Techniques in Mountaineering Bill March (Cicerone Press).

Modern Snow and Ice Techniques Bill March (Cicerone Press).

Mountaineering Alan Blackshaw (Penguin Handbooks).

GENERAL INTEREST

From a vast list of titles the following are particularly worth searching out on the library shelves as they offer a unique insight into the various aspects of mountaineering via selected writings and unsurpassed photography:

Classic Rock compiled by Ken Wilson (Granada).
Hard Rock compiled by Ken Wilson (Granada).
Big Walks compiled by Richard Gilbert (Diadem).
Cold Climbs compiled by Ken Wilson, Dave Alcock and John Garry (Diadem).
Games Climbers Play edited by Ken Wilson (Diadem).

MAGAZINES

Climber & Rambler (monthly). All aspects of climbing at home and abroad. Best magazine for club listings and classified ads on courses, accommodation, etc.

High Magazine (bi-monthly). As above but more comprehensive on rock climbing information.

Mountain (bi-monthly). International magazine reporting on major ranges but little home news or relevance for beginners.

One of the great classic mountain rock climbs, Jones' Direct, on Scafell Crag in the Lake District.

a member of the Cairngorm Mountain Rescue Team since 1977. When her son Neil became diabetic she turned this apparent setback to the family into a success story. Making sure that Neil ate little and often and always had his glucose tablets in his pocket, she arranged for him to be taken up to the snowline to practise cross-country ski-ing. He came home excited and happy, his confidence in life restored. In 1981, to raise funds for the British Diabetic Association, Ann walked 300 miles alone across Scotland, from Peterhead, furthest east, to Ardnamurchan, furthest west.

Cross-country or Nordic ski-ing is an activity that now offers exciting new possibilities to families. With safe, modern equipment and the growth of centres offering expert tuition the technique is quickly learnt. "Nordic ski-ing," writes Ann Wakeling, "is a means of travel across the snow-covered countryside which can be as energetic as you like to make it — a cheap and safe activity for the whole family." What a marvellous way to make winter fun!

Ann Wakeling lives with her husband Edwin and two sons Ian and Neil at Aviemore in the Spey Valley. She has been associated with the Highland Guides (started in 1970 by Iain Hudson) for the last 10 years. She leads walks in the Cairngorms in summer and teaches cross-country ski-ing in the winter. She qualified as a Grade 3 Instructor in 1982 and has been

Cross Country Ski-ing

ANN WAKELING

The first time I skied was from necessity. We lived five miles from the nearest village and the road was blocked, so the shop could not deliver our groceries. We would have to go and collect them from the Old Manse at the end of the glen road. It was only three miles each way — a pleasant stroll on a nice day — but it had been snowing hard for the last two days and now it was getting on for knee deep. It would be very hard work going that distance on foot. Why not use the skis? Edwin, my husband, had been ski-ing for four years but my experience only amounted to an hour or so slithering about on a slope in a field. Would I be able to manage? We set off, carrying rucksacks.

Edwin broke trail all the way, the tips of his skis just breaking the surface of the snow as he pushed forward. I followed in his tracks. It had stopped snowing and the day was cold and bright. The whole valley was quiet, the birches laden with snow. The road down the glen was gently undulating but, as it approached the junction at the Old Manse, it steepened before a sharp bend with an old stone wall at one side. I was wearing Edwin's skis — light and springy — and I glided beautifully as I reached the hill. Not that I particularly wished to. I was getting too fast. I overtook Edwin, whistled down to the bend, the wall loomed up, I shied away and was at the bottom, sitting down, skis in the air! Edwin laughed as he always did when I sat down in the snow. We arrived at the Manse, dug our box of groceries out of the snow and filled our rucksacks. Edwin took the eggs . . .

Returning up the hill past the farm we saw the shepherd, with feed for his flock. He scorned our skis; obviously he preferred to be on foot. True, going up the hill he was faster, with snow up to his knees leaving a great furrowed wake behind him. But once more on level ground we left him far behind as he trudged slowly along. We hardly sank in at all on the homeward trail, gliding along in our own tracks. The track went down a steep bank to our house and again I soared past Edwin to land in an undignified heap. I struggled out of the rucksack straps and out of his way as he glided down and stopped neatly by our gate. The eggs were safe with him. From that moment I was hooked.

When I tell people I go cross-country or Nordic ski-ing, the reaction is either "Oh, you must be really energetic", or else complete ignorance that there is any form of ski-ing other than downhill, with expensive lifts and tows to take you back up because you cannot walk far in rigid plastic boots. Nordic ski-ing, using long narrow skis, is a means of travel across the snow-covered countryside which can be as energetic as you like to make it, a cheap and safe activity for the whole family. It is very much like cycling in a way, quite hard work going up hills but grand free-wheeling down the other side. If you wish you can just potter along peacefully on your skis, keeping to fairly flat country, and teach the children. (Watch out — they are so quick to learn they will soon be teaching you!) If you like competition you can join a club and progress to racing. When the children are very small you may be limited in the distances you can cover, but as they grow up and gain experience you can go on longer tours, perhaps from one centre or across country from hut to hut.

Why do I enjoy this form of ski-ing so much? Well, I am in the open air, getting out and about and really seeing the country-

Exploring the winter countryside with the family.

side which can be so beautiful with the effects of frost and snow, and full of surprises. One day last winter when I was out with my husband and son tacking our way up a broad slope, I saw hare tracks going uphill. I altered my line to alongside. Looking ahead I saw the line of an old fence. I could not see the tracks going on beyond it. Curious, I followed the trail until it ceased at a little tunnel, by one of the fallen fenceposts. I knelt and peered in and there was a twitchy nose and whiskers, and the bright eyes of a hare solemnly regarding me, only inches away. My son followed me and peeked in too. We had never looked a hare in the face before — it was quite a thrill.

HOW TO BEGIN AND WHERE TO GO

For absolute beginners I would recommend hiring equipment and trying a short course, perhaps over a weekend or half term. Hire and try before you buy. Look in *Climber and Rambler*, *Footloose*, *The Great Outdoors*, and *Ski Magazine* for the current adverts., and see the list of courses at the end of this chapter.

EQUIPMENT

DEVELOPMENT

When I made that first trip down to the Manse 20 years ago, the bindings were a cable and spring clip device, the cable running under a couple of pairs of hooks on the side of the ski. For touring you released the cable from the rear hooks, so the heel could lift; for downhill both hooks were used. The development of downhill skis concentrated on holding the heel down more firmly, leading to the invention of release bindings and the use of stiffer

boots, resembling hiking boots, square at the toe to fit into the adjustable toe-piece. The Nordic Norm was introduced and boots and bindings were made in standard widths — no more adjusting the bindings to each individual boot. Then three-pin bindings, or 'rat traps', were imported from Scandinavia and these are now in common use.

BOOTS AND BINDINGS

Boots range from a light low-cut shoe for racing, through light boots for general touring, up to a heavy boot with a Vibram

Spring sunshine on Carn Ban Mor in the Scottish Highlands. Note the light boots.

sole for mountain touring. The boot needs torsional rigidity, that is, it must not twist from toe to heel, but it should be flexible in that direction.

The boot is attached to the ski by the binding. In the three-pin binding the pins protrude to locate with the pin holes under the toe of the boot and a spring bail holds the boot in place. Nordic Norm can be 50 mm for racing or 75 mm for touring. Make sure your boots are the same width as the bindings. A new type of binding has recently been developed by Salomon which can only be used with their own special boot. Salomon Nordic system has a central ridge in the foot-plate which mates with a groove in the boot sole to aid control. The toe of the boot has a metal loop protruding, which slots over the binding and is held firmly in place with a spring lever. With either type of binding the heel is free to rise and this flexibility means even severe falls rarely cause injury.

SKI STICKS

These may be of cane (which are the cheapest but rather heavy), fibreglass or aluminium alloy. Sticks are used for propulsion, not only to prop you up, and the correct length will just fit under your armpit.

SKIS

Nordic skis are long and narrow. Reach up, holding your skis, and they should reach to your wrists. As you travel across the countryside you will be going up and down hills. A ski will readily slide down a hill but how do you climb? You can use waxes for grip or you can buy a special non-wax ski.

Fibreglass skis can be waxless, having a fishscale, step-cut pattern, mohair strip, or mica base to provide grip when going uphill. This type of ski is simple — you put it on and away you go. So it is often the beginner's choice and very easy for children to use. Non-wax skis are particularly useful in 'transition' conditions, when it is around freezing and difficult to wax skis correctly, or when weather conditions are changing rapidly. However, a waxing ski will give a better performance *if* it is waxed correctly. A better performance means it will go faster and further for less energy and that counts at the end of a long day. There is a simple two-wax system with which you can start. You can progress to one of the 'colour coded' systems later on. It is wise to stay with one manufacturer's waxes and become familiar with them.

Fibreglass skis have almost completely replaced wood although a good pair of wooden skis is still worth having. Wooden skis take more looking after and need to be treated with 'base' wax before waxing for grip.

Your choice of skis depends on where you are going to use them. If you are taking your holiday in Scandinavia you will find many miles of marked trails with cut tracks. The ski will tend to stay in the track, turns will mainly be gentle, and you will need only light equipment. Light skis can be used for making downhill turns on an open slope, but only in very good light snow unless you are a real expert. On open hillsides and untracked moorland the ski must bite into the snow to maintain direction or to initiate a turn, especially in hard or icy conditions. You will need a heavier ski with a metal edge which will cost a little more. However, metal-edged skis will enable you to cope with varying conditions, including icy slopes and with ski-ing downhill.

ROLLER SKIS

Used originally by racers for pre-season training, roller skis are becoming increasingly popular. They are like elongated roller skates, with a ratchet arrangement so that they can run backwards. During autumn 1983 roller ski races were scheduled for Aberdeen, London, Aviemore, Glasgow, and Harrogate. More than eighty people attended the races at Aviemore. In England, owing to the lack of snow some seasons, roller racing is becoming a sport in its own right with inter-club competitions being held. A list of clubs in Britain will be found at the end of this chapter. The chart will show you the range of equipment and help you to select the type you need.

Once you have your own equipment you can ski anywhere with sufficient snow: forest trails, on the common, the local park or golf course. For a family holiday in Scotland I would recommend the Spey Valley — I am biased, I live there! If you are thinking of going abroad, I suggest Norway or Sweden.

CLOTHING

Don't buy special clothing to begin with. Most children (and parents) these days have a tracksuit; use that, with a pair of long-johns or pyjama trousers underneath if needed. Dress using the layer system; several thin layers are not only warmer than one thick one, but are also adjustable. This is very important; as you warm up you can take off a layer, rather than getting sweaty and wet which will cause you to chill when you stop. It is better

Robert Hovey, chairman of the Lakeland Cross-Country Ski Club, guides a blind member, Jennifer Hodkinson, who is trying out her roller skis. Jennifer has now won a certificate and badge by ski-ing 4 km in 53 minutes against the allowed time of 70 minutes. Ski holidays, with guides, in the Alps and Norway, are organised for the disabled by the British Ski Club.

to have a dry layer ready to put back on. Taking off and putting on means you need a small rucksack to put things in, and "Mum, can I have a bit of chocolate now and will you look after my gloves?" also has to be catered for.

TABLE 1

Where to ski	Type of skiing	Ability	Activity type	Equipment	Weight	Width in mm at tip and waist	Cost
(Roads)	Roller	Intermediate—expert	Race training	Roller ski; Light low-cut shoe			£60—70 £30
Low ground; prepared tracks only	Racing	Intermediate—expert	Runners and competitive people	Very light ski; light low-cut shoe	1200 gm	42/44	Up to £90 £30
Low ground; prepared tracks and easy terrain	Cross-country	Basic—advanced	Joggers and sporty keep-fit people who ski for exercise	Light ski; High-cut shoe	1500 gm	51/49	£25—90 £30
Low ground; untracked forest trails and open terrain with moderate slopes	Touring	Basic—advanced	Ramblers who ski for recreation	Medium ski; may have metal edge; Light medium-cut boot	1900—2100 gm	59/54 59/54	£38—50 £38—50 £25—45
High ground; untracked mountain and moor; any terrain or snow condition	Mountain touring	Intermediate—expert	Hillwalkers and backpackers; exploration and winter travel	Heavy ski, full metal edge; Medium boot—heavy boot, vibram sole, can take crampons	2200—2700 gm	65/55	£55—90 £45—£70

Bindings £5—10   Poles £5—10 (racing poles up to £30)   Total for set: £50—180

For comparison:

Where to ski	Type of skiing	Ability	Activity type	Equipment	Weight	Width in mm at tip and waist	Cost
Untracked mountain terrain in any conditions	Alpine touring	Advanced—expert	Hillwalkers and backpackers; exploration and winter travel	Downhill type ski, skins for climbing, release bindings with heel lift; Rigid plastic boot, vibram sole, can take crampons, suitable for snow and ice climbing. Poles	4000 gm	85/65	£100—200 £30 £60—90 £90 up £15—30

Total for set: £300—400

Ideal clothing for a cold day's touring.

The outer layers of clothing ideally should be windproof with a separate lightweight waterproof cagoule and over-trousers. When you are moving you generate heat and a waterproof layer will trap this as condensation. The waterproof trousers will be needed a lot to begin with, as you will probably sit down fairly often — it is one positive way of stopping! Only use the waterproof top when it is snowing wet snow or, perish the thought, raining.

Gloves tend to get wet and soggy, so take several thin pairs of woollen gloves or mittens (mittens are warmer) rather than thick leather gloves, which take a very long time to dry. I have even put small plastic bags over the children's gloves if the snow is wet, as they tumble in it a lot. When a chill wind blows a scarf adds comfort, and do make sure everybody's hats can cover their ears. In springtime remember your sunglasses; the glare is hard on the eyes and could be dangerous, leading to 'snow blindness'. In deep snow gaiters can be useful: they don't have to be bought ones; you can improvise with a pair of old socks with the feet cut off, pulled up over your tracksuit. They keep the snow out of your boots and are easily pulled off before going indoors.

LEARNING TO SKI

If you are a beginner you can just put on your skis and plod away, which is fine for the first 10 minutes! Then try to go along with a spring in your step, more like a jogging movement. As the ski is bounced down by one foot the other ski is slid forward in a glide and weight transferred to it ready for the next stride. Swing your arms and use your poles to help push you along. This is called the diagonal stride and is the basic movement. Always slide the ski forward, don't lift it, and as you stride out lean forward a little and push your knee forward over the binding.

On an uphill section a more emphatic bounding stride will carry you up. If the slope is too steep or long you can zig-zag when the ground is open, or use the herringbone if you are confined to a track. Splay out the tips of the skis and edge them to form a 'V' by pushing your knees forward. Lift your skis, moving your feet directly forward, crossing the tails of your skis and making a herringbone pattern. Keep your sticks behind to stop you slipping back. An even steeper section can be side-stepped. Be careful to keep your skis across the fall line (the line a snowball would take if you rolled it down the slope), and using your sticks for support, step up sideways.

For the descent in a straight run, adopt a flexible relaxed attitude, skis almost shoulder-width apart, knees flexed, leaning slightly forward, hands low . . . and push off. Try to find a gentle downhill for your first attempts, with a safe run-out area

Below and opposite: Learning how to ski, jump and land correctly

where you can glide to a stop. The other way of stopping is generally known as a 'bumstop', self-explanatory, and used pretty often to begin with! Getting up is easy. Put your skis across the slope, roll on to your knees and stand up. If the snow is deep you may need to put your sticks down on the snow in a cross to have something to push up on, or put your hands on to the skis to push up.

If you are gliding too fast, use a snow-plough for brakes. Sink down, bending your knees even more and pushing out on the heels to make the skis form a 'V' with the tips about six inches apart. That is the gliding plough. Now roll the ankles inward to edge the skis on to the inside edge — gently. You should stop in control. Learning tip: practise first on a very gentle slope.

To turn, the gliding plough is the first

movement for snowplough turns. Did you know you have a 'magic button' in your knee? Go into a gliding plough and reach your hand down to your right knee and press. This will bring more weight on to the right ski and it will take control. It is pointing to the left so you will turn left. Straighten up (equal weight) and glide forward, then lean over and try the other way. It works like magic!

Children tend to learn very quickly as they do not think about what they are doing and just copy. Adults worry whether they have the technique quite right, so they are stiff and tense. It is best not to think too hard, but relax and play games on your skis. You can try the old favourite, touch tag, or slip a scarf through your belt and try not to let anyone close enough to pull it out. Or you could play throwball. (The ball is more likely to be someone's hat or a bum-bag.) Make the play area as big as you need for the number taking part, using everyone's sticks to mark the boundary and rucksacks or anoraks to mark the goal. You can have up to four goals; all you need to know is which one you are defending and attack all the others. Were you worried about falling over? Soon forgotten in the excitement of the game. All games should be played without sticks. You need your hands free, and milling around at such close quarters with sticks would be dangerous. Practice without sticks, as in games, is very good for everyone. It will improve your balance and help you to establish your stride.

MAKING PROGRESS

When you have learnt the basic movements of ski-ing, what next? Short trips are all you can do with very small children; they tire quickly, especially when it is cold. Then they fall over more often and that is tiring too. Remember to brush the snow off them, or it will melt and make them wet and unhappy. A short rest in a sheltered place can work wonders, but do not stop for too long or you and the children will chill, and lose the benefit of the break. Always sit on something, your waterproofs, a bit of Karrimat, your gloves if nothing else is available. When my two were small I used to carry an extra large plastic bag which opened along the side, and four of us could just sit in it. At least the middle ones were properly sheltered! Nowadays on mountain trips I carry an emergency tent, a home-made job which goes up on a couple of pairs of skis and which has on occasion sheltered six adults.

FURTHER AFIELD

If you are going out into untracked moorland or mountain areas, what should you know? I assume that by now you will have mastered the basic ski-ing movements, and the family are setting off for the day. You have been up on the moors in summer, you have your map and compass and, I hope, know how to use them. If there has been a heavy snowfall the stream beds may be filled in, paths and tracks covered. So it will be far more difficult to recognise these features. And should the mist come down the winter wonderland becomes a much more exacting environment.

With all the energy you use in ski touring remember you need a good packed lunch, and a bit extra at the bottom of the rucksack in case you take longer than expected on the way back.

When you go further afield and on to higher ground you will need to know more about looking after yourselves, how to dig a snowhole for instance, should conditions become desperate and you decide to stay put rather than exhaust yourselves trying to push on into a blizzard. When there is a strong wind the effective temperature will be much lower than the actual thermometer reading. This is called the wind chill factor. The wind will take heat from your body as fast or faster than you can produce it; spare clothing will be required, and extra food for the energy to keep yourselves warm. If you are exposed to a freezing

Right and below: Ski-ing on the Great Moss in the Monadliaths.

soon rewarmed, can go deeper and become frostbite. Shelter out of the wind, and place warm hands on the affected part of the face. Hands can be put under the armpits or in the groin to rewarm. Feet can be rewarmed, the manual says, 'on the stomach of a friend'. Prevention is obviously better than cure (ask the friend!). Do not lace boots too tight, or you will restrict circulation. If there is not room inside for an extra sock, use an overboot or even an old sock over the boot itself.

HOLIDAYS

A centre-based tour is ideal for your first ski trek holiday (you will find some useful addresses at the end of this chapter). I was once fortunate to have the opportunity to be an assistant leader for such a trip in Norway, based on an hotel in Sjusjoen. We explored the trails around Sjusjoen, making longer trips as the group's standard improved. There were so many marked trails that we hardly covered any ground twice. The week was gone far too soon.

Then you might try an organised hut-to-hut tour. I can do no better than tell you about my first, again in Norway, in the Rondane National Park. We had come up to the road end at Mysusetter by bus. Some of us wandered off to watch children taking part in the Saturday races. I stepped off the beaten track and immediately sank up to my thighs! I realised why ski-ing was invented here, in Norway, probably 4000 years ago, and why everyone from toddlers to grandmothers goes around on skis.

It was 11 km to Rondvassbu hut and uphill nearly all the way. No passenger vehicles are allowed in the National Park, but as a Weasel — a tracked motor vehicle towing a couple of sledges — was to bring our kit up later on, we had only to carry our light rucksacks with our immediate needs. The way began steeply and our party soon spread out. As we breasted the first rise we came to a group of summer huts and heard a hubbub of chatter. A school party was taking a breather. Children of around ten or twelve, each carrying a small rucksack, accompanied by a teacher who was dragging a pulk — a type of small sledge — with the rest of their gear, were on their way up to Rondvassbu for the weekend.

Later, as we settled into our four-bunk room we heard them again. Shrieks of laughter, challenges and dares came from the steep slope beside the hut which made a convenient practice ground. A couple of them came down the slope on sledges, some on skis, the rest on their backsides, tumbling, jumping and enjoying themselves until it was dark and the supper bell sounded.

We spent several days in the hut, making day trips and improving our technique before setting off for the next hut with all we needed in our packs. Our leader, a young Norwegian, had strapped avalanche probes and a shovel to his pack. The shovel came into frequent use. At our first lunch stop he made a wall to shelter himself from the breeze. When we arrived at the unstaffed huts we often had to dig out the woodstore and out came the shovel again.

It was a wonderful trek. I enjoyed moving on each day into fresh country and the evenings sitting round the glowing stove after our meal, swopping yarns, and drinking cup after cup of coffee to counteract the dehydrating effect of the dry mountain air. A trip like that would be quite feasible for an older family with a fair amount of experience.

A FINAL NOTE

I still feel a thrill when I look out and see the soft flakes floating down, the first snow of the season. Will there be enough to ski by morning? The Monadliaths are my back door territory and I like to roam there whenever the snow is suitable. They lie on the opposite side of the Spey Valley to the Cairngorms, and rise to wild moorland at around 2000 feet, with a few peaks of 3000 feet around Newtonmore. In spring there is still ski-ing to be had on the Cairngorm plateau which rises to over 4000 feet. But it is no place for the inexperienced. The weather, as on any mountain range, can change with alarming rapidity, and make demands on your navigation as well as your ski-ing. The Eskimos have something like fifty words for snow. It can come in so many forms, dry or wet, soft or firm. The varying conditions you may encounter are a challenge that you will learn to cope with by experience. As my husband said when I asked him why he enjoyed ski-ing, "It's testing your experience and skill against the terrain and the prevailing conditions." Make sure that your skill matches the challenge of the mountains.

Learning to ski on the artificial ski slope at Plas y Brenin in Wales.

NORDIC SKI CLUBS

Scotland

Aberdeen University X-C S.C: N. Spinks, Butchart Recreation Centre, University Road, Aberdeen. Tel: 0224-40241, Ext. 5544.

Edinburgh Nordic Ski Club: Sec. Gordon Peckham, 17 Cherry Tree Park, Edinburgh EH14 5AQ. Tel: 031-449 3735.*

Edinburgh University Nordic S.C.: The Secretary, E.U.N.S.C., Students Union, Edinburgh University, Edinburgh.

Kirkaldy Ski Club: Finlay S. Taylor, 10 Kirkriggs, Forfar, Angus DD8 2AT.

Livingston Ski Club: Miller Anderson, Deans Community High School, Livingston, West Lothian.

Nordic Ski Club of Scotland: Sec. Tom Mowat, Cochran Croft, Kincardine O'Neil, Aberdeenshire. Tel: 033-984 245.*

Strathspey Nordic Ski Club: Sec. S.N.S.C., Inverdruie, Aviemore, Inverness-shire PH22 1QH. Tel: 0479-810729.*

Tayside X-C Ski Club: Pres. Tony S. Campbell, 16 Rossie Park Drive, Inchture, Perthshire. Tel: Inchture 426.

England

Hexham Nordic Ski Club: Sec. D.C. Spearman, 11 Shaws Park, Hexham, Northumberland NE46 3BJ. Tel: 0434-604093.

Lakeland X-C Ski Club: Sec. Susan Foster, 9 Windermere Road, Kendal, Cumbria. Tel: Kendal 26494.*

London Region Nordic S.C.: Sec. Hilary Field, 21 Dinorben Avenue, Fleet, Hampshire. Tel: 02514-21214.

Manchester X-C Ski Club: Sec. c/o Nick Estcourt Outdoor Sports, 84 Stamford New Road, Altrincham, Cheshire WA14 1BS.

Newcastle University X-C S.C.: Sec. Athletic Union, Students Union Building, Kings Walk, Newcastle upon Tyne. Tel: 0632-28511, Ext. 267.

Tyneside Loipers X-C Ski Club: Sec. Sylvia Dowse, 95 Queens Road, Whitley Bay, Tyne & Wear NE26 3AT. Tel: 0632-521816.*

Yorkshire Dales X-C Ski Club: Secretary, 71 Station Parade, Harrogate, N. Yorks HG1 1ST. Tel: 0423-62874.*

Norway

Kvitavatn Nordic Ski Club: Sec. Roderick Tuck, Kvitavatn Fjellstoge, 3660 Rjukan, Norway. Tel: Rjukan 036-91174.*

OTHER USEFUL ADDRESSES

For Scottish and UK Cross-country race calendar (snow and rollers): Andy Main, 10 Mossmill Park, Mosstodloch, Morayshire. Tel: 0343-820936.

For English and UK race calendar (roller and snow): Eric Wooley, E & H Adventure Sports, 71 Station Parade, Harrogate, N. Yorks. Tel: 0423-62874.*

For the North Wales scene: Noel Hulmerston, 'Fron Deg', Fron Park Road, Holywell, Clwyd. Tel: 0352-713238.*

* after phone numbers signifies they are willing to give snow condition reports for their area and nearby hill and mountain region.

Snow condition reports can also be obtained by ringing the numbers listed below:

East and S.E. England (N. and S. Downs, Chilterns): Met. Office 01-246 8091.

S.W. England (Dartmoor, Exmoor and Cotswolds): Moorland Rambler, Exeter 0392-32681.

Central England (South of Sheffield): Rowland Wood, Prestidge, Derby 0332-42245.

N.W. England (West Pennines and Lakes): Mountain Centre, Broughton-in-Furness 065-76 461.

Southern Scotland (S. Uplands and S.W. Highlands): Nevisport, Glasgow 041-322 4814.

W. Central and N.W. Highlands: Nevisport, Fort William 0397-4921.

SKI-ING COURSES AND HOLIDAYS, HIRES AND INSTRUCTION

Cairdsport's Aviemore Ski School: The Aviemore Centre, Aviemore, Inverness-shire PH22 1PL. Tel: 0479-810 310. (H)

Carrbridge Ski School: 'Mafeking', Carrbridge, Inverness-shire PH23 3AS. Tel: 047984 246. (H)

Highland Guides: Inverdruie, Aviemore, Inverness-shire PH22 1QH. Tel: 0479810 729. (H,C,I)

Cameron McNeish, The Birches, Kincraig, Inverness-shire. (I)

Peter Nicol, Aboyne, Aberdeenshire. (I)

Ramblers Holidays Ltd.: Longcroft House, Fretherne Road, Welwyn Garden City, Herts. AL8 6PQ. Tel: 07073 31133. (A)

Scottish Norwegian Ski School: Speyside Sports, Aviemore, Inverness-shire. Tel: 0479810 656. (H)

Ski Road Skis: Inverdruie Visitor Centre, Aviemore PH22 1QH. Tel: 0479810 922. (H)

Scottish Youth Hostels Association: 161 Warrender Park Road, Edinburgh EH9 1EQ. Tel: 031-229 8660. (C)

Waymark Holidays: 295 Lillie Road, London SW6 7LL. (A)

Eric Wooley, E & H Adventure Sports, 71 Station Parade, Harrogate, N. Yorks. Tel: 0423 62874. (H,I)

Key: H hires, C courses, I instruction, A holidays abroad.

Scottish Mountains on Ski Malcolm Slesser (West Col 1970) (touring).

Ski Technique and Instruction Manual (Book 1. Basic Ski System) Editor: Doug. Godlington (B.A.S.I. — British Association of Ski Instructors). Manual for downhill ski-ing — excellent illustrations of downhill techniques, but not all applicable to cross-country.

MAGAZINES

Climber & Rambler, Footloose, The Great Outdoors.

PUBLICATIONS

BOOKS

Cross Country, Downhill and other Nordic Ski-ing Techniques Steve Barnett (Pacific Search Press 1979) (touring).

Nordic Touring and Cross Country Ski-ing Michael Brady (Dreyer) (basic).

Spur Book of X-C. Ski-ing Terry Brown and Rob Hunter (Spurbooks) (basic).

The New X-C Ski Book John Caldwell (Stephen Green Press 1973, possibly out of print) (basic).

Mountain Navigation Peter Cliff.

On Ski in the Cairngorms V.A. Firsoff (Chambers 1965) (touring).

Cross Country Ski-ing Ned Gillette (The Mountaineers 1979) (basic).

Ski-ing Pierre Laplame (downhill).

Nordic Ski-ing Cameron McNeish (Cicerone) (basic).

Cross Country Ski-ing John Moore (British Ski Federation) (basic to race training).

Wilderness Ski-ing Lito Tejada-Flores (Sierra Club Book 1972) (touring).

Backcountry Ski-ing Lito Tejada-Flores (Sierra Club Book 1981).

ing business, Ellis Horwood Limited, of Chichester. She lives in a cottage in West Sussex with her writer husband, two Jack Russell terriers and three mongrel cats. The family's beloved Welsh cob pony mare, Rusty, lives on a farm close by.

Riding, trekking, perhaps owning a pony of your own, provide hours of enjoyment for the whole family and need not be expensive. Sue Gibson explains all that a beginner needs to know in this warm and loving introduction to the world of horses.

Sue Gibson is a freelance journalist specialising in equestrian and racing subjects. She began her career writing for the *Sporting Chronicle, Horse and Rider* (then *Light Horse*) and *Pony* in 1975, and has written regularly for these publications ever since. She is the author of the delightful *Rusty's Foal* which was published by Ellis Horwood Limited in two editions in 1981 and 1982.

She was editor of *Horse and Rider* for a time and March 1984 saw the publication of *Glorious Uncertainty* by Jenny Pitman and Sue Gibson (Collins Willow). This is the autobiographical story of the first lady to train a Grand National winner, as told to Sue. Sue is currently engaged on an informative dressage book with Olympic rider Jennie Loriston-Clarke.

Sue is a director of her family's publish-

Riding, Trekking and Owning a Family Pony

SUE GIBSON

Riding with your family is a lovely way to spend a weekend morning, riding out, away from the town, into bridleways and open country, sharing special moments. Wild creatures are not worried by the sound of hooves: you will see a fox out hunting for food for its young, rabbits enjoying an early morning nibble of grass, perhaps a badger family having a game before they retire for the day. You will see the first cowslips on the downs in mid-May, early primroses and pale wild violets. Sharing these pleasures with your family is very, very satisfying. Riding regularly, you watch the seasons change. You become sharply aware of the months coming and going. Tiny details in nature will tell you when spring is on the way.

Riding is enjoying an increasing popularity today. It does not need to be an expensive activity and it is now becoming more common for a family to keep one, or even two ponies or horses of their own. Ponies, incidentally, are less than 14 hands 2 inches (14.2), a hand being 4 inches, measured from the ground to the highest point of the withers, and horses are over this height; but there are many specific pony breeds, individuals of which may attain a height greater than this. Two ponies mean that parents and children can share even more fully in the very real pleasure to be derived from riding and caring for horses. Of course, pony owners — as opposed to pony riders — are in a minority. Most riders are well content with a weekly Saturday or Sunday 'hack' out from the local riding establishment. You do not have to live in the countryside. Right in the heart of London's West End, one minute's walk from Hyde Park Corner and the roar of a thousand cars, is a riding school called Lilo Blum's which houses around forty horses. They ride in Rotten Row through Hyde Park, or else 'box' horses out into the countryside to hack or hunt. Lilo has run her establishment in Grosvenor Mews for around fifty years.

CHOOSING A RIDING SCHOOL

The suburbs of London and of most big towns and cities have riding schools. They vary widely in quality and if you have never ridden a horse before it is wise to contact the British Horse Society at Stoneleigh in Warwickshire. The BHS has an approval scheme for riding schools and trekking centres throughout the country and can tell you where your nearest 'approved' establishment is situated.

To begin with, go out and inspect a few riding schools. You need very little experience to be able to tell roughly the kind of quality they offer. Rather as you would turn your nose up entering a restaurant where the tables are grubby, the ashtrays full of cigarette ends and the waiters untidy and careless, so when you enter the riding school yard you will see whether the place is fairly spic and span, whether the horses are standing in clean fresh straw and whether they look half starved. It's a matter of commonsense. The manner of the proprietor will also give you a clue. If he is friendly and greets you with a smile you are on the right track. If, on the other hand, he sits there with a cigarette hanging from one corner of his mouth, his feet up on the desk and says, "What do you want?" then forget it.

The most obvious giveaway in a riding stables is the dung heap. A good yard will have a tidy dung heap swept into a neat shape, not sprawled all over the place, tripping people up.

Explain to your chosen proprietor exactly how much or how little riding you have done in your life. Riding is a most delightful occupation, equalled by few others for the bond it offers between horse and man, but horses aren't motor cars. They don't have dual braking systems, they have minds of their own and when frightened by a noisy lorry or by sudden stirrings in the hedgerows can take off at an alarming speed before you know what is happening. This is fine, provided you have already done a lot of riding and have established your 'seat', in which case you are unlikely to fall off. But if you have pretended to the riding school that you are rather good, and they give you a fairly lively animal to ride, you can hardly hold

A class at Walton Heath Livery Stables.

them responsible if things go wrong. Riding schools are most anxious that things should *not* go wrong, as they prefer as few accidents as possible. So be scrupulously honest, tell the man that you haven't actually been on a horse since you were 17 years old, and they will mount you accordingly.

Listen to everything they tell you very carefully. Ask a few pertinent questions about the horse you have been given for your ride. You may like to know where he came from, how long he has been with the riding school. You'll be surprised how many riding schools keep the same horses for years — a very good sign indeed. They trust the horse to carry their clients in safety, and the horse in return can give them many years of reliable service. What is his name? How old is he? Suddenly, you find yourself riding a 'character' with a personality of his own, rather than just a horse.

YOUR FIRST LESSON

Your first lesson will probably take place in the school's own manège, or riding paddock. There is infinite wisdom in this. To begin with, as with riding a bike, you may feel unsteady and peculiarly high off the ground. It seems a long way down and you might possibly experience some natural apprehension. Now you will appreciate the value of having been honest about your riding ability! Suddenly, you feel beneath you a vibrant, living creature — and you don't want him too vibrant to start with! A spritely creature dancing elegantly about is fine for the experienced person, but unnerving, to say the very least, if this is your first ride.

The instructor will show you the correct way to sit, and how to hold the reins. Do not imagine this is all for show — there is a reason for sitting upright, with your heels pressed firmly down and your toes pointed forwards. Not only will you look smarter than the man slouched in his saddle with his feet sticking out like sore thumbs, but you are safer in the event of unexpected movement. The forward-tipped rider is already half-way towards coming out of the saddle, and those pressed-down heels give you security when you move off. Keeping the reins in a firm but not vice-like grip ensures that you are in control of the pony, and not he in control of you.

NOW TO GO SOMEWHERE

The 'aid' or signal for walking will be shown you, and you will find yourself learning to balance in the centre of the saddle, concentrating considerably on all the things that the instructor says. It seems endless at first, like driving a car. So it is with riding — heels down, toes forward, back straight, look ahead, grip firm but gentle, squeeze gently and don't kick him forward, and after a couple of circuits of the paddock you will find things slotting into place.

Now for something faster. Trotting is a unique two-beat pace in horses, which requires a 'posting' action by the rider: called rising to the trot, this involves 'sitting down' in the saddle on one beat, and rising (not too high) from the saddle on the other beat. It may take a little while to get the hang, and you may bump precariously around for a short spell — until the penny drops and you are circuiting happily at a rising trot.

It is highly unlikely that you will canter

Leaving Bramble Hill Riding Centre.

on a first riding lesson. Be satisfied the first time with learning to 'apply the aids' carefully and enjoy the response from the horse beneath you as you ask him for a change of pace. Relax, but keep alert, and content yourself with this first time out. Next morning you may find yourself a little saddle sore. You will have been using muscles that haven't seen the light of day in years, and they will complain fairly noisily next morning about all this sudden work they have been asked to do. Take no notice of them. They soon pipe down and within a day or so you'll be back to normal. Just remember — next week they won't mind being worked nearly so much!

YOUR SECOND LESSON

Your second lesson may be on the same horse, or the school may let you try another. But if you were happy on the first lesson, it is wise when booking the next lesson to ask for that horse again. A friendly face, a familiar back upon which to ride, can make riding that much more pleasurable — you know this horse's name, and a little about him, and can get to know him quite well after another lesson or two.

The progression from trot to canter is, for the apprehensive beginner, quite momentous. OK for those without a single nerve in their bodies — some people take to riding horses like ducks to water — but the majority of newcomers to the sport, quite rightly, feel somewhat nervous. However, once your cantering is mastered, and you are able to change from one pace to another and back again with reasonable confidence, the time has probably come for your first hack.

HACKING

The pleasure to be gained from merely hacking out across country or in quiet lanes has no price on it. Provided you have learned the basics and are accompanied by a proficient person, you should find your spirits soaring as you first ride out of the yard and into the countryside.

Wait until you turn off the lane into a leafy bridleway, where you must duck occasionally to avoid overhanging branches, and you will see the countryside as you have never seen it before from a car or on foot. You enjoy views over hedges that you didn't know existed. You turn away from traffic, head deep into woodland, cross common and moor. You watch rabbits scurrying for their burrows as you come near. Squirrels sit quietly in branches above your head, for some reason unafraid of riders and horses, and watch cheekily as you pass beneath them. As the traffic

Away from it all, deep in the heart of the countryside.

noises fade you grow accustomed to new sounds and new feelings . . . the rush of the wind about your ears as you canter across an open stretch . . . the sound of a river which you ford on horseback . . . the strength of the horse beneath you, his head down as he pulls up a gradient, working every muscle. It's like magic. And the satisfaction you feel after your ride, as you turn back into the stable yard with a clatter of iron shod hooves on concrete is immeasurable. You just can't wait for next Sunday morning.

DOBBIN'S DAY

But what of the horse, between now and next Sunday morning? You may wonder what his week will entail. The day after, if it were a Monday, might be his day off. Riding school horses work much harder on Saturdays and Sundays, as you might expect. So on Mondays they are usually turned out to graze in a paddock, stretch their legs, roll contentedly on their backs and kick their legs up. If it is summer, however, they will probably spend the day indoors where they are safe from the unwanted attention of a million flies buzzing round their heads. They may be asked to take a passenger out for an evening ride. They will spend the night out, when it is cool, where they can graze in peace — grazing is an essential part of a horse's mental wellbeing. Like relaxation is for the human.

In winter the horse will probably be brought back into his stable before dark and given a nice warm 'tea' of oats, bran and possibly sugar beet pulp, which he adores and scoffs with noisy relish. Then a nice large fragrant haynet, stuffed full to keep him contented and munching most of the night.

Tuesday morning he will be 'mucked out', that is, have his stable cleaned out, and possibly be given a small breakfast an hour before he is required to do any work. Horses take some time to digest oats or 'hard' feed, and can become quite ill if asked to work on a stomachful. His week will continue this way, depending upon the time of year, until Saturday morning comes round again. He may be asked to work three rides before lunch, and a further three in the afternoon — assuming each to be an hour long. Sundays will be the same, and you will appreciate him all the more for knowing how hard he works.

A great deal of pleasure is to be gained from taking an interest in stable management, which means looking after a horse properly. Each stable has its own methods and routines, but most riding establishments really welcome the pupil who comes half-an-hour before the ride to help prepare his or her horse, and who stays for half-an-hour afterwards to help untack and feed him.

The riding school horse upon whom you have just enjoyed your look at the countryside must rest a little while between rides, and have his tack removed. You may enjoy helping to brush him down, comb his mane and tail through, and pick his feet clean. You can learn the correct way to put on his saddle and bridle, and if you are ever to consider buying a family pony it is essential to know what you are doing, so these riding school lessons can prove invaluable.

When the lesson is over watch his feed being mixed. See the way his tack is carefully removed, and the 'saddle marks' brushed away. His water must be checked — carrying you was thirsty work — but he must not be allowed too much if he is hot, or after he has been fed. You will notice that some riding schools only permit a half-bucket of water per horse after feeding. The reason for this is quite simple. The horse, hungry from work, eats his food with obvious pleasure and doesn't toy with it. If he drinks too much on top of the meal the food can swell in his stomach and give him what is known as a colic, or bellyache. He can't belch the wind up to relieve the indigestion. He cannot be sick if he 'overdoes' it and so he starts to roll to try and relieve the pain. This could cause him to twist a gut and, I'm afraid to say, there's not much a vet can do with twisted guts. Sadly, it means destruction. So riding schools withhold excessive water until the food has been digested properly, when he can drink his fill. Then another munch on some hay before his next pupil arrives to ride him. The pleasure gained from learning about how horses are kept is to some people almost as great as the pleasure gained from riding itself. More of this later.

WHERE TO RIDE

Having learned the basic art of staying on board, and gained some knowledge about riding, you may well feel when planning your summer vacation that a riding holiday would be fun. Quite right. There is a vast range of centres all over England, Wales, Scotland and Ireland — and indeed abroad — to which you can go as a family. Any members of the family who perhaps do not enjoy riding can often take part in other outdoor activities instead.

A good way to sift through the holiday and trekking centres is to buy one of the equestrian monthly magazines such as *Pony* or its 'big sister' *Horse and Rider*. (These should be available from your local newsagent or from 104 Ash Road, Sutton,

Grooming a pony after a ride.

Surrey.) These magazines carry advertisements from recognised and established centres, and as the people who write for the magazines occasionally spend weekends at these centres they can personally vouch for most of them.

Possibly the loveliest riding country close to London is the New Forest. Here you can ride over miles and miles of sweeping heathland dotted with herds of semi-wild pony mares, usually accompanied by their foals if you go after June, or along clearly marked paths through thick woods. The Forest is partly on a sandy soil which gives well-drained ground for most of the year and there are few riding restrictions, which is wonderful.

Exmoor is unrivalled for beauty as riding country; nearby are the Quantock Hills, famed for picturesque villages and farmhouses. To the west you can explore the wild beauty of the North Devon coast. Further south you can discover the even wilder Dartmoor. You can visit Widecombe-in-the-Moor, but unlike Old Uncle Tom Cobley, who had to share his grey mare with so many tipsy friends, you will find a wealth of trekking and riding centres on Dartmoor, able to provide each member of the family with a horse of his own.

Bodmin Moor is another unspoilt part of the West Country with several riding holiday centres. The vast tracts of rolling moorland that Daphne du Maurier describes in *Jamaica Inn* do not appear to have changed in centuries. You can find the real Jamaica Inn, no longer noted for smugglers and highwaymen, more for its tourists and trekkers enjoying the local ales!

The Cotswolds are perhaps more 'civilised'. Deep in the valleys between thickly-wooded hillsides you will find glorious villages built of local grey stone. Westward lies the Forest of Dean, still so unspoilt and most attractive for the holiday horseman.

Wales provides one of the most extensive areas of natural beauty for the rider and a nice idea is to rent a cottage and ponies for your holiday. Obviously, this would only appeal to a riding family who know a good deal about ponies.

Add to these the Yorkshire Dales, the whole of Scotland, the Lake District, Norfolk (splendid riding holidays as well as sailing) and Ireland, where the Guinness will help to make your holiday even more enjoyable! Of course, every county has special areas of natural countryside to offer but the regions I have mentioned are among the best.

You can expect most trekking centres to accommodate entire families, offering bed, breakfast and evening meal, and making sure that each member is provided with a suitable mount. In the average family, with two children, there will be the need for a hunter-type for father, a more gentle type of riding horse for mother, and reasonably fit and well-behaved ponies for the children. Trekking centres are fully aware of the importance of matching horses to people and indeed would soon go out of business if they were not.

On a trekking holiday you can often find tuition as well as hacking, and the more imaginative centres will also organise weekly gymkhanas and shows. You will find out more about stable management and become far more involved with the horses themselves than you did at your local riding school. Here is another world — horses fill your morning, afternoon and evening. You will find yourself helping the trekking centre's grooms, fetching horses in from the fields, learning to pick stones from their feet and how to tack

Pony trekking along a quiet forest track.

up correctly.

On longer rides you will discover that the trekking pony, although an extremely fit and sturdy beast — he would not be able to work unless he were — needs to rest his back once or twice during the ride. You will stop for a picnic lunch, miles from any sound but the wind and the buzzards searching the heather for their lunch, the horses untacked and grazing close by while you rest in the sun. They often enjoy rolling from side to side on their backs after several hours' weight-carrying, walking and cantering up and down hill.

An alternative form of holiday is to hire a horse-drawn caravan and just take off on your own with the family. You should read a book on harness beforehand because although tuition is naturally given before you drive away, it is advisable to know *why* a harness is shaped the way it is. It is best to know about the sores that badly-fitting tack can cause, and avoid them, rather than find yourself 50 miles from where you started and the horse in pain because everything has been done up too tightly.

Riding outside the United Kingdom is a very exciting prospect but the extra expense added to possible language problems could present the beginner with difficulties.

SAFETY FIRST!

Most trekking centres never let riders take their horses out without the supervision of a member of staff but there sometimes may be occasions when you are permitted to ride out unaccompanied. There are some unwritten laws of the countryside where horse riding is concerned which make the activity safer and more pleasant for all. Bridleways (marked by red dashes on the Ordnance Survey maps) are specially for horse riders, although walkers use them too. Footpaths are the special province of walkers. People who ride horses on footpaths can be very unpopular.

Before riding across farmland, ask the farmer's or landowner's permission. Some dislike riders in general because of the inconsiderate behaviour of the few who leave gates open and let sheep and cattle out on to main roads, or gallop over young crops and ruin strips round the edges of fields. So ensure that your family closes gates and does not damage crops.

If you ride on roads you may find you are unpopular there too! Some motorists understand the nuances of horse behaviour but many do not. They cannot understand why you should need to take up the width of a car with your horse or why you must make them slow down before they pass you. If you ride single file along main roads — which appears sensible — it is an invitation to uninitiated traffic to whip past, almost blowing your hat away as it skims between you and the opposing stream. But you can do a great deal to help. Remember to thank *every* motorist who slows down for you and your horse. You should, the BHS advises, ride two abreast in main road situations so that cars coming up behind you are obliged to slow down, but once they have slowed tuck yourselves in a little and if the way is clear, wave the cars behind you politely past. Thank them and spare them a smile. You will be helping to make riding, and motoring, safer for all.

Quiet country lanes may not be as quiet as they seem. Tuck yourself out of danger in good time — remember the motorist cannot see you from around the bend a hundred yards ahead.

All this may make riding appear nerve-racking, but if you take lessons at a reputable riding school and watch how a good, experienced rider behaves both on the roads and in the country then all will be well. Your riding will become the highlight of your week. That a promise!

The average riding school or pony-trekking animal is not going to be frightened of traffic. Generally, you will ride in groups of between three and ten. Horses are gregarious creatures by nature and herd animals since time immemorial. They are not cats who walk by themselves! Having other horses around makes them feel safe. This is one reason why I personally rarely ride alone. Our pony, Rusty, is probably one of the safest family ponies in the country, though she is not a 'slug' by any means: little worries her. But even on Rusty I am careful. A dog can rush up behind us barking madly, and flight — instant and uncontrollable — is the only defence mechanism a horse possesses. So the only time I permit myself a solitary

ride is early on Sunday morning, around six or seven o'clock, when I creep out of the house, tack Rusty up and enjoy a potter through the village High Street back up to the house. Sometimes we set Rusty free in the garden where she 'weeds' the strawberry patch for us or grazes our lawn. Then I enjoy an early cup of coffee with my husband in her company before a quiet ride back to the farm where we keep her, again very early, and home for breakfast. If I were to fall off Rusty in the village then I would be within sight and sound of someone who would, hopefully, come out and help me. And if we were separated Rusty would probably just head off back to her field and early on Sunday morning she would be unlikely to meet heavy traffic tearing through the village street. But if Rusty were to accidentally 'drop' me somewhere in the hills close to the farm where we keep her, she would head for home and I would be left until someone found me, which could be a long time!

Riding in pairs is far more fun, riding as a family the best fun of all. Your horse is less likely to gallop away should you part company with him. His instinct is to stay close to his equine companions. If you are hurt the others can tie your horse up and get help.

RIDING CLOTHES

Riding clothes are designed with a specific purpose. First of all, you need a hard hat. This is no decorative piece of equipment, it is the most important item you will need for riding. Not that you intend to make a habit of falling on your head, but it is always a possibility.

Next, you must protect your legs, so

wear a pair of leather or very strong rubber boots. Anyone who has knocked their legs against a gatepost while riding through will know the sense of this. Jodhpurs, made from stretchy material and close-fitting, are a wise buy. I learned this the hard way. Once, in my ignorance, I wore jeans rolled up 'Pirates of Penzance' style with my riding boots. This I imagined looked pretty 'hip' for a horsewoman. Silly me. One May afternoon I went down to the farm with a non-horsey friend after a pleasant and rather alcoholic lunch to turn our mare back out into her field. Inspired by the wine I leapt on to the mare bareback, hatless and with my jeans rolled up. As we went through the gateway, the rolled-up part of my jeans caught on the catch of the gatepost. They held firm as the mare calmly continued on her way into the field. Next thing I was hanging inverted from the gatepost, much to the amusement of my friend and a group of other people irresistibly drawn to the scene. I could not help laughing myself but a small part of me said, "Thank God she's a quiet mare and didn't kick up her heels."

As well as being safer, jodhpurs are more comfortable than jeans which can cause chafing. Jods can be obtained nowadays in practical colours including black, navy blue, dark green and chocolate brown as well as white, beige and canary yellow. The lighter colours are generally reserved for shows as you will need to wash them after every wearing — somehow they always get marked, no matter how careful you try to be. They are well worth their price and the better makes will give you longer service.

For hacking, a checked jacket looks smart, especially over a polo-necked sweater, or for more formal occasions a shirt and even a tie. In summer wear a short-sleeved cotton shirt; in winter a thermal tee-shirt under your thicker shirt does not go amiss, with an extra sweater if it is cold.

The more casual sort of riding wear includes quilted anoraks and vests, which keep the cold and light rain out. Very smart dress involves a dark blue or black showing jacket — expensive unless you intend to wear it often.

Riding in the rain need not be unpleasant. Various riding macs are available — from the expensive, smart white heavy variety, through plastic, to light nylon. Although not as elegant, the cheap nylon is almost as effective as the expensive kind and will fold up to almost nothing to stuff in a pocket. Some come in their own little bag which can be tied to the rings on the back of your saddle.

An essential to carry when you are riding is a small fold-away hoof pick. Horses often trap small sharp stones in their feet and can go instantly lame. It is a matter of hopping off the moment you feel any difference in your horse's 'action', and inspecting each foot in turn to find and remove the offender. Experience will teach you whether it is a hind or fore leg in trouble. (Like cars, horses have a near side and an off side to which you refer in much the same way as a sailor talks of port and starboard. Near is left, off is right.)

That's *you* all dressed. Now, what about the horse?

TACK

First the horse needs a saddle and a bridle. The saddle for hacking is called general purpose, and is sometimes worn with a shaped pad, known as a numnah, underneath to make it more comfortable (for him, not you). The saddle is held in place by a girth which should be tight enough to stop the saddle slipping without taking the horse's breath away. It usually needs tightening once you have mounted — you will be shown the correct way to do this — and again after about 15 or 30 minutes' riding, when it may have stretched.

The horse's bridle is more complex. It has a bit which runs through his mouth across his tongue and rests on his jaws. This must fit correctly. It is attached to the reins with which you guide him left or right. The bit is held in place by the cheek strap, running around his head behind his ears, and the browband which runs in front of the ears. Some wear a noseband. A drop noseband runs behind the horse's chin and helps keep his mouth from opening too wide. A cavesson noseband fits higher, and can be worn with

A few final adjustments before the ride.

or without a sheepskin cover — sheepskin nosebands suit some horses better than others. The other piece of leather is the throat latch which runs under his jaws and must not be too tight.

Horses may also wear 'brushing boots' on their legs, which prevent them from kicking one fetlock (ankle) with the opposite hoof. Remember a horse wears iron shoes and brushing boots prevent this kind of self-inflicted injury. 'Over-reach boots' which you see on some show jumpers' front legs are to prevent their forelegs from being cut by their hind legs.

other paraphernalia belong to the realm of the more experienced owner. For a beginner, there you have the basic outfit.

By now, you and Dobbin should be looking smart and feeling comfortable, enjoying your hacking and your lessons. So much so, in fact, that you may even be considering a very dreamy idea — a horse of your own . . .

A HORSE OF YOUR OWN

Owning a family pony is an Experience! No other animal that you ever buy will be quite such a challenge, be quite so demanding or provide so much pleasure. Pony and horse ownership brings special rewards but special responsibilities too.

It is essential to find out as much as you can about horses before you buy one and advisable to keep your first horse at a livery yard. These vary enormously. There is the extremely up-market yard, where it can cost around £30 to £35 a week to keep your horse in elegant conditions. This price would include two or more feeds a day, unlimited good quality hay, grooming, exercise, mucking out and bedding of straw or woodshavings. You can expect shoeing bills (£15 or more per set each six weeks) and veterinary attendance to be charged as extras.

Then there is the opposite end of the scale, the grass livery, which means that for £4 or £5 per week you can put your horse in a specified field. Boxes (stables) are also sometimes available. You can use your box to keep the horse in by day during the summer months — away from flies — and he can live in there by night in winter. In spring, when the grass is very lush and the animal may get top heavy through consuming it in large quantities, the box is a useful place to help him keep his figure in nice shape. As spring grass can also make ponies more frisky than is good for them or their rider, the stable has an added benefit.

The grass and box livery system is cheap, but means the owner has to do the work himself. He must get up every morning in winter to muck out the box, feed the pony, and turn him out into the field for the day. He must go back at night, make the pony's bed, fill the haynet and the water bucket, and fetch the pony back indoors again. In summer the process is reversed. A friend with a pony at the same livery will be invaluable. You can take it in turns to do the animals, or one can do the morning shift, and the other take over in the evening.

Some yards have an ideal compromise, a part do-it-yourself, part we-do-it-for-you arrangement. The cost naturally falls somewhere between a full livery and a grass livery, and means that your horse is neither a total stranger which you dress up and ride out on a couple of times a week nor is he a total burden to you. You could arrange to see to the horse's needs in the morning, and leave the yard to take care of him for the remainder of the day. The possibilities are several, and it is up to you to discuss them with the owner of the yard.

Livery yard addresses are available through the British Horse Society, through your local papers or by word of mouth from horsey friends. At livery there are usually plenty of knowledgeable people to advise you and to help when things get out of hand — as they can.

The first question must be what kind of horse to buy and for most of us price is the deciding factor. (Remember the initial purchase price is just the beginning.) There is always someone at your trusty local riding school, preferably one of the instructors, who can advise you. But let us imagine you have a £500 windfall and would like to buy a pony with it. For £500 at the present time you can buy a fairly decent, cob-type animal which will give the whole family a lot of fun. The word 'cob' signifies a tough, hardy, sturdy pony or horse. The average height for an animal of this 'native' type is around fourteen hands, two inches. The word 'native' covers the entire range of ponies which originate from semi-wild areas such as the New Forest, the Welsh mountains, the Highlands, Fells, Dales, Dartmoor, Exmoor, and the Connemara hills of Ireland — and the Shetlands. The ponies are named after the area whence they came and many shows have breed classes to which you can take your native pony in due course.

The Welsh cob Section D type offers an ideal family pony. They have a good temperament and can live out all winter, or live in equally happily. They really need only bulk hay in winter, but they do not get overheated temperament-wise when given 'hard' feed, such as oats and barley. Most of the native breeds have these

New Forest pony.

Welsh cob cross thoroughbred.

traits and all can carry adults and children equally well — except perhaps the Shetland! Though I know adults who do ride even them occasionally!

You cannot be too careful in choosing your pony as there are a great many doubtful varieties on the market, of indistinct breeding and unknown heritage. The vital questions to ask yourself are: is the pony 100 per cent, or as near as possible, safe to ride on the roads? Is he sound and unlikely to give you trouble with endless veterinary bills? Is he 'kind' to handle, quiet about the stable, well-mannered enough for all the family to ride?

Don't get carried away by a beautiful chestnut head with a flaxen mane or a fanciful thoroughbred-type animal which has in all probability become too much of a handful for its previous owner. Look for that special something in the eye — as you would possibly judge a person. A kind eye, believe me, is one of the biggest giveaways of a horse's temperament. Not that you want an ageing slug, either, because you will be disappointed. Something that is not too fiery, not too slow, has a welcoming eye, and stands reasonably still and calm while you inspect him, is what you should aim for.

Where to find such a paragon of virtue? It's difficult and very few of us get it right the first time. There is a way to avoid buying an unsuitable horse and that is to ask the seller if he would mind you taking it for a month's trial first.

Any genuine horse-seller will agree. The loving family whose children have outgrown the pony, a working owner who no longer has time for a horse, these are the people who will want the best possible home for their old friend. You may indeed find them asking you questions — what kind of grazing have you arranged for their precious family pony? How experienced are you? Are you planning to keep him for a reasonably long period? Can we come and visit him occasionally?

Word of mouth is the usual way of hearing about horses, at least in villages and horsey communities. The local riding school instructor is bound to hear frequently of horses and ponies for sale, and the chances are he can find out a few things about the pony's history, habits and price before you get involved.

The riding school is obviously pleased to help because when you have bought a pony there is a strong chance that you may keep it at their establishment. This can often be a perfect solution since you have the benefit of experienced help, riding school facilities and round-the-clock care for your pony. Some schools will take your pony at livery for quite a small sum, provided they can use it in the riding school for other riders. Whether or not you fancy beginners or other riders on board your pony is up to you.

Then there are pony agencies which keep a register of horses for sale and put potential buyers in touch with sellers. You could also try the dealers. Good dealers make their reputation by honesty, getting the right pony for people and even in due course 'trading' the pony for something bigger or more adventurous. They are usually happy to permit a month's trial. Again, your local riding school may help you sort out the good dealers from the bad.

There are several guidelines to follow when you are seeking out a pony and going to inspect it. Ask that the pony be out at grass when you arrive and watch them catch the pony without tricks like buckets and sugar lumps. See for yourself whether he comes easily to hand, or whether he runs off at a naughty trot to evade capture. If there is one thing that will frustrate you it's the horse you cannot catch — how can you get pleasure from such a beast?

Having seen him caught, ask to see him groomed over lightly and handled. Does he lay back his ears when brushed, kick when his feet are picked up, refuse to stand quietly tied up whilst these things are being done? If so, that's probably the very reason why he is being sold and you had best forget him. Horse's habits, owing to human misuse, can last a lifetime.

Ask to see him tacked up and watch his behaviour now. Does he open his mouth willingly for the bit or shake and toss his head to avoid the bridle? A horse shaking his head can knock you flat! Watch his face when the girth is being done up. If he looks nasty and about to turn and bite remember he will always do so, even to you who would love him so much! Try another pony.

Now he is ready to be ridden and it may be all you can do to say calmly, "Can you please put him through some paces for us to watch?" But say it. Any unwillingness on the part of the seller to ride the horse is an instant giveaway. He is frightened of the horse and you, possibly a beginner, could end being frightened too. If the horse is the type to take advantage of a nervous or slightly apprehensive rider — it's quite true, they know by instinct if you are a beginner — he will do you and your family no good whatsoever. One fall can be enough to ruin a beginner's confidence — you want a pony that will not drop you on the road.

If you like the way he goes with his present owner, try him yourself. Then, if you are satisfied that the pony is naturally

well-mannered and obliging, the next step is the vet. He will inspect the horse thoroughly if you ask, and although you may have quite a bill for this service it can save you hundreds of pounds and a great many tears. Provided the pony is passed sound, provided your riding school instructor gives his seal of approval and you have a one-month trial period agreed, you have a horse at last!

Take him back to your livery yard and on his first night try and stable him and worm him. The vet will provide you with worm medicine and may dose the pony for you. Check the horse's last tetanus injection — they need regular protection. I am in favour of the annual September booster which can be done at the same time as rasping his teeth which grow quite long and sharp in summer. All three done together will put your mind at rest.

A stable gives your horse dual protection. One, against the bitter cold rain, wind and snow of winter — bring him indoors at 5 p.m., turn him back out around 8 or 9 a.m. — and two, against intense summer heat — bring him in around 10 a.m. and put him out for the night around 6 p.m. In spring and early autumn the grass has what is known as a 'flush' and too much of this high protein diet can cause not only overweight but a nasty condition known as laminitis, a swelling of the inside membranes of the foot. Bring your pony in for half the day, let him have old dry hay to nibble and don't give him hard feed.

Always keep your pony on clean straw or clean woodshavings (you can also get shredded paper now). He needs mucking out at least once a day when he is living on the combined 'in-and-out' system. Straw needs the droppings carefully lifted

Mucking out the stable.

by fork, the wet straw removed, and the clean piled into one corner. Swill the floor with water and disinfectant, sweep clean and leave to dry until he comes back in again. When he does, put the piled-up straw back on the floor, and add a fresh bale on top to give a clean bed. You may not always need a whole bale.

Top up water buckets, which **you** will wash out regularly and **leave upside** down when not in use, to **dry. Fill a haynet**, and the bed is ready for Dobbin.

With shavings, you need only muck out once a week, since the droppings lie on top and may be lifted with old gardening gloves and a shovel. The wet soaks through to the bottom — you need at least a 9-inch deep bed, of course — and the top remains dry. Rake the dry top layer 'smooth', and that's that. Once a week you will need to rake the dry top layer right back against the four walls, and with a shovel, dig out the 'wet' bottom layer. Having done this, swill the floor and sweep clean, and leave all day to dry. When dry, rake the old top layer down, smooth it out, and put a fresh bale of woodshavings in on top, ready for another week.

The methods depend upon how much time you have each day. Working owners find shavings ideal, since they can muck out in the mornings in winter, and perhaps rely on a good friend to bring Dobbin in at night to his bed. If the water buckets and haynets are filled in the morning, that's all that is required.

Avoid possible accidents to your pony in the stable. His water bucket needs to be soft, so that if he gets a foot through it, it will give. The manger, if one exists, needs smooth edges and should be boxed in so that Dobbin does not get his head stuck under it when he lies down. A hayrack, should one be fitted, must be at the height of his head. Too high, and hayseeds fall in his eyes and set up infection. Too low, and he bangs his head on it while getting up or down. Window glass must be covered with a grill to prevent cut noses. Protruding metal and wood must be removed. Stable doors must be secure from the clever pony who can undo top bolts but cannot reach them at ground level outside. Stable top doors need a device to fasten them back to stop them blowing in his face or yours in the wind. And the stable needs to be big enough to allow him free movement. He can get 'cast' or stuck down on the ground in a small stable. Then he will start threshing in a panic which can result in lameness or even, if he should twist the gut, in death. Horses invariably get cast in the small hours when no human help is at hand. Ten feet square is the smallest you should consider for the average 14.2 hand cob.

The native pony, living out, will grow his own long, thick winter coat. It starts growing in August or September and is composed of a coarse outer layer which sheds the rain, and a softer, downy underlayer which adds warmth. Provided you feed him about 10—15 lbs of hay, given in two lots, morning and evening, plus a tummy-warming hard feed at night to fuel his central heating system, he will survive happily. However, you may, like me, be too soft to leave him out. How could I enjoy a decent night's sleep if I thought our beloved Rusty was out in the rain?

Feeding a horse is really commonsense. In winter the pony needs up to 15 lbs of good quality hay. Never buy cheap hay, it is usually musty and carries spores which can set off allergic coughs. Once coughs like that start in a horse they are difficult to cure. A small feed of perhaps a pound of pony nuts mixed with a pound of damped-down bran and a small pan of sugar beet pulp is an ideal winter feed for the family pony. Bran should never be fed dry and oats should be avoided altogether. Oats are for thoroughbreds, broodmares, growing youngsters, very aged ponies and show animals. They will transform your placid family cob into a fire-breathing dragon!

Barley is good for fattening thin horses and is less 'hot' than oats. Maize flakes are helpful in very cold weather, as is boiled-and-cooled linseed. Sugar beet pulp is a marvellous feed — you buy it, soak it for 24 hours in cold water and feed it to keep the cold at bay.

Hay is fed in haynets as a rule, though some horses prefer it on the ground. However, as most of the horses I have ever known mash it around, tread on it and even dung on it, I invest in a hayrack. But the net suffices, provided it is correctly tied. Fill it, draw the strings in and loop the string through an iron ring or round a stout post at horse's head level. Pull the haynet up, push the strings through one of the holes at the bottom of the net. Draw the strings tight, and make a loop-knot and it should hold all night. In an emergency — perhaps the horse may get his foot caught up in it — just pull the end of the string and it will free itself at once. Never tie a haynet in complex knots.

Now you have your pony, you have learned the basics of horse care and want to start riding him. May I suggest again that you always go out in company and ride alone only when at home. When you have gained experience together, then you can venture out alone safely. But always let someone know where you plan to ride, just in case your horse comes back without you. Then the search party will know where to start looking for you.

Take riding lessons on your pony, privately if necessary, to gain elementary schooling knowledge. Learn to conquer any bad habits your horse may acquire, such as 'napping' (constantly turning for home), or spooking at 'fairies' (you can't see them, he can) in hedgerows. Learn with confidence, always think forwards, and carry a stick (don't over-use it, it's more a warning than a weapon). Above all, *enjoy* riding. If, after your first month's trial, you don't like the pony — it can happen — then nothing is lost. You have gained priceless experience and there should be no hard feelings. Explain to the seller your reasons for not wishing to buy him, and look for another pony.

There is a system of loaning ponies between friends. A family who has had a 14.2 h pony from the age of four may not want to sell him when he is 14 and the family have outgrown him. You may hear

of such a pony and offer to take him, sometimes free, sometimes for an agreed price. You are responsible for the pony's wellbeing and for his insurance and you have the pleasure of riding him. When you feel you have learned something about riding, stable management and horse care, you may be ready to return him to his owners and buy a pony of your own.

Consider all costs carefully. Apart from the pony itself you will need to buy a good saddle (£200, although some ponies are sold with their own tack), bridle (£50), and a grooming kit consisting of several brushes, a hoofpick and a curry comb (£10). Prices for keep vary all over the country. Shoes, about £15 a set, need replacing every six to eight weeks. You should insure him (£25 for a £500 horse for ordinary purposes). You can insure against death by accident or disease, theft, straying and permanent loss of use. You can insure against him creating damage and you can insure against veterinary fees up to a point. You can also insure your tack — it often costs as much as the pony!

GYMKHANAS

Adults and children can enjoy gymkhanas which are always fun. Although I had to wait until I was 27 before I owned my first pony I was not too late to join in. Activities range from potato races (you are given potatoes to drop into buckets from your pony's back as you gallop past at high speed), through sack races (you wear the sack and lead the pony, not the other way round) to the game which is my special favourite. In this you gallop from one given point to another — where a mug of something good to drink is waiting — before

A young winner.

galloping back to base. I usually come second in this event as I generally compete against one of my husband's friends who can drink his Scotch quicker than I can!

If you enjoy jumping there is Chase-Me-Charlie. A single jump is the centre of attention, starting at about one foot in height. Usually, all the competitors clear it comfortably the first time round, but are gradually eliminated as the jump creeps upwards. It isn't always the smartest and nimblest pony who wins. At the last gymkhana I attended, an ageing Nowegian Fjord pony named Olav did best of all in spite of ring-bone and his advancing years. He had a unique method of bringing himself to a complete standstill before the jump, rearing up to the required height, launching himself rear-end first, and sliding

over the pole like a snake. This rather different approach brought him a bouquet of winner's rosettes.

There's usually clear-round jumping — you pay a small competitor's fee, get round as best you can, and are presented with a rosette. And also you may find a 'minimus' which is a course of low jumps. I like 'minimus' as Rusty does not approve of jumps over eighteen inches. Fancy dress is often the order of the day at a gymkhana and you will find ponies and riders disguised as fairy godmothers, frogs or toadstools!

BREEDING

Finally, what about breeding? Just how difficult is it to breed a foal from your beloved family mare? The most important point to consider is finance. Can you, as a family, afford to keep a second horse? If you can, then carefully consider the type of foal you want to breed. If you have heeded earlier advice about buying a sturdy cob-type family pony, you must now apply the same thinking to its offspring. Unless you are breeding a part-thoroughbred for a specific purpose, I would advise against using a thoroughbred stallion. A part-bred stallion is a good compromise. Ask a knowledgeable friend or your vet to recommend a good sire. A Welsh cob crossed with a part-bred Welsh cob would give you an animal with possibly one-quarter thoroughbred breeding, enough for some good looks and paces, but not too much breeding for you to handle.

Having selected the stallion, arrange with the stud for your mare to be boxed to them. They may require a certificate from your vet to say that the mare is disease-free and this will cost you at least £20. It is wise to find a stud fairly near

home to avoid excessive travel expenses for the mare and enable you to visit her. She will need at least six weeks with the stallion. During her first 'season' at the stud she will be 'covered' three or four times and then left to see if she comes into season again after a further three weeks. Mares are in season for about five days, then have 21 clear days before coming into season again. If the stud finds the mare does not come back into season after a month it is usually safe to assume she is in foal and she can come home. Otherwise, she will have to stay longer.

When the mare comes home make a big fuss of her. Don't exactly wrap her in cotton wool, but remember that the first three months are special. It is supposed to be better if she is grazed with mares only as geldings have a reputation for causing pregnant mares to abort. She will be capable during those first three months of average hacking but she should not be ridden excessively or used for jumping.

After about six months you will find her beginning to round out and she will be looking very pregnant indeed by nine months. Mares carry their foals for 11 months and you can work out her foaling date by adding eleven months and four days to her last service date, which the stud will give you. It usually works. However, be alert for telltale signs from at least two weeks before the 11 months are up. She will begin to 'bag up', an expression which means that her milk bag starts to swell. About thirty-six hours before the foal is actually due you will see white or yellow secretions from the teat which form waxy blobs. This is known as 'waxing up' and is a sign that foaling is imminent.

A cob and newly-born foal.

Try to leave her in peace as much as possible. Mares prefer to foal without human presence and if you hang about all night watching for the miracle to occur you may cause problems. The mare could instinctively try to hold back from foaling and that's when problems arise. Keep an hourly check, as quietly as possible, if you wish. Personally, I agree with our vet that the normal broad family pony is quite capable of producing her offspring without any assistance. When the deed is done she will be proud to show you her baby!

If the foal does not suck immediately still leave them in peace. The mare will strip the caul from the foal herself and lick her baby clean and dry. Eventually when the foal is strong enough to find its legs — about three hours — it will suck of its own accord. Even a 'maiden' mare will be unlikely not to feed her young. Call the vet to come and check the mare once her foal is born. He will give you sound advice about the first few months of the foal's life.

Learn to handle the foal from the first day. I brushed Nanette, Rusty's first foal, the day she was born. (If you have any worries about foaling then read my small book about Nanette called *Rusty's Foal* which should put your mind at rest.) Nanette had her feet picked up and cleaned out at three days. Any earlier and she might have fallen over! She was led from the age of two days in a small 'foalslip'. In fact, it was easier to lead the foal and let Rusty follow. She wasn't going to let her baby out of her sight for a moment!

A small covered yard or a grass-free paddock are ideal for keeping the mare during her post-foaling season. The foal can run free and learn to use its legs without falling over, feeding adequately from Mum at the same time.

All the time Nanette was with us we taught her new lessons. She had her feet trimmed, took injections without fuss, let herself be led quietly and when required stood tied up without fidgeting. We introduced her to traffic including farm tractors. She went to Hickstead at five weeks and won a Best Foal rosette. I smacked her on the neck when she bit people, as nipping is a naughty foal habit which must be checked. In training the foal you use the same approach as you would with a human youngster. Allow some freedom but not too much. Make life fun and learning a pleasure. Let the foal see as many new sights as possible. Handle it every day so it never turns wild. All these things will make it easier to manage when it has grown into a full-sized horse with a mind of its own.

Fun should be the keynote of all your riding activities. If there are some aspects of riding you don't enjoy, don't be persuaded to do them. If all you want to do is plod quietly then let no one make you do otherwise. Riding should be, above all else, a pleasure, a safe hobby, and a joy.

PUBLICATIONS

BOOKS

There are so many books available on equestrian matters that it is best to write to the Book Shop, The British Horse Society, National Equestrian Centre, Stoneleigh, Warwickshire, for a full list.

The editors have enjoyed two of The British Horse Society's publications: *The Manual of Horsemanship* and *Training the Young Horse and Pony*.

Equus Books, 99 King Street, Cambridge, are specialists in horse books, new and old.

Also recommended by the editors are *All About Riding* by Dorothy Johnson (Stanley Paul), and *Keeping a Pony* by Jane and Melinda St. Clair (Sphere Books).

MAGAZINES

Horse and Rider (monthly). For the sophisticated older reader and keen youngster.

Pony (monthly). For keen young readers.

Horse and Hound (weekly). *The Times* of the horse world.

Riding (monthly). For all ages.

Horse and Pony (fortnightly). For the less sophisticated young reader.

Rusty and Nanette with friend Sarah.

Whernside Manor, the National Caving Centre in Cumbria. You will then discover at first hand the magical hidden world Rob Palmer evokes so vividly in this chapter.

Rob Palmer has caved for 14 years. For three of those he taught caving at outdoor centres in Yorkshire and Wales. He holds a Cave Leadership Certificate and has led several major caving expeditions abroad. He is one of the world's foremost cave divers and is a keen underground photographer. He lives in Bristol.

Man has reached the moon but, as Rob Palmer tells us, there are unknown regions still to seek beneath the earth: "Cavers still have their boundaries to discover. No one may ever know the world's deepest cave or the longest, but you can be sure they haven't been found yet." That is only part of the attraction of the mysterious world underground.

Caving is not an activity for the uninitiated but there are many fascinating caves you can easily visit with the family. Perhaps the most exciting is Gaping Ghyll in North Yorkshire where, at Whitsun and August Bank Holidays, members of the Bradford and the Craven pothole clubs arrange a bosun's chair to carry you 360 feet down into the earth to explore Britain's largest underground chamber. If this whets your appetite the next step may be to join a club, or attend a course as a family unit at

Caving

ROB PALMER

A FIRST VENTURE

The ladder rattled as it uncoiled down the gaping hole in the ground. Below, in the dim distance, the sound of a stream could be heard rushing noisily over rock, more than fifteen metres beneath the sunny fellside. I looked at Tony, and at the solid looking rock that the ladder was belayed to.

"Down there?" I said uncertainly. He nodded, grinning at my obvious nervousness. I checked the bowline knot on my lifeline, took a deep breath, and went over the edge. It wasn't quite as easy as it looked; the thin 'electron' ladder seemed to have a life of its own. Remembering Tony's advice, I wrapped my arms behind it, pulling it towards me. That did the trick. Balance restored, I moved on down as Tony paid out the lifeline from above.

A few moments later a quick shock of cold water on my feet told me I was down, and standing in the stream. Only a dim daylight filtered down, and my unaccustomed eyes could see little yet. Above, Tony arranged the lifeline so that I could safeguard his descent from below, and he was soon standing beside me, at the bottom of the entrance shaft of Calf Holes, near Pen-y-Ghent, in Yorkshire.

"OK?" he asked. I grinned reassurance, certain that this was going to be fun. He peered downstream, his eyes following the river into the darkness . . .

"That way." We bent, and filled our carbide lamps with water. Tony cupped his hand over the reflector and flicked the flint. A long flame shot out, making us both jump. Lamps burning brightly, we left the gleam of daylight behind and I set off into my first cave.

The passage was roomy, three metres wide and four high, and the stream ran over a bed of small rocks. This was easy, I thought. Looking too closely at a beautiful bed of fossils exposed in the wall was my undoing. I gasped as I stepped unwittingly into a deep pool, the water rising over my thighs. Tony laughed.

"That'll teach you to watch where you're going!"

Soon the cave roof began to drop lower, and the stream gurgled off down a narrow crack on the left side of the passage. I looked at it in horror.

"We don't go down there? You couldn't get a rat down that!" Tony smiled at the look on my face, shook his head, and pointed on down the main passage.

"No, there's a way round that, down here. Not quite as bad. It's a bit of a wriggle, then we go through the Letterbox, then it gets a bit bigger again."

The Letterbox. Cavers seemed to have a habit of giving names to exceptionally uncomfortable bits of cave. As an experienced mountaineer with a love for wide open spaces, I found this black humour a bit perverse.

Soon we were flat on our stomachs and the nice clean overalls I'd scrounged from somewhere were looking far from new. I wondered if this sort of glutinous mud washed off easily. I must have said something of the sort because Tony, up ahead, muttered something about having a shower before we went out of the cave. I shook my head in pity for the guy and, banging it on the roof, felt grateful for the helmet I wore. I wondered what new evil he had in store; I'd never thought of him as a sadist before.

There was a muffled grunt up ahead, and the pair of boots I'd been looking at suddenly turned into Tony's muddy face. Good trick, I thought, wonder how he did that? Teeth glinted through the lumps of mud in his beard.

"Now it's not very hard, this bit. You want to sort of turn on your back as you're halfway through, and drop down. Then your legs won't get stuck."

"We could always turn round and go back the way we came in," I muttered rebelliously. "Then I won't get stuck at all."

The jeer that followed hit a rapidly dwindling point of honour. Through narrowed eyes I looked at the 'Letterbox'. I could see how it got its name. A hole in the floor dropped into a passage a couple of feet below. The hole was only half a metre or so across and the passage on either side seemed barely big enough to lie flat in.

I thought about it for a minute or so, then went for it. The wrong way. Heels stuck on the roof, and shins on the edge, I hung upside down as Tony chortled below. I glared at him, not amused. He suggested through the sniggers that I turn over, and try again. A cynical sneer came to my lips. Turn over . . . how?

Looking back on it later, I wondered why I hadn't felt claustrophobic, as I had expected. There I was, stuck underground in a passage barely a foot high, trying to get down into a similar one through a ridiculously small hole. Nightmarish! That's the way it goes underground . . . when the conditions suggest claustrophobia you are usually too busy wondering how to get through to worry about nerves.

I can't remember how I did it then; I certainly find it easy now. It's all a matter of technique. I seem to remember it was something to do with losing my temper, my light, and my hold on the roof. I found myself in an upside-down heap in a small chamber, glaring up at a cheerful Tony. A drip of water fell from the ceiling and found my eye with unerring aim. I cursed. Tony dissolved into a fit of laughter, and I found myself joining in despite myself. Suddenly it was fun again; the ridiculousness of it all was just too appealing.

A short wriggle, a careful climb down a narrow cleft, and we were back with the stream, just below a roomy hall. The water cascaded down from above in an underground waterfall and provided the

An underground stream in Bridge Cave, South Wales.

shower that Tony had promised. We left our carbide lamps on a rock, illuminating the chamber, and washed the mud away.

Clean again, if rather wet, we went on. The cave got bigger. We were out of Calf Holes by now, having passed through the underground connection with Browgill Cave, from which the river resurged into daylight. Clambering over a huge rock that had fallen from the roof an age before, Tony told me to look up. On the flat roof a thousand droplets of water twinkled — tiny stars in the stone sky of the cave.

We scrambled round the next corner, climbing along the sloping wall to avoid a pool, and saw a glimmer of light ahead. A moment or two later we were standing once again in the June sunlight, listening to a blackbird singing in a nearby rowan tree. In the distance the graceful curve of Ingleborough Hill rose against the clear blue sky. I could smell the thick summer scent of the outside world.

I looked back into the cool, inviting mouth of Browgill Cave. I turned to Tony. "Where next?" I was hooked!

THE LURE OF CAVING

That was almost fifteen years ago, and since then I have been through Calf Holes— Browgill many times, and down a countless number of caves elsewhere, far harder and more spectacular than that first trip. But Calf Holes will always have a special place in my memory and I have used it in my turn to introduce others of all ages to the sport. If a caver is asked why he or she goes caving, a variety of reasons may be given — the challenge, the chance of making a new discovery, the beauty, the quiet. But most of these can be reduced to one main reason. It is simply good fun. There are few sports that allow adults to get legitimately wet, muddy, excited and exercised — to swim, climb, walk, crawl and scramble in the underground obstacle course that is a cave. And the reward for this primeval fun and effort may be the sight of a splendid crystal chamber, or the knowledge that you have tested your prowess and skill in one of the most challenging environments nature has to offer.

Caves come in all shapes and sizes (as do cavers). Formed by the slow movement of water through limestone gradually dissolving the rock along the lines of greatest weakness (and generally leaving the strongest bits behind), they offer a surprisingly varied challenge to the explorer.

Many caves still contain their original rivers but some are dry, the water moving elsewhere in much the same way as a surface river changes its course. They can be entered in a variety of ways. In some the entrance for man is where the water goes underground — the 'sink' or 'swallet'. Sometimes the easiest way in is where the water comes out — the 'resurgence'. Often it is in between, where nature or man has created another entrance to the cave. These entrances come in a variety of sizes. There are those you could drive a bus down and others barely big enough to get your shoulders in. The latter usually provide the most fun . . . at others' expense if not your own.

Caving is the ultimate sporting leveller of people. It is very hard to maintain any real dignity when your rear end is half-stuck in a narrow opening, or when sitting in a pile of glutinous and strangely smelling mud deep underground. Age and social barriers soon disappear and as a way of really getting to know your family, caving is hard to beat!

HOW TO START

So how do you start? There are several ways of going about it. You could just go off with the basic equipment and do a simple cave, though that is not recommended. What is a *simple* cave exactly? What would you do if your light went out, or something happened to a member of your party? No, as in all outdoor sports, there are better and safer initiations than the do-it-yourself approach.

One of the best ways is to join a caving club. There are scores, some better than others. Most big towns will have at least

The massive stalagtites in the main chamber of Llethrid Swallet, Gower Peninsula. 'Curtains' of calcite run down the roof of the chamber away from the huge formation.

one or two. The advantage of joining a club is that you can call on a pool of existing experience to teach you all the basics and share the cost of the more expensive equipment . . . ropes, ladders and the like. Also, if there are other enthusiasts about, it is easier to get the required number for a 'trip' as cavers call a venture underground.

Some landowners demand that a caver be a member of a recognised club before he or she is allowed down a cave on their land. This attitude, which at first may seem a bit heavy-handed, is quite justifiable, unfortunately, as in the past a cowboy element in the sport has been responsible for damage not only to caves, but to the land above. The disadvantage of club caving is that few clubs cater for family caving. Insurance reasons often dictate that a minimum age is required for membership, and in any case, many club meets would be a bit serious or strenuous for young children. It is, however, possible to find people in most clubs with the same problem, and so it is relatively easy to arrange private meets to easier caves, where permission is less of a problem. The caving club is still one of the best introductions to the sport, and for the older members of the family is thoroughly recommended. Contacting the National Caving Association (address at end of chapter) will bring you the name of a reputable club in your area.

If for some reason a club doesn't appeal, or you want to try the sport first and join a club with some experience already under your belt, then another option is to enrol for a course. Though quite a number of other outdoor centres offer caving as a part of a course, without a doubt the best place to learn is Whernside Manor, the National Caving Centre. Situated in the beautiful valley of Dentdale, on the edge of the Yorkshire Dales, the Manor offers a wide variety of courses at all levels in almost every aspect of caving. On a weekend or longer course, you can learn about the

The graceful 'columns' of Ogof Fynnon Ddu in South Wales reveal one of the hidden rewards of the underground world.

sport from some of the most experienced cavers in the country.

You will learn how to move underground, how to recognise the hazards, what basic equipment you need for simple exploration, and a lot about the caves themselves, how they form, what to look for and where to go.

This is possibly the best way to start if you are a complete novice, learning the game from someone you know you can trust, in one of the classic caving areas of the country. An added advantage is that most of the specialised equipment can be supplied by the centre; all you will need is some old, warm clothing. And a final bonus: the family can go as a unit on one of these courses.

WHAT TO WEAR

What do you wear? A random delve into the old clothes cupboard is no use. Some clothes, old or not, are entirely unsuitable for caving. Try and avoid nylon shirts and denim, which don't keep you warm and can be positively dangerous when wet. Exposure is even more dangerous underground, and doesn't need any help. You can lose a lot of body warmth through such clothing, and a lot of pleasure by being cold and miserable. Wear old woollens if you have them, with an overall over the top to stop jerseys and shirts rucking up during squeezes and crawls. Otherwise you could end up with bare skin in close contact with mud and rock ... not pleasant! Overalls also keep a lot of the mud off; it is much easier to hose down one garment than several at the end of the day.

This type of clothing has its disadvantages for serious caving. It is bulky, and heavy when wet. Wool retains a lot of water. Neoprene wetsuits are commonly used in wet caves, the best ones having an inner lining of nylon material to make them stronger. Double lined suits, with a nylon lining on both sides, are expensive, and though visually attractive are stiffer to move around in. Flexibility is an important factor underground. A 4 mm or 5 mm thickness is quite adequate, and suits can be one- or two-piece; each has some advantages. In dry caves fibre-pile under-suits are often worn beneath a waterproof oversuit. This combination is more comfortable than a wetsuit, warmer when dry, and provides a measure of protection against water.

A helmet is necessary, to protect the head from bumping and scraping the roof more than from falling rocks. Caves are surprisingly stable places when treated with care. The helmet must have a secure inner cradle to help cushion blows and to give a close fit, and it also needs a good strong chinstrap to hold it on. An adapted workman's plastic helmet is OK, but there are several makes of special caving helmet, like the Petzl, which are safer and stronger.

Footwear is important too. Boots that protect and support the ankle are imperative, and they should have a good Vibram or similar cleated sole. Nails are no good; they damage the cave, and slip on mud. Wellingtons are suitable as long as they are strong, close-fitting and have a good cleated sole. Ribbed 'fireman's' wellies with an internal steel toecap provide some of the best underground footwear, though you will hear as many recommendations as there are cavers. Leather boots are fine, but should be kept well-dubbined to avoid the damage caused by limestone water drying out (the leather becomes very stiff

and the boots are then both hard to get on and uncomfortable to wear until wet). Many cavers wet such boots before they start. Climbing boots with lace-hooks are a menace, the hooks are just the right size for catching in the wires of electron ladders, making them potentially dangerous for the wearer. Whatever boot you use, make sure that it is in good condition. Your life can depend on good footwear underground, so don't hang on to old boots once they start to wear out!

Gloves are an individual choice. They actually tend to keep your hands *cold* when wet, though they do offer some protection against cuts and small scrapes. Neoprene gloves are expensive, and don't last long down caves.

Finally, you need a belt. An easy item to forget, but important for carrying your electric lamp, and holding your garments together round your waist. It is worth getting a proper, load-bearing one from a caving shop, which can act as a belay-belt for lifelining on pitches, saving hours of tying knots with cold fingers. Check that the material used in the belt is not affected by the type of light you use. Nylon is seriously weakened by acid, so don't use a nylon belt with a lead-acid battery pack (like an 'Oldham'); use terylene instead.

LIGHTING

Caves are pitch black. Absolutely dark! The light you bring with you is your only source, and so it must be dependable and robust. Bicycle lamps or non-waterproof hand torches have no place underground. They don't like water, and they don't last long. It is important to leave your hands free, and so you need a lamp that will fix easily to your helmet, following your eyes automatically whenever you turn your head.

The old favourite, the carbide lamp (known as a 'smellie' for obvious reasons to any caver who has used one), has been almost completely replaced by the miner's electric cap lamp. Carbides are still available, and are initially much cheaper to buy, but they have many disadvantages. They are a nuisance to maintain, they smell, last for less time on one charge, and leave you with a small pile of mess when reloaded. Leaving the waste carbide in a cave seriously affects the natural balance of the cave and is very unsightly. Such lamps are banned from many major caves for conservation reasons.

It is worth the extra money for a good electric light and these can often be picked up second hand from good caving shops. They will last longer (a new Oldham will last around 14 hours before it needs recharging) and are generally more reliable and robust. There are several types in common use, some with lead-acid batteries (Oldham), others with alkaline cells (Edison, Nife, Ni-cad). Alkaline ones generally have a longer life but are more difficult to obtain.

Such are the basics. I would add to this equipment a good waterproof box (old Army-type ammunition box, or BDH container) to take spare food, emergency lighting and a small first aid kit for safety's sake on each trip. Ropes and ladders are more specialised equipment, and proper training and instruction in how to rig them properly and use them safely should be sought before they are used.

WHERE THE CAVES ARE

There are four main caving areas in mainland Britain: the Yorkshire Dales, Derbyshire, South Wales, and the Mendip Hills. There are several other smaller areas but these have few major caves. Ireland, both north and south, has many major cave systems, notably in Counties Clare, Fermanagh and Sligo. Each area has its own special attractions.

Yorkshire is *the* classic area, with the greatest variety of caves. The longest cave system in the UK, the Pippikin—Easegill system, lies just outside its western border, however. The system is at present almost 50 km long, in a labyrinthine underground maze of passages beneath Leck and Casterton Fells. It forms the basis of the hypothetical 'Three Counties System', a single cave system linking the counties of Yorkshire, Lancashire and Cumbria underground which would be the northern caver's dream, and one of the longest caves in the world. That most of this system exists is known through hydrological links but much of it has yet to be entered. One of the main fascinations about caving is the real possibility for any caver to discover an unknown cave and to tread in a place unseen before by man. Several caving families have been involved in the discovery of new caverns and such an experience seems to create rather a special bond.

One of Yorkshire's most spectacular trips can be made by anyone. Twice a year, at Whitsun and August Bank Holidays, the Bradford and the Craven pothole clubs respectively erect a winch over the deep vertical shaft of Gaping Ghyll, where the waters of Fell Beck run off the slopes of Ingleborough and disappear 365 feet down the cave entrance to enter Britain's largest underground chamber in a spectacular waterfall. Diverting the water for the occasion into another nearby entrance further up the beck, the two clubs lower visitors in a bosun's chair down the shaft. This safe and tremendously spectacular trip includes a tour of the massive chamber beneath and, fortunately, a winch back out. Tradition has it that the descent is free but a small charge is made for the ride back to the fell above!

Derbyshire is the home of 't'owd man' — the lead miner of past generations. Often cave explorers will break into what they think is a new cave passage only to find broken clay pipes, clog-marks in the mud, or a pile of old, rotting pit props. T'owd man had been and gone, following the veins of ore, breaking into the cave from an unnatural direction, his way in long forgotten and lost. Recently a cave-diver (cave diving is a highly specialised and dangerous branch of the sport) passed through a long and very awkward underwater section deep inside Peak Cavern near Castleton to reach the most isolated region of the cave. Leaving his diving equipment beside the water's edge he set off to explore the new, dry cave passages beyond. Round a corner he found a set of initials carved on the wall. T'owd man had beaten him to it!

South Wales has the country's deepest cave, Ogof Ffynnon Ddu (Cave of the Black Spring) in the Tawe valley north of Neath. An explored depth of 308 metres and length of 32.5 kilometres, and three entrances, provide some of the country's most dramatic 'through-trips', using the minimum of equipment. The cave also contains some of Britain's most spectacular formations, the 'Columns', delicate calcite pillars that have formed slowly over tens of thousands of years in a recess of the cave. For conservation reasons, access to these is now restricted and trips to see them have to be arranged well in advance.

Across on the other side of the valley the entrance to Dan-yr-Ogof show caves conceals another extensive cave system beyond the well-lit walkways of the tourist section. Cavers of the future have, at a conservative estimate, the same distance of cave left to discover before the sinks for the water are reached, several kilometres away on the fell above. The boulder-choked and flooded passages at the end of the cave still hold their secrets for a new generation to discover.

The Mendip Hills of Somerset are the nearest caves to London and Bristol, and so they generally see tremendous traffic at weekends. Some of the country's best-known caves are here. Swildon's Hole is one: a classic cave where water sinks to emerge more than five kilometres away as the River Axe from the dramatic Wookey Hole caves.

Wookey Hole is perhaps the country's best-known show cave. A tour through the cavern, following the Axe back into the hill, ends in the ninth chamber. Further progress is impossible without diving underwater into flooded passages that continue upstream. Wookey was the birthplace of cave diving. A visit ends with a trip through the museum, which not only traces the history of the cave and its connections with mankind (including the curious story of the witch who used to live here), but also contains the nearest the country has to a 'museum of caving'. Perhaps the gentlest family introduction to the sport is to come here, to view the story of Wookey and take a guided tour of these easy but very atmospheric underground caverns.

THE RULES OF THE SPORT

Caving has few rules but many guidelines. The first concerns access. It helps everyone if you make sure that you have permission to go down your chosen cave, especially if the entrance lies on someone's land. Please pay any nominal 'goodwill fee' that may exist; it makes things easier for those following after you! Remember the Country Code on your surface walk to the cave — shut all gates, and don't climb over dry-stone walls, a prominent feature in all

The shadows and shafts of light contribute to the otherworld atmosphere of caving.

limestone areas.

Make sure that your party is fit, and capable of the trip you plan to do. Make sure that their equipment is satisfactory too. Never be tempted to use a cave as a 'testing ground', or use a trip to show off your own skills at the expense of others. That merely means you aren't really capable of leading it safely, and you put others at risk. (I'm sure you wouldn't dream of doing such a thing!)

Always leave word of where you are going, who is in your party, when you are due back, and your home address. If your route to the cave involves a long overland walk, leave details of that too. It's amazing how many parties surface in the evening to a mist-covered fellside, and promptly proceed to get lost and need to be rescued! Don't get caught out! Always check back with the person you left your details with, be it police station, pub, outdoor shop or whoever. If you don't, a lot of people will be giving up their evenings looking for you when you are snug at home in a hot bath. In the unlikely event of things going wrong underground the details you leave above are often the only guide to your whereabouts, and the very efficient cave rescue service will find you that much more quickly if they know where to look.

Never cave with fewer than four in your party, two of whom should be adults. Then if something does happen, one person can stay with the injured whilst the other two go out for help. Make sure whoever goes out knows exactly which cave you are in, whereabouts in the cave you are, and what has happened.

Having worried you with all that, some words of comfort. Few parties ever need rescuing, especially if they go about their trip sensibly. Genuine accidents are rare underground, probably because we all realise the environment we are in needs extra care. Most rescues involve people who haven't followed the basic rules — not checked the weather and been caught by floods — not used a lifeline on a ladder or climb — not taken adequate lighting — overestimated their own ability — or simply got lost! Common sense and care will avoid all of these.

Do remember to check the weather before you go underground. Conditions down a cave can alter dramatically and without warning. Remember the walk back to the car afterwards. If your party is tired and wet, and the weather is very bad, then things like exposure are possible. If you are unsure about what effect the weather will have, check with someone who knows. Not just a local inhabitant who may well have less of a clue than you, but the police or a local outdoor centre or outdoor shop. I know of a schoolmaster who asked an old local if it was safe to go down one of the classic beginner's caves in Yorkshire. The old guy had never been down a cave in his life, but had seen people down this particular cave before — in dry conditions. Notwithstanding the fact that rain was due to fall on deep snow, the old man said it was safe, the teacher believed him, and the party ended up at the wrong end of a very close call.

So much for the gloomy side of things. Once underground, happy that someone knows where you are, have fun. The cave is yours for the day and there is a lot to look for. The small static rock pools contain microscopic life. The cave walls and floor often reveal a cross-section of a fossil bed where the corals and shells that help form the rock can be seen in graphic detail. Stalactites hang from the roof, and stalagmites grow from the floor, sometimes joining to form graceful columns of crystal calcite, their many colours stained by minerals within the rock.

Remember the maxim 'Take nothing but photographs, leave nothing but footprints', and care for your cave. Don't leave litter, or mark or break formations — they take many thousands of years to grow, and others want to see them too. A careless hand or muddy foot can cause an unsightly stain that may be calcited into a stalactite or stalagmite, so use every opportunity to wash mud off in a stream, provided you don't get unnecessarily wet or cold. Think about your movements underground. Most come with practice — a sort of sideways crouch gets you through low sections easily, and there are other obvious ways of negotiating obstacles that you will learn through experience. Always use a lifeline on ladders. Your technique may be excellent, but the belay may not. Avoid loose rock wherever possible, in whatever form, and take care in uneven streamways and deep pools. Unless you have wetsuits, water underground is best avoided. It is too much of a problem, unless you are very near the end of an otherwise unstrenuous trip. Make sure that everyone in the party takes the cave seriously, and try not to force people, especially children, to do anything they really don't want to do. A caving trip should be primarily fun, not too much of a testing ground. A certain anxiety is all part of the eventual 'buzz', but real fear can be a danger to all.

So then, have fun. That is what caving is all about, and once the guidelines above are second nature — which won't take long — caving is one of the most exciting and challenging adventures around. Exploring the underground world of cavern, streamway canyon, crawl and lofty chamber is a fascinating and addictive pursuit. The rules won't interfere with your enjoyment of it at all.

FURTHER READING

There are many good books on caving and reading a few of these will give you a much better grasp of the sport. The best factual books on basic caving techniques are *Caving and Potholing* by Arthur Champion and David Judson, and *Basic Caving Techniques* by Chris Bradshaw. These books cover equipment and techniques and are a must for beginner and expert alike. For the historical aspects of caving the classic books of Norbert Casteret, the great early French caver, are unforgettable reading if a little dated. *Ten Years Under the Earth* tells the story of early caving and provides the background to his later work. Jim Eyre's new classic *The Cave Explorers*, a ribald and often touching account of the author's involvement with caves in Britain and elsewhere, Mike Boon's autobiographical *Down to a Sunless Sea*, and Martyn Farr's dramatic history of cave-diving *The Darkness Beckons*, are all armchair guides to the mysterious and awe-inspiring world deep underground.

There are two regular magazines which cover recent discoveries and include articles on new equipment and world-wide caving. *Descent* is the longer established but the newer *Caves and Caving*, the magazine of the British Cave Research Association, is also becoming a very popular periodical. The BCRA is a popular and wide-reaching organisation that exists mainly to disseminate information to cavers. It holds an annual conference at which all the year's news is discussed, and films, slide-shows and lectures tell of the exploits of cavers at home and abroad over the last year.

THE FUTURE

Caving is one of the sports than can truly be said to have a future. Though the highest mountains have been climbed, the world circumnavigated both ways by lone sailors, and the remotest corners of its surface mapped, cavers still have their boundaries to discover.

know the world's deepest cave or the longest, but you can be sure they haven't been found yet.

Caves exist throughout the world, in jungles, in deserts, in mountains and underneath the sea. They offer as varied a challenge as can be imagined and new techniques are being developed each year which help to push the borders of the unknown farther and farther back. This is the real challenge of caving — the exploration of a new world. This is what could develop from your family caving trips — it has happened before and it will again. Everyone has to start sometime. Who knows where that first, hesitant step into the darkness might lead?

USEFUL ADDRESSES

Whernside Manor Cave and Fell Centre, Dent, Sedbergh, Cumbria. For caving courses and instruction at every level — you can attend as a family unit.

National Caving Association, c/o The Geography Department, University of Birmingham, Box 363, Birmingham 15.

British Cave Research Association, 30 Main Road, Westonzoyland, Bridgwater, Somerset. This is a popular and wide-reaching organisation that exists mainly to disseminate information to cavers. It holds an annual conference at which all the year's news is discussed, and films, slide shows, and lectures tell of the exploits of cavers at home and abroad over the last year.

PUBLICATIONS

BOOKS

Caving and Potholing by Arthur Champion and David Judson (Granada).

Basic Caving Techniques by Chris **Bradshaw**.

Caves by Tony Waltham (Macmillan).

The Darkness Beckons by Martyn Farr (Diadem).

MAGAZINES

Descent (bi-monthly), £1.00. Published by Ambit Publications, 6a College Green Gloucester. Editor Bruce Bedford. National and international caving news, articles, features, including new equipment.

Caves and Caving 80p. Published by British Cave Research Association. Obtainable from B.M. Ellis, 30 Main Road, Westonzoyland, Bridgwater, Somerset. Editor Juan Corrin. National and international caving news, articles, features.

to panning for gold and searching ghost towns in Arizona. He has followed the 'treasure trail' in many different forms and to many different places.

Greg is editor and publisher of *Detector User* magazine. He lives in Chelmsford.

You no longer have to charter ships to sail the seas, risking the perils of pirates and desert islands to find buried treasure! There is treasure right here beneath your feet, perhaps even in your own garden. With the advent of modern detectors all the family can share in the fun and excitement of finding it. And there is more. "An interest in history and a curiosity about the past is deep within all of us," Greg Payne writes. "So, too, is the romance of going out looking for treasure buried in the ground. Add one final ingredient, electronic gadgetry in the form of a metal detector, and you have a hobby with universal appeal." Good hunting!

Greg Payne has been an active treasure hunter for twelve years. His appetite was probably whetted, he says, by his love of history and reading books like *Treasure Island* as a child. His fascination with the hobby has led him from digging for bottles and clay pipes on Victorian rubbish dumps,

Treasure Hunting

GREG PAYNE

To anyone who has read *Treasure Island*, treasure hunting may conjure up visions of reckless bands of adventurers sailing to some tropical island to dig for pirate chests full of gold and pieces of eight. But today's treasure seekers — over a quarter of a million of them in Britain alone — are people of all ages and occupations whose hobby is to use an electronic detector in the search for buried metal. Ownership of a parrot, eye-patch and wooden leg is quite optional! But in some ways the *Treasure Island* idea of the hobby is not so far from the truth. Modern life can be very tame sometimes and deep within us all is a need for adventure and excitement. And who does not thrill to the idea of digging up buried treasure?

Today the 'treasure' could simply be an old and interesting coin, badge or button to add to one's collection. Of course, some detector users are lucky and do find valuable coins, lost hoards of jewellery, and items of great historical interest, but to the majority of detector users the enjoyment in the hobby itself counts for more than any financial considerations. For example,

a friend of mine, Les Clayton (founder of the Medway Detector Club), recently found a unique hammered silver penny of King Stephen's reign (AD 1135–1154). He was offered £10 000 for this coin but refused it, stating that although he was willing to make the coin available for study or display, no sum of money on earth could induce him to part with it permanently.

In the same way, very few detector users are willing to part with the coins, buttons, badges, and so on, that they have found. The excitement and joy of having made the find gives the object far greater worth to the finder than any cash value it might possess.

Returning to the idea of those treasure chests, today's enthusiasts are certainly luckier than the treasure hunters of yesteryear. Nowadays, going on a treasure hunt has the same excitement but does not involve months or years of danger and hardship. It is a pursuit that can be carried out in as short a period of time as a lunch break, or an hour before or after work.

A FAMILY HOBBY

Treasure hunting can be satisfying for every member of the family. Most of us are curious about the past and the way our ancestors lived. Then there is the excitement of never knowing quite what we may find. Add one final ingredient, electronic gadgetry in the form of the detector, and we have a hobby for everyone.

It is true that to be able to find the older coins and artefacts (dating perhaps from medieval or Tudor times) does require the development of technique, but for the beginner to unearth Victorian coins no special skills are required, and certainly no high degree of physical fitness. Anyone can use a detector, from children of seven or eight to old age pensioners.

Nor do you need expensive equipment. To make a start you require no more than a £40 detector and a garden trowel. On outings, members of the family can take turns using the detector, whilst the others dig up the finds, examine and note them. Later on each member of the family may have a detector of his own.

Older members will find detecting very relaxing. Listening to the signal has the same effect as watching the float when fishing. It requires concentration and this takes the mind completely away from everyday worries and concerns.

Children benefit from the hobby in quite a number of ways. It provides them with excitement, fresh air and exercise, but most important of all it endows them with a real interest in history. Learning dates and the names of kings and queens from textbooks can be very dull, but the finding and handling of an actual artefact is another matter. The unearthing of a single musket ball can lead to a hundred questions. Was it fired in a Civil War skirmish between Roundheads and Cavaliers? Does it indicate the presence of a nearby camp where soldiers trained in Georgian times before going to fight at Waterloo? Did a duel take place on the field? Any of these things could be possible. Adults can gain similar benefit. People who had a positive dislike for history when at school suddenly find it coming alive for them.

Although a large part of the hobby is concerned with outdoor activities, there is always something to do in the evenings or on rainy days. A fair amount of research is necessary in old newspapers, local history books and Ordnance Survey maps. This is something of a treasure hunt in itself, and diligent detective work is involved in finding and piecing together clues. For example, from reading 1890s copies of your town's local newspaper, perhaps in a reference library, you may find mention that 'For the tenth year running St. Andrew's Fete will be held on Bridge End Fields'. If the site could be located it is quite likely to produce some Victorian coins and jewellery. However, the field names may have been changed and further research may be necessary to pinpoint the place exactly. More indoor work is also involved after a successful outing such as the enjoyable task of sorting, cleaning and identifying finds. Such a diversity of objects are found with the detector that one or other is bound to appeal to the collecting instincts of each member of the family.

In the first year or so of detecting, it is usually a case of sampling everything and amassing all sorts of finds. After a while, however, specific interests develop and collecting becomes more specialised. At this stage sites are chosen that are most likely to produce the desired items. They may be coins, tokens, lead seals, buttons, buckles, bells, horse accoutrements, military badges, bullet heads, cartridges, rings and jewellery, farm relics, book clasps, weights, lead toys, pipe tampers, spoons — to name only a few.

WHAT CAN BE FOUND?

Virtually every square yard of soil in Britain over which people have lived, worked, played, fought, or travelled contains some item of man-made metal. The object could be anything from a rusty nail or a 1p piece lost yesterday, to the most priceless Roman or Saxon treasures. All have one thing in common: they are out of sight of the naked eye and in 99% of the cases could not have been recovered by digging alone. The surface area of earth in this country is far too great for random digging. Dig up a small area of earth knowing that it contains a metal object and even then you are unlikely to spot it. Metal detector users have aided archaeologists by

Treasure hunting is fun for all the family.

searching spoil heaps and recovering many hundreds of coins and other artefacts missed by even the most stringent methods of digging and sieving. Since people first began to use metal, it has been lost, discarded, or purposely buried.

Small metal objects are very easy to lose. Coins slip through holes in pockets. A

woman is feeding ducks; as she throws the bread her wedding ring flies off her finger into the pond. People are swimming in the sea; the cold contracts the fingers making their rings a loose fit. The splashing of the hands in water is all that is necessary for rings to come off. In many cases the loss is not discovered until later, and the chances of recovery without the aid of a metal detector are very slight.

Our ancestors were no different from ourselves. In the last 3000 years untold millions of items have been lost in everyday life. Added to this are an even greater number of items lost in battles or skirmishes, or discarded because at the time they were considered worthless. Even today, with our efficient police force, a great many robberies

Left: Ten gold 18th century coins found at Rapparee Cove.
Below: Part of the Prince John hoard of 80 silver coins found on the banks of the River Shannon.

take place. In the lawless times of the past the situation was far worse, and banks were not available to the general public until around two hundred years ago. Before that time the individual with any savings hid them in the house, garden or near vicinity — often burying them in the ground. Through mishap or the death of the hoarder they were never recovered, and are still there to be found today. Highwaymen, robbers, and footpads would also bury their loot, perhaps because they were being chased, perhaps until it was 'cool' enough for them to sell. Many were caught and hanged before they could retrieve it, or having buried it at night they simply forgot where it was hidden!

As you will find out when you start using a metal detector, there is not much ground in Britain that does not have some item of metal in it. A shoe or brass decoration lost in Victorian times by a plough horse; cannon shells ejected by aircraft during a Battle of Britain dogfight; coins purposely thrown into rivers by the Romans as propitiatory offerings to their gods — both the reasons and the list are endless.

WHERE TO SEARCH
INLAND SITES
In spite of the modern spread of urban development, there are still many thousands of acres of land in Britain available to be searched with a metal detector. In fact, if every inhabitant of Britain was to own and use a metal detector, it would still take hundreds of years to search all the available area.

'Coinshooting' is the name given to searching for Victorian to modern coins and jewellery. For this a beginner has no better place to start than his own back garden. Gardens have obviously seen a great deal of activity. During the summer months people spent a great deal of time in what is a comparatively small area — with the resultant concentration of losses. The older the house the greater the chances of making finds, but there are few house gardens in Britain that do not contain at least one or two coins.

The back garden is also an excellent place to start practising neat digging — essential when moving on to the searching of nicely turfed parks or commons. To recover objects located with a metal detector all that is necessary is a garden trowel. On grassland this should be used to cut three sides of a square (a 'U' shape). The fourth side is left as a hinge, allowing the turf to be flapped back. A piece of sheeting (such as a plastic carrier bag) is then placed at the side of the hole and the earth dug out and placed on this. Having extracted the coin the earth is tipped back into the hole and the grass flapped over and trodden down. With a practised digger it is difficult to see any disturbance.

Having started off by searching your own garden, the obvious progression is to move on to those of neighbours, friends, and relations. The gardens of large Georgian or Victorian houses can be very productive, so if you have any of these in your locality it is well worth seeking search permission. Such permission is usually not too hard to obtain once you have proved to the owner that you can dig neatly and not make a mess of his lawn. Treasure hunting etiquette also dictates that an offer should be made of dividing up any finds on a 50/50 basis.

The variety of sites is almost endless and the research involved in finding them can become almost as enjoyable as the actual detecting itself.

The following list represents just a few ideas to begin with; further ideas will occur as involvement with the hobby increases: parks, commons, footpaths, bridle paths, fields used by funfairs, the edges of football pitches, orchards, 'pick your own' fields, old military training areas or ranges, and woodlands.

If you are looking for older artefacts such as medieval buckles or hammered silver coins, then research is vital. Productive areas include the sites of ancient fairs and markets, drovers' roads, and the routes used by pilgrims to visit famous religious shrines such as Canterbury or Walsingham. Articles on the methods of research needed to find such sites are regularly included in the magazines *Treasure Hunting* and *Detector User*.

INLAND WATER SITES

It takes little stretch of the imagination to envisage the wealth and variety of artefacts lying submerged under Britain's waters. The beds of rivers, ponds, lakes, canals, and streams throughout the country hold 2500 years' accumulation of lost, discarded, sacrificed, or deliberately concealed items. Besides such rubbish as bike frames and old prams, our shallow waters hold hoards, guns, coins, jewellery, swords, safes, cashboxes — the list is almost endless. In 1978 the plug was accidently pulled out from the Chesterfield and Stockwith canal. The short stretch of exposed bed yielded a mass of items which ranged from Victorian bottles to a silver tea set; from Coronation china to gold sovereigns. The canal concerned has no particular historical associations to account for so many finds being made. Canals throughout the country must be capable of producing similar finds. To select specific locations on the canals, look for bridges, pubs, or houses, and other signs of habitation or activity. These will be marked on a large-scale early series Ordnance Survey map of the area.

Ponds and lakes are common in almost every county in Britain and can be the most interesting of all the watery sites. They have always been the quickest and easiest places to hide anything — once the surface of the water has closed over the object no trace of disturbance remains. Many weapons have been disposed of in ponds in this way and even — in one instance — church treasures.

Rivers, like beaches, tend to conform to certain natural rules which govern the resting places of objects lost or thrown into them. Finds will not be evenly distributed. All heavy objects will tend to come to rest in one area while smaller and lighter articles (such as coins) will lie in another place. The factors involved are the strength of the river's current in relation to its shape. The winding bends in rivers are often caused by the current eroding one bank and depositing the material swept away on the opposite bank. The current always deposits on the concave side of a bend where the water will be shallower and the current weak.

Although any place on the bed of a canal, river or stream could contain objects of interest, it is also likely that vast areas will contain very little except light modern rubbish. To increase the chances of success, therefore, specific areas need to be researched and chosen. Perhaps the easiest and most productive area to locate and search is a ford. The positions of fords are marked on any Ordnance Survey maps (the best to consult are the Victorian series of 6 inches or larger scale). When searching fords it is a mistake to stick strictly to the

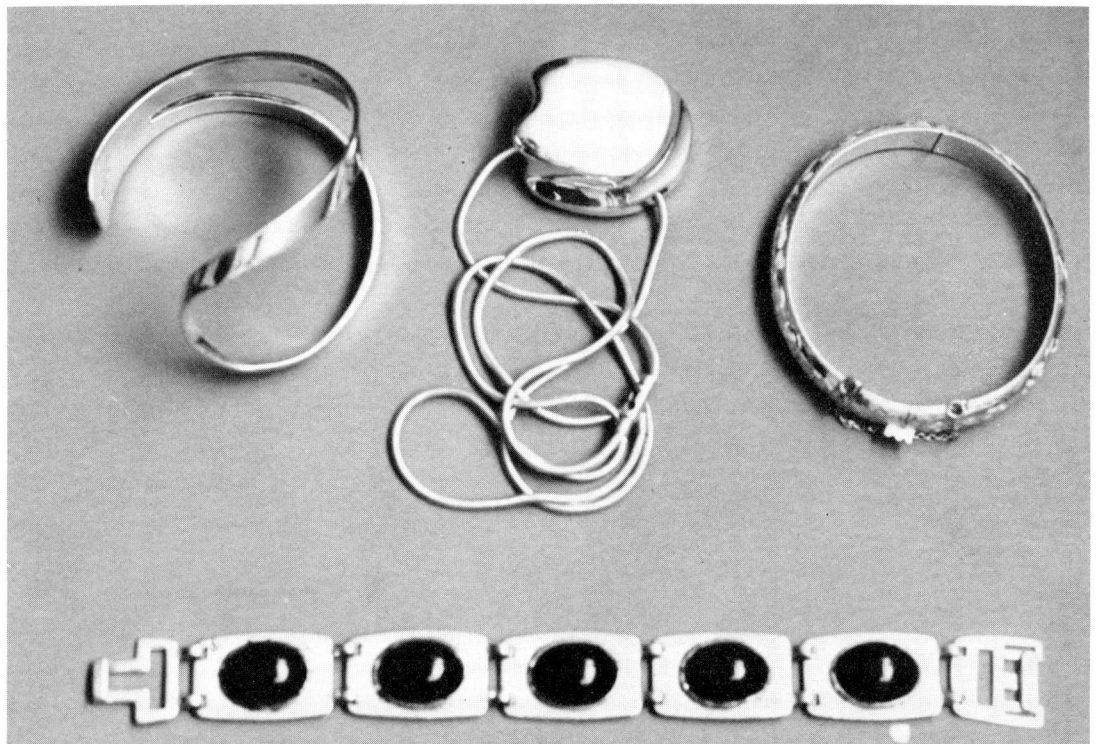

A hoard of silver jewellery found near a disused entrance to a country estate, probably the proceeds of a robbery.

designated area. A road's width may be the main fording area and can be extremely rich in finds, but this should not be the only area to be worked. The area upstream or downstream for at least 20 feet can be just as productive. On many occasions fords were crammed — the traffic was two-way on quite a narrow lane — and bypassing at a ford was commonplace. During these bypass operations many accidents occurred. Coaches and wagons overturned, some became completely stuck in the riverbed and people were often drowned. The accident rate was, in fact, surprisingly high. Expanding the width of the search area therefore to either side of the main lane (where most of the accidents would have happened) will make fords a very interesting shallow water area. Also, search areas around (and under) bridges, where footbridges cross streams or where foot-

paths lead to a definite part of a stream for no apparent reason.

Many turnpikes — which can be traced through older records — were placed on or near bridges, and the watery areas near these should be carefully worked as many have proved to be 'glory holes' for finds.

Not all searching in rivers and canals needs to be undertaken with a detector. Although when detecting on land iron can almost always be equated with 'junk', this is not true with underwater recoveries. The searching of watery sites with a magnet and rope has all the thrills and excitement of fishing without the need to throw your catches back! Items recovered with trawled

magnets have included pistols, swords, watches, lighters, cashboxes and cannon balls. One of the most widely used magnets for searches of this type is the purpose-built 'Sea Searcher Recovery Magnet'. This is small enough for easy handling and casting but strong enough to lift 140 lbs on clean contact (available from Nauticalia, 121 High Street, Shepperton, Middlesex).

BEACHCOMBING

No permission is yet required to search public beaches and digging for finds is quick and easy. On inland sites digging a neat hole with a trowel for a deep item could take up to five minutes. On the beach, using a sand scoop, an item at the same depth could be recovered in a matter of seconds.

Treasure hunting at the side of a river using highly sophisticated equipment.

Most beaches are rich in coins and jewellery. It seldom takes more than a few minutes to uncover your first modern coins with a detector. It is obvious why beaches should be so rewarding — thousands have flocked to the coast since sea water bathing became popular in Georgian times. And in sitting down, lying down, changing their clothes, running, playing and swimming, people lost a great many coins and other valuables. Anything dropped in sand is quickly covered up.

For modern coins and jewellery beaches can be searched between the months of June and September. These would be very recent losses, for by November a coin lost in June could have sunk down in sand to a depth of 5 feet or more. Areas to search during the summer months are places where money changes hands — kiosks, piers, cafes, deck chair hire areas for example; also, permanent fixtures such as beach huts, and sea walls and break-waters where people would shelter from the wind. On the beach itself the best places are low areas of sand, and the high tide and low tide lines.

The most effective detectors to use on the beach are TR discriminators, but these are limited in depth to 10 inches or so. The problem is that objects lost in Regency or Victorian times could be lying on the actual bedrock of the beach — perhaps under a build-up of 30 feet or more of sand during the summer. Serious searching for the older coins therefore usually takes place in the winter months of November and December, when the storms and tides are ripping away the sand and often exposing the bedrock.

Although hoards do not turn up on beaches, this type of site has an equivalent — 'glory holes'. These are spots on the beach where the action of the tides brings objects of a certain weight and metal together. One person lucky enough to find a 'glory hole' recovered over ten gold rings (besides countless coins). As well as comparatively modern finds, beaches have produced far older items. These include Portuguese and Spanish silver and gold pieces (washed in from offshore wrecks), and Celtic and Roman coins that have fallen from the cliffs as a result of erosion.

Beachcombers have their own national event known as the 'Brighton Beach Clearance'. Once a year, just before the start of the summer season, a group of Sussex Treasure Hunting clubs get together with Brighton Corporation and organise this day-long event. An open invitation is extended to every detector user in the country to join in. On arrival each participant is provided with a dustbin bag which they fill with all the silver paper, iron, coke cans, bottle tops, and so on, that their detector registers on the beach. This may not sound very exciting, but whilst doing this they are finding modern losses of coins and rings . . . and something else. A few hours before the event the organisers travel the beach burying marked metal tokens. Each one of these can be exchanged at the end of the day for the prize it represents — anything from accessories to detectors of up to £400 in value. What a splendid way to introduce your family to detecting!

METAL DETECTORS

Metal detectors of a crude type were known as early as the 19th century. They saw later development, as mine detectors, through the two World Wars. Although such detectors were capable of finding large iron objects at reasonable depth, their sensitivity to small objects such as coins was very limited. As their circuitry was based on valves, their weight was also a problem and it was said that to use them you needed one man to carry the detector and two men to carry the batteries!

It was not until 1954, and the development of the transistor, that detectors could be produced light enough and cheap enough for the hobby of treasure hunting to evolve. This took place in the United States during the 1950s, with a few American-made machines being imported into Britain by the early 1960s. By the late 1960s, hobby electronics enthusiasts in this country were starting to build their own detectors,

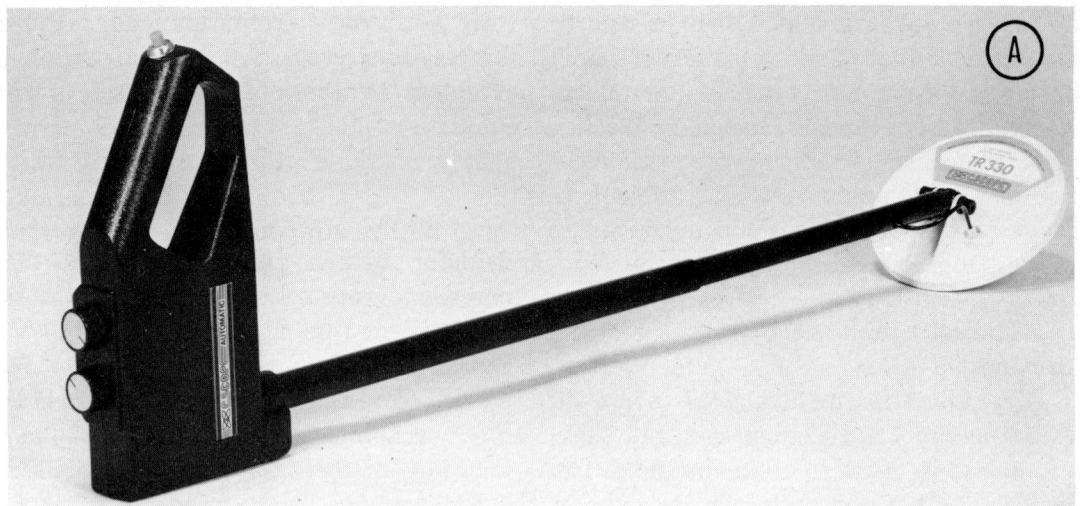

supplemented by a few imports from the States. As simple as these BFO (Beat Frequency Oscillator) detectors were, and as limited in depth (they could detect coins at depths of only a few inches), they quickly proved the potential of Britain for coin and relic hunting.

For enthusiasts taking up the hobby in the early 1970s it was very easy to make finds. It was not unusual to recover 200 or 300 coins from a common in a single day's detecting, in addition to perhaps a ring or some other item of jewellery. Coins in Britain date back over 2000 years and it was not long before 'treasure' (in the normally accepted sense) began to be found. The finding of these hoards of coins — Roman, Saxon, medieval — made news headlines which in turn further stimulated an interest by the general public in the hobby of metal detecting. So by 1971 factory production of metal detectors was under way in Britain.

Today, it is no longer possible to take such large quantities of coins from the local common. Most (but not all) the shallow coins and relics have been recovered from such sites. The enthusiast joining the hobby

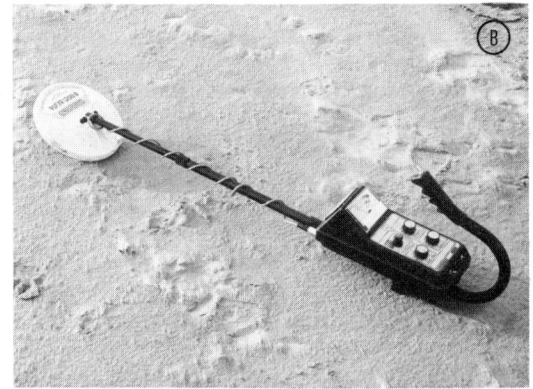

(a) Basic TR detector with push-button memory tuning.
(b) Typical mid-range detector.
(c) Top-of-the-range detector.

at the present time, however, has one big advantage — modern detectors are far more sophisticated than they were 12 years ago. At that time it was unusual to find coins or artefacts earlier than the Victorian period; in this age of the micro-chip it is possible, on the right site, to find hammered silver coins of the medieval period, or even Roman ones.

Not only will today's detectors search deeper, but they have other advanced features such as fully-automatic tuning. Some detectors even have the facility to predict the type of coin, and its depth, before you dig it up!

HOW DETECTORS WORK

The search head of a metal detector contains a wire coil. When an electrical current is passed through this an electro-magnetic field is produced. If a metal object comes within the influence of this field it creates a disturbance which is processed by the circuitry of the detector and relayed to the user as an increase in audio volume through the detector's loudspeaker or headphones.

Advances in electronic technology have allowed detectors to be manufactured fairly cheaply, and a good — but basic — TR (Transmit-Receive) detector can be purchased for around £40. Such detectors usually have simple two-control operation — very much like a pocket transistor radio. One control turns the detector on and adjusts the volume; the other control is for tuning. Unlike a radio where you would tune for a station, the detector is tuned to 'threshold', the point where a faint signal can just be heard.

A further refinement on the basic TR detector is automatic push-button tuning.

This works very much in the same way as a push-button channel selector on a television set; pushing the button in brings the detector back to the pre-selected tuning point — 'threshold'.

Without doubt basic TR detectors can certainly make finds and have been responsible for the recovery of a number of large coin hoards. They are a good detector with which to serve an apprenticeship, and should you, after six months or so, feel that you have outgrown it, there will always be a member of the family or a friend to take it off your hands (treasure hunting is infectious!).

The basic TR detector has one disadvantage — it will detect *all* metal. The soil of Britain is littered with desirable buried coins and artefacts, but it is also littered with scrap iron, bottle caps, silver paper, and ring pulls. The basic TR detector will register these 'junk' items in the same way as a coin, and digging is the only way to find out which it is.

The next class of detectors — TR discriminators — to a large measure overcome this problem. Good TR discriminators can be obtained for £100 or less and these can be set to reject iron, silver paper, and even ring pulls. By doing so, however, some depth and sensitivity is lost and the golden rule is always to set the discrimination only to what the site demands (that is, if very little silver paper is encountered, the detector should be set only to reject iron).

For £100 upwards it is possible to purchase a detector with 'ground cancelling' abilities. On certain sites where the soil contains a high degree of mineralisation (iron ferrite), these detectors are capable of searching to a greater depth than a normal TR discriminator.

Some of the top range and higher priced

detectors (selling at £400 or more) do need some experience to operate and a beginner is advised on a first machine to go for a basic TR or TR discriminator. Either one, I am sure, will provide many hours of enjoyment.

Unfortunately, space does not allow for a complete review of all the detectors available and their abilities, but consideration is given to current models in 'Field Test Report' included each month in *Treasure Hunting* magazine.

TREASURE FOUND!

Since the inception of *Treasure Hunting* magazine in August 1977, its pages have included hundreds of stories of treasure which has been found. Some concern treasure valued at over two million pounds; others tell about finds of little intrinsic value but of high historical significance. All have one thing in common — they were found by ordinary members of the public with no special training in archaeology. Now here are some of the stories to whet your appetite!

Mr Holbrook was detecting on a Kentish hillside when he received a signal. Digging down with care (the site had already yielded an Anglo-Saxon shield boss and two ring brooches), he unearthed a beautiful 6th-century Anglo-Saxon brooch made of silver gilt set with garnets.

Mr Halewood unearthed a hoard of six Bronze Age axe heads in the Vale of Glamorgan area. The axe heads dated back to around 700 BC.

Peter O'Nions uncovered one of the largest coin hoards ever to be found, in South Yorkshire at Maltby. He found 3800 Roman bronze coins snugly concealed in a brown earthenware pot.

Sixth century Anglo-Saxon brooch.

Britain's biggest coin hoard was found by Peter Humphries and John Booth in a field at Mildenhall, near Marlborough. They found over sixty thousand Roman coins — silver and silver-washed antoninianii — in a large earthenware urn, only 12 inches beneath the surface.

At Brandon, Tony Langwith found a 9th-century gold plaque, now in the British Museum.

Michael Webb of Clonmel and his son were detecting on bog land at Derrynaflan when they uncovered what has come to be recognised as 'the most significant Irish archaeological and historical find of the century'. The find, dating back to the 8th century, consisted of a chalice, wine strainer, stand and tray — a Eucharist set buried by monks as protection against plunder by the Vikings. The hoard was in a shallow hole and protected by a battered bronze basin. It had lain untouched for 1000 years and, had it not been for metal detectors, would have remained buried for all time. The chalice is similar to the famous Ardagh Chalice. This was unearthed in 1868 and has been listed until now as the most beautiful chalice in the world and one of Ireland's most important works of art. The treasure is thought to have a total value of at least two million pounds!

Arthur and Greta Brooks were searching with a detector in a field near Thetford, Norfolk, when they uncovered what has been described as 'the most important historical and archaeological find in Norfolk for thirty years'. The hoard (the first find in Britain with a metal detector likely to be worth over one million pounds on the open market) consisted of 77 Roman objects of gold and silver including 33 silver spoons, gold finger rings, ear-rings, pendants, necklaces and bracelets. There was also a gold belt buckle that appeared to have been made abroad.

At an Inquest, during which the find was declared treasure trove, Dr Timothy Potter of the British Museum concluded that the objects were the stock of a jeweller. They had been buried around AD 390–

The Derrynaflan chalice, unrestored.

400 at the very end of the Roman occupation of Britain. An award was made to Mrs Greta Brooks for the find which she subsequently shared with the landowners.

A hoard of silver pennies which could add a new chapter to the history of Wales was uncovered in a South Wales wood by two brothers. The coins were uncovered at a depth of only three inches near the site of a 'camp' in the Wenault Mountains. The hoard, described by a National Museum of Wales expert as 'breath-taking', was thought to have a value of more than £100 000. It comprised 86 whole coins and 16 fragments of coins from the 12th century, and throws new light on the civil war involving King Stephen and the Empress Maud (Matilda). Seventy-two of the coins bear the mark of the Empress Maud, trebling the number of coins of this type which are known to exist in Britain. The group of coins was struck at a mint in Cardiff, the first indication that South Wales may have sided with the Empress in her efforts to claim the throne from Stephen. Four of the coins were minted in Swansea (Swensi) and these bore the imprint of Maud's father — Henry I. She was Henry's only legitimate child and came to Britain to claim the throne from her cousin Stephen. A number of other British mints are included in the collection, which was declared treasure trove.

Jeremy de Montfalcon, the finder of a hoard of 97 gold sovereigns and guineas near Winchester in 1978, also discovered two rare and valuable silver Viking coins of the reigns of Aethelred I and King Burgred of Mercia. The coins were amongst a number of ancient artefacts recovered from a building site Jeremy was searching. His other finds included a decorated brooch of the Anglo-Saxon period which is of extreme rarity and value, tin staters, a Roman spoon, Georgian buckles, a spear head and buttons of various periods.

Upon discovery of the first Viking coin, which was of the Aethelred I period, Jeremy declared it to Portswood police station who passed it on to the British Museum. The coin was declared not treasure trove but was said to be of very high quality silver which was used only in the early part of Aethelred I's reign, and it is therefore of great interest to coin dealers and collectors. The King Burgred coin and the Anglo-Saxon brooch were both said to be in 'very fine' to 'extremely fine' condition.

Jack Basham uncovered a fascinating pre-Roman bronze brooch of a perpendicular Omega design. Dating from the first century BC, it probably originated in Saal-burg, Germany. The only similar brooches known had been found on Augustan and Claudian sites in Britain and on the Continent. For Jack, the whole thrill of treasure hunting is "in the hunt and not knowing what is going to turn up".

And you don't have to look far! Jimmy Ellis was searching the edge of his games pitch at Breeston Hall School, Cromer, when he unearthed an axe head. He took it to his headmaster and together they used the detector to reveal 16 more axes and a spear head. Andrew Lawson of the Norfolk Archaeological Unit was consulted; he believed the objects to have been buried by a smith in the ninth century BC.

The Omega brooch found by Jack Basham.

TREASURE HUNTING CLUBS

Joining a treasure hunting club holds a number of benefits for the detector user, and most enthusiasts do belong to one or other of Britain's 300 established clubs. The popularity and advantages of the club scene can be appreciated from the fact that at least two or three new clubs are formed every month. Clubs vary in size from the very small — with no more than five or six members — to the very large and well-organised (such as the Ipswich and Plymouth clubs) with over two hundred members. These clubs are formed into Regional Federations which in turn are affiliated to the National Council for Metal Detecting. Wherever you live in Britain, there should be a club not too far away from you.

Besides the social events most clubs organise, joining a club provides the opportunity to talk to 'old hands' who will be only too willing to pass on their experiences of using detectors, locating sites, and identifying finds.

Clubs usually hold meetings once a month, at which there is a very friendly and informal atmosphere. Events vary, but often include talks by museum curators, coin experts, detector manufacturers, or experienced treasure hunters. The meetings also give members a chance to display their latest finds, and there is often a 'Find of the Month' competition. Outdoor meetings are also held, including searches of club sites, and organised outings to a local beach, or coach outings to not-so-local beaches such as those of Calais or Boulogne. The larger clubs also organise National Rallies of which there are about six a year. Members of other clubs are welcome to attend these events at which there are treasure hunts for buried tokens, the prize often being a metal detector worth £300 or £400. A further major advantage of club membership is that clubs are able to get permission to search sites that would not be open to the individual. Club membership is open to men, women, and children and most clubs offer a reduced subscription for family membership.

Not everybody can join a club, and for these people an organisation has been established called the Federation of Independent Detectorists. Members receive regular newsletters, gain many of the advantages of club membership, and by F.I.D.'s affiliation to the National Council can have a voice and be represented in the hobby.

An up-to-date list of all treasure hunting clubs in Britain can be obtained by sending an s.a.e. to *Treasure Hunting* magazine, Sovereign House, Brentwood, Essex.

CODE OF CONDUCT

The following Code of Conduct for metal detector users was drawn up with guidance from the Department of the Environment, when treasure hunting was beginning to become widely popular in 1971. The Code, although self-imposed, has been adopted by the National Council for Metal Detecting, by every treasure hunting club, and by *Treasure Hunting* magazine. By carefully adhering to it, detector users should run no risk of upsetting either Authority or the general public.

1. Do not trespass. Ask permission before venturing on to any private land.

2. Respect the Country Code. Do not leave gates open when crossing fields, and do not damage crops or frighten animals.

3. Do not leave a mess. It is perfectly simple

to extract a coin or other object buried a few inches under the ground without digging a great hole. Use a sharpened trowel or knife to cut a neat circle or triangle (do not remove the plug of earth entirely from the ground); extract the object; replace the soil and grass carefully and even you yourself will have difficulty in finding the spot again.

4. Help to keep Britain tidy — and help yourself. Bottle tops, silver paper and tin cans are the last things you should throw away. You could well be digging them up again next year! Do yourself and the community a favour by taking the rusty iron and junk you find to the nearest litter bin.

5. If you discover any live ammunition or any lethal object such as an unexploded bomb or mine, do not touch it. Mark the site carefully and report the find to the local police.

6. Report all unusual historic finds to the local museum and get expert help if you accidentally discover a site of archaeological interest.

7. Familiarise yourself with the law relating to archaeological sites. Remember it is illegal for anyone to use a metal detector on a scheduled ancient monument unless permission has been obtained from the Secretary of State for the Environment. Also, acquaint yourself with the laws of treasure trove.

8. Remember that when you are out with your metal detector, you are an ambassador for our hobby. Do nothing that may give it a bad name.

PUBLICATIONS
BOOKS

Treasure Hunting on the Coast by E. Fletcher. Available from Treasure World, 155 Robert Street, London NW1, price £1 + 35p p & p.

Treasure Hunter's Directory and Guide by E. Fletcher. Treasure World. £1 + 35p p & p.

Complete Book of Treasure Hunting by Kate Johnson. Available from C-Scope Ltd., Wotton Road, Ashford, Kent, price £1.50.

Buckles Identified by John Webb. Available from Historic Publications, 38 Colet Road, Hutton, Brentwood, Essex. Price £2.25.

Go Metal Detecting by Val Singleton. Available from C-Scope. Price £2.50.

Gold Panning is Easy by Charles Garrett. From Treasure World. Price £2.75.

Successful Treasure Hunters Site Guide by John Webb. From C-Scope. Price £2.75.

Successful Treasure Hunting by Roger Johnson. From C-Scope. Price £2.75.

Electronic Prospecting by C. Garrett and R. Lagel. From Treasure World. Price £2.75.

Successful Coin Hunting by C. Garrett. From Treasure World. Price £3.50 + 75p p & p.

Complete ULF/TR Metal Detector Handbook by C. Garrett. From Treasure World. Price £4.50 + 75p p & p.

Detector User from Bright Star Publications, 12 Recreation Walk, Ramsden Heath, Essex.

MAGAZINES

Treasure Hunting from Sovereign Publications Subscriptions Department, 513 London Road, Thornton Heath, Surrey. Price £13.80 for one year's subscription.

BRITISH METAL DETECTOR MANUFACTURERS

Arado: Arado Electronics, 59 Pound Street, Carshalton, Surrey SM5 3PG. Tel: 01-773 1210.

C-Scope: C-Scope Detectors Ltd., Wotton Road, Ashford, Kent TN23 2LN. Tel: 0233-29181.

Saxon: Essex Treasure Hunters, 33a South Road, South Ockendon, Essex. Tel: 04025-7249.

Fieldmaster: Young Electronics Ltd., 19 The Broadway, The Bourne, Southgate, London N14 6PH. Tel: 01-882 5579.

Hightec: Hightec Electronics, Warren View, Mardens Hill, Crowborough, East Sussex. Tel: 08926-62978.

Viking: Rimatron, 79 Moorgate Street, Blackburn, Lancs. BB2 4NY. Tel: 0254-55887.

Whites: Whites Electronics (UK) Ltd., 13 Harbour Road, Inverness IV1 1RY. Tel: 0462 223456.

IMPORTERS OF AMERICAN DETECTORS

Garrett: Treasure World, 155 Robert Street, London NW1. Tel: 01-387 3142.

Fisher and Teknetics: Joan Allen Electronics, 184 Main Road, Biggin Hill, Kent. Tel: Biggin Hill 71255.

For details of your local stockist (and types and price range of detectors held), phone any of the above companies or consult a current issue of *Treasure Hunting* magazine.

OTHER USEFUL ADDRESSES

Federation of Independent Detectorists: Colin Hanson, 26 Lewell Avenue, Old Marston, Oxford.

Nauticalia: 121 High Street, Shepperton, Middlesex.

Windsurfing — or boardsailing as it is also known — is the new family sport. You can adapt the activity to suit yourself. The real enthusiast will enjoy the challenge of the big waves and the thrill of speed, but, says Simon Bagge, "for many people the real pleasure of windsurfing lies in just pottering about on the water, in control of a sailing machine at once so simple and so effective".

Simon Bagge has sailed dinghies from an early age and then developed a keen interest in boardsailing. After six years as a newspaper journalist he joined *On Board* magazine of which he is now the editor. The magazine caters for the growing number of people taking up this exciting activity.

Windsurfing

SIMON BAGGE

Few sports have become as popular as windsurfing in such a short period. Since it burst on the leisure scene in the early seventies it has captured the imagination of hundreds of thousands of people all over the world — people of all ages and abilities and from every walk of life.

Windsurfing — or boardsailing — is here to stay. For the real enthusiast it offers almost limitless challenges, among them big waves and adverse conditions and the thrill of speed. For many people, the real pleasure of windsurfing lies in just pottering about on water, in control of a sailing machine at once so simple and yet so effective. Others enjoy racing their boards around set courses in events as organised as big yacht races. This side of the sport has been endorsed by its inclusion in the Olympics for 1984 — a sign that windsurfing is not a passing craze.

GETTING STARTED

Holidays are ideal for learning to windsurf — especially if you're going somewhere sunny and warm such as the Mediterranean.

Many people get their first taste of windsurfing abroad and come back hooked. But often I have heard people say: "I tried windsurfing on holiday but I just kept falling off — I didn't seem to get anywhere." Generally, there is one simple reason for this: they had no proper tuition.

To get the best out of windsurfing when you are an absolute beginner, it is essential to have proper lessons. True, you can teach yourself, but will spend hours floundering around in the water before you discover what you would otherwise have learned in a few minutes of instruction from a qualified tutor. In Britain there is a growing number of boardsailing schools giving professional tuition through a scheme recognised officially by the Royal Yachting Association (RYA). If there is a lake or any stretch of water near you where sailing takes place, there is probably a boardsailing school there too.

Costing around £20, the RYA-recognised course will teach you in a day all the basics you need to know about how to windsurf. You will learn the essentials of windsurfing on a dry land simulator (which saves a great deal of time and energy spent in the water) together with basic sailing theory and safety. Then you will have the opportunity to take to the water on a board which may be tethered at first (to stop you floating away while you find your feet), before experiencing the thrill of doing it all by yourself. At the end of the day (it might be two if the course is split) you will come out with a certificate which shows you have achieved a basic degree of competence. You should also have a big smile on your face!

THE BOARD AND ITS PARTS

Seven component parts and a few lengths of rope add up to the essential gear which gets you going on the water. They are:

The Board. Usually made of glass fibre or tough plastic, boards are filled with foam which makes them very buoyant. In general, the longer and wider a board is, the more suitable it is for a beginner. Short, narrow boards are used by the experts for high-wind sailing and wave-jumping.

THE BOARD AND ITS PARTS

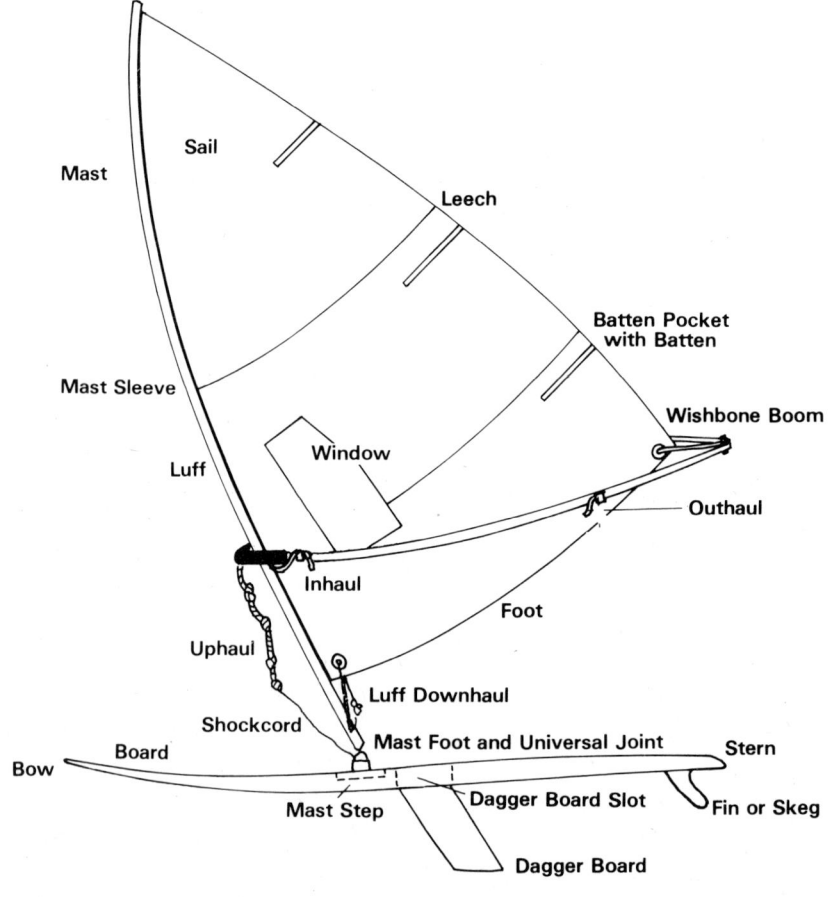

The Sail. Made of light, synthetic material such as Dacron. Experienced boardsailors may own sails of differing sizes to suit varying wind conditions. A large sail would be used in lighter winds.

The Mast. The sail fits snugly onto the mast through a long pocket sewn into the sail's leading edge (the luff). The mast is usually made of tapered glass fibre or aluminium.

The Mast Foot. This is used to attach the mast to the board, and incorporates a flexible joint (the universal joint) which allows the mast to be tilted at any angle.

The Boom or Wishbone. Two tubes of aluminium joined with plastic end fittings make up the boom. One end is lashed to the mast while the other supports the sail. The boom is used by the boardsailor to control the rig and board.

The Daggerboard. This slots through the board and helps promote forward movement rather than sideways slippage when the board is being sailed across the wind or upwind.

The Skeg. Known also as the fin, the skeg is screwed under the rear of the board. Its purpose is to keep the board sailing on a straight course and to promote turning.

Four lengths of rope accompany these basic components: the inhaul, the outhaul, the downhaul, and the uphaul.

The Inhaul. Simply the lashing which ties the boom to the mast.

The Outhaul. A length of rope which runs from the sail to either side of the boom. This is used to tension the sail horizontally.

The Downhaul. Attached to the foot of the sail and tied to the mastfoot, the downhaul tensions the sail vertically. It also keeps the mastfoot inside the mast tube.

The Uphaul. A thick, knotted rope attached to the boom at the mast end and used by the boardsailor to lift the rig clear of the water. The dangling end of the uphaul is secured to the mastfoot with a piece of shockcord.

The terminology and the bits and pieces may seem a little daunting at first, but once you are familiar with them you will be amazed at their simplicity and effectiveness.

HOW IT ALL WORKS

Books and books have been written about how to windsurf and the theory of sailing. If you're really keen, it's well worth finding out how and why a board moves in the way it does in relation to the wind. Here are a few facts to help you along.

A board achieves forward motion from the power of the wind in the sail coupled with the sideways resistance exerted by the daggerboard in the water.

The further a board is turned away from the wind, the less the daggerboard is needed while sailing.

A board cannot sail at an angle much closer than 45 degrees to the wind direction. This means that to sail upwind (towards the direction from which the wind is blowing), the board has to be sailed on a zig-zag path.

On the water, the theory all falls into place — if it doesn't, you fall off and get wet!

A sailing dinghy has a rudder to control direction and sheets (ropes) to trim the sails. A board has neither — the trim of the sail is controlled directly by the sailor grasping the boom. The course of the board is altered by tilting the mast forwards or backwards. Tilting the mast forwards (over the front of the board) will make it turn away from the wind; tilting it back will turn it into the wind.

HOW YOU MAKE IT WORK

This is what should happen when you're out there ready to make the most of that light breeze on a warm summer's day. If you don't get it right first time, persevere — you will in the end.

The wind is blowing over your back as you stand with feet either side of the mast on the board. You bend down and grip the uphaul and, leaning back, draw the sail out of the water.

As the sail flaps in the wind, you transfer your forward hand to the boom. Moving your other hand to the boom, you angle the rig forward and pull in with your back hand to stop the sail flapping. Then whoosh . . . you're off. Keep thinking about the position of the rig — if you angle it back too much the board will simply luff up (head into the wind) and you will stop.

Of course, when you want to sail back in the other direction, you will want to luff up anyway. Angle the rig backwards slightly and the board will turn into the wind. Now grab the uphaul or boom handle with your back hand, walk around the front of the mast, change the position of your hands and sheet in to sail off on a new tack.

If you are saying to yourself: "But I can't possibly do all that!" don't lose heart! Once you have had basic tuition it

Pulling the sail out of the water.

all fits into place. This is an introduction, not an instruction manual for prospective windsurfers.

SAFETY

Windsurfing is a very safe sport — as long as you bear in mind a few rules which keep it safe. Most people learn to windsurf inland, on flat water where help is close at hand if anything goes wrong. At sea it's a different matter. If you get tired or your equipment fails, you could be in real trouble.

Quit while you're still ahead — don't sail yourself to the point of exhaustion. Keep warm — that could mean wearing a full wetsuit even in summer. Wear a buoyancy aid. Never leave your board. These are some of the points which will be impressed upon you as a beginner.

TAKING IT FURTHER

Having reached a basic level of competence, you may wish to take windsurfing further — and you can progress as far as your enthusiasm and technique will allow. You might try freestyle, go into racing at a local club, or learn to sail a short board for high-wind fun.

Freestyle is using the board and sail to perform tricks. Experts have evolved complicated, gymnastic routines for competitions, but for the average boardsailor freestyle offers the chance to improve balance and have a lot of fun in light winds. You might learn to sail the board on its edge (railride) or with your back leaning against the mast (back to sail).

You could join a local club to take part

Children can learn to sail using 'mini-rigs'.

in racing or to pick up tips from more experienced sailors.

Short board sailing opens up a whole new field. You have to learn new techniques to get to grips with this end of the sport. But everybody you see in the action shots screaming along and jumping off waves started as a beginner — and often not very long ago, either!

WHAT IT COSTS

If you have a car and a roofrack, an outlay of between £300 and £600 will set you up with a new board. But remember, you also need a wetsuit (say £50), a buoyancy aid (£20), and a lock to keep your board on the roofrack safe from the hands of thieves. Insurance against theft and third party accident liability costs about £20. It all seems to add up to a lot, but once you have laid out the initial capital you will find you have a package which costs little or nothing to maintain and will last for years.

USEFUL ADDRESSES

Royal Yachting Association: Victoria Way, Woking, Surrey GU21 1EQ. Tel: 04862-5022.

United Kingdom Boardsailing Association (UKBSA): Masons Road, Stratford-upon-Avon. Tel: 0789-299574.

PUBLICATIONS

BOOKS

The Complete Guide to Windsurfing by Jeremy Evans (Evans Brothers Ltd.). £7.95.

Sailboarding. Basic and Advanced Techniques by Peter Brockhaus and Ulrich Stanciu (Adlard Coles).

MAGAZINES

On Board Windsurfing Magazine, 60 Station Road, Draycott, Derbyshire DE7 3QB. Tel: 03317-4731.

Left: Club racing.

Right: Freestyle. Sailing the board on its edge (railriding).

Below: Wave-jumping.

of Kent.

Now, as a full-time Mum and part-time writer, she 'dabbles with odd journalistic jobs'. To date these have included boat testing, editing, broadcasting, and television work, which included being one of the presenters of the 1983 Boat Show. She has teamed up with husband Mike to write three books: *Dinghy Racing* and *Practical Sailing* (Ward Lock), and *Sailing* (Sampson Low) which is one of the range of handbooks used in the Duke of Edinburgh's Award Scheme.

'Just messing about in boats' covers a range of activities to suit all ages. You don't have to race them to have fun — though of course you can! Wendy Fitzpatrick suggests you might like to join a club and take part in organised activities or you may prefer taking your family day-sailing, exploring quiet creeks and waterways. If you are a beginner, Wendy shows you how to get started and how to choose the right kind of boat for your family.

Wendy Fitzpatrick has raced dinghies for 20 years. Despite putting many types of boat through their paces during her career as a yachting journalist, she still prefers to do her sailing in a thoroughbred racing dinghy

She began to turn her hobby into a profession when she joined the staff of *Yachts and Yachting* in 1967. Ten years later she left to further the Fitzpatrick lineage in an elderly rectory in the heart

Dinghy Sailing

WENDY FITZPATRICK

A boat brings to the family the exhilaration of a versatile outdoor life, friends of all ages and occupations, and an enviable suntan! There are many who will tell you that the phrases 'young family' and 'dinghy sailing' are mutually exclusive. For a while, I confess, I tended to agree. Sitting on a stony beach with two toddlers whose calling in life seemed to be to clean up the foreshore by sucking the dirt off each individual pebble was not my idea of fun. Far better to let them run riot at home, with all their toys to hand, whilst Dad went sailing. So, for a while we were not a sailing family. Mike managed to snatch time off to compete in the occasional club race. I bought a lawn mower. But that novelty soon faded; once a dinghy sailor, always a dinghy sailor. Now, once again, we spend our weekends at the sailing club. And once again, non-sailing friends have stopped issuing invitations to social events during daylight hours: "No point," they say, "they're bound to be sailing." And we are — all of us. Even if you have yet to experience the joy of going places in small boats there is no reason why you and your family should not learn to sail and become as addicted as we are.

FIRST STEPS

So you would like to answer the call of the sea but don't know where to start? If you have a friend who sails, all your problems are answered. If he is willing to take you along to his sailing club as a guest member for a day or a weekend, you will be able to meet his sailing friends, go for a sail, and generally size up this new way of life. But if you are on your own, don't be daunted. Making the first approach to a club full of strangers need not be an ordeal. If it is, you have chosen the wrong club.

DO I HAVE TO JOIN A CLUB?

No, of course not. It's a free country and there is nothing more free and plentiful than the wind which you'll use to power your boat. But having a club as a home base has a lot of advantages. For a start, there is the constant exposure to other sailing folk. You don't have to see a lot of them but it's very pleasant to swap comments and yarns as you meet on the beach, in the dinghy park or at the bar. A club gives you somewhere to park the boat, so you won't have to take it home with you each time you sail. There are changing rooms with hot showers, a club room with bar (usually!), and frequent informal social evenings. And in the club lounge you'll be able to read all the latest sailing magazines — an inexpensive way to decide which one you will ask your newsagent to deliver on a regular basis.

A thriving family club will almost certainly have a thriving cadet section for the under-18s, with a special cadet club night and probably special sail training weekends where the youngsters may improve their sailing, among their friends and in a spirit of friendly competition.

WHICH CLUB?

There are sailing clubs and there are yacht clubs; clubs based on the coast, clubs on inland waters; ostentatious clubs, clubs on the bread-line; clubs which are exclusively Big Boat, clubs which cater primarily for dinghies. Don't worry, you'll soon learn to spot the difference.

It makes sense to join a dinghy sailing club if you plan to sail dinghies yourself. Look for a large population of sailing dinghies in the club's compound. Be impressed by a general air of activity, be wary of signs of neglect such as mildewed covers full of rainwater, ropes flapping in the wind, long grass growing up around flat trolley wheels. A large percentage of abandoned boats in a club's dinghy park can reflect a general air of apathy in the club as a whole.

A good introduction is to visit the nearest clubs on a popular club night. A telephone call in advance is courteous. Ask for the secretary or a Flag Officer (a sailing club committee will consist of Commodore, Vice Commodore, Rear Commodore, and various sailing and social secretaries). Make yourself known, explain that you are a novice and see what happens.

It is at this stage that you will begin to learn whether this is the right club for you. Sailing clubs tend not to be 'cliquey' though there is usually a healthy rivalry between devotees of the different designs of boat. The collective term for several boats of the same design is a class (as in motor racing, not as in 'Upper Middle').

It shouldn't be long before somebody offers to take you out sailing, probably as their crew in a club race. This is a marvellous way to learn which ropes do what and an excellent introduction to different types of boat. And there's no substitute for going out on the water and 'having a go' to gain you instant acceptance by long-standing members.

THE MORE FORMAL APPROACH

Some clubs run training courses, though all too frequently these are aimed more specifically at the junior members. Some large firms have a sailing section within their sports club. But perhaps the best instruction a family could receive is from a good sailing school. There are so many schools that it is an easy matter to spend a successful family holiday in your favourite part of the country and learn to sail at the same time. It is worth carrying out some research before booking. Some establishments merely tolerate children on their adult courses, others bend over backwards to make the kids' instruction

adventurous and enjoyable. Like that first ski-ing holiday, or that first week of pony-trekking, the sailing holiday can be great fun for you all from start to finish. It also gives you an opportunity to sail a variety of boats, experience which will guide you in choosing your own first family boat later on.

Many people have learnt to sail in the 13 ft 2 in Enterprise.

THE ROYAL YACHTING ASSOCIATION

A loose collection of blithe spirits like this country's sailing folk is not easily administered. However, there is a national body that makes an excellent job of doing just that — the Royal Yachting Association.

Just about every sailing club is affiliated to the RYA and most sailing schools have its official approval. Choose a sailing school from the RYA's own list. And, if you don't know the address of your nearest sailing club, the RYA will be able to advise you. It is possible to become a personal member of the RYA for something like £8 per annum and this is quite a good investment if you are starting to sail in earnest. The RYA publishes a magazine and a great many excellent booklets, some of which are available free to members. The address is The Royal Yachting Association, Victoria Way, Woking, Surrey. Tel: 04862-5022.

WHY CAN'T I GO IT ALONE?

You can. Many do. But at the beginning of your sailing career, it's a gamble. Buying a dinghy blind, without any knowledge of boats or sailing them is a risk. You could be lucky, but you could more easily spend too much on an unsuitable boat which will prove a disaster in unskilled hands. The result may be the indignity of having to be towed home by a passing fishing boat, a local club rescue boat or even the lifeboat. So please don't do it! The rescue services are voluntary. It is better that they spend their limited resources on genuine emergencies, not on ill-considered expeditions.

EXPANDING HORIZONS

Even when you have left your sailing class with flying colours — perhaps even gained the RYA's Elementary Dayboat Certificate — don't be tempted to rush out in all weathers. There is still a great deal to learn. The sea is a harsh environment. Learn to respect it. There is no substitute for time spent on the water, time spent in the boat, time spent learning to recognise and anticipate all the variations of water and weather. Inland waters can be tricky, too. The wind blowing round buildings or trees can be unpredictable. On a gusty day it's very much a case of the quick and the wet.

RYA teaching methods and learn-to-sail books are excellent primers but you must have a feel for the boat, too. Remember the Prussian officer in 'Those Magnificent Men in Their Flying Machines'? The time-honoured way to become familiar with a

The 10 ft 10 in Mirror dinghy is an ideal first boat for children or adults.

variety of sailing conditions and techniques is to crew for another, more experienced helmsman. If he is competing in a club race you will probably learn more quickly than if he is merely pottering. There is more urgency in all your boat-handling manoeuvres if another competitor is threatening to sail past the moment you do something wrong. Your mentor really comes into his own when the wind is blowing hard. Before you risk your family's safety you must yourself be confident in a blow. But how are you to gain heavy weather experience if you are not sufficiently expert to go out in heavy weather? Try 'odd-jobbing' for others during the first season. The whole family will gain confidence and experience and you will form a clearer idea of the type of boat you would like to buy for yourselves.

DAY SAILING

A few hardy souls go cruising in dinghies, making quite long passages in small, open boats equipped with all that is necessary for self-sufficient camping. It is a rewarding way to explore little-visited creeks in sheltered, shallow waters, free from the ties and costs of civilisation. But it may not be for everybody, especially families with young children.

Day-sailing a dinghy is quite different, however, and an ideal form of relaxation with the family. You can either base the boat at a given launching site and potter along the shore to chosen picnic spots, or trail it to a different launching site each weekend to explore new sailing grounds. Rush and worry slip gently out of your life as you launch your boat and feel the wind begin to fill your sails.

A few of our established racing dinghy designs make very good dayboats because they are roomy and relatively stable. The Wayfarer, for example, is a truly multi-purpose boat. Sixteen feet long, she will carry a crew of four, race with a crew of two, and has a good sailing performance with excellent sea-keeping qualities.

More beautiful — though less fast — is the famous Drascombe Lugger. She is an 18-foot open boat with plenty of space for stowage and camping, and probably the precursor of the current wave of traditional-looking craft which use modern materials.

Kenneth Duxbury, who writes for the *Sunday Express*, bought one of the very first Drascombe Luggers and now there can be few places where Ken and 'Lugworm' are not known. His two books for Pelham, *Lugworm on the Loose* and *Lugworm Homeward Bound*, describe his journeys to, through and back from the Greek islands. Regrettably, they are out of print, but no doubt still on your library shelves. A third book, *Lugworm Island Hopping*, is still available in the Cornish Library series of Anthony Mott Limited and this one brings us closer to ventures we might undertake ourselves one day — cruising around Cornwall, the Isles of Scilly, and the Hebrides.

RACING

It isn't necessary to be super-competitive to enjoy racing a dinghy. In fact, it is a logical extension of joining a sailing club. As club races rarely last more than a couple of hours and the buoys used as turning marks of the racing course are usually within sight of the clubhouse, members of the family left ashore can take an interest in what is happening. They can, that is, if they are not doing anything more productive. Frequent visitors to a sailing club rapidly become part of the 'hard core' which involves itself in anything and everything which is going on. There's always a helping hand needed, whether it be for repainting the changing room, helping to make soup for returning mariners, timing the finishers across the line or putting a new engine in one of the rescue boats.

The only drawback with racing as a family involvement is that it will usually mean buying more than one boat. Racing dinghies are designed either for single-

The Laser singlehander gives a fast, exciting ride and is an ideal racer.

enough time at playgroup during the week and that they were entitled to some of Daddy's time at the weekend. If they did think this, they didn't show it. And we certainly benefited. But it isn't long before most children want to take an active part. Sitting in a boat as a passenger is of momentary interest; really helping to sail it is a wonderful experience. And there is no reason why an easily-handled small boat such as a Mirror dinghy should not have a six- or seven-year-old as a crew, provided Mum or Dad at the helm know what they are doing and avoid sailing in bad weather.

But however keen the small crew may appear, don't be disappointed if he's had enough after the first half-hour. The will to see a race through to the end probably will not come until the age of eleven or so.

Once a youngster does decide to devote his energies to sailing, he'll be unstoppable. Every free moment will find him at the club or on the water. And boat-handling learned at an early age, usually among a peer group with an element of competition, is learned very easily. There are dinghies which are designed especially for children. The most popular ones are not always the most attractive because their reputation has been built up over many, many years and they could by now have become a little dated in design or construction, even though they may have been quite revolutionary in their time. The best possible design for a young helmsman or crew is one which has a devoted local and national following. With a thriving class association to back it up there will be opportunities such as summer camps and family rallies, as well as organised class racing both at the home clubs and around the country — sometimes even internationally, too.

handed sailing or to take a crew of two. If the children are very young the chances are they will enjoy a few minutes afloat every now and again, but won't want to spend a long time involved in what may seem to them a pointless occupation. If the club, or group of sailing friends, run a crèche during racing hours you are likely to find the children are quite happy left ashore with their friends whilst Mum and Dad race. It took us quite a long time to take this step. We were worried that the children might consider they had spent

ONWARD AND UPWARD

After the initial fear of 'mixing it' in the local club race has been conquered and the basic rules of sailboat racing have been assimilated it is time to move on, even if only to the next club's annual regatta.

Each class has its own comprehensive fixtures list. If there are, say, half a dozen crews in the same class racing regularly at their own club, they will naturally want to visit other fleets and encourage other fleets to visit them. The clubs like this, too, because a sudden influx of temporary members and their families for an open meeting is a good excuse to hold a social

Below and right: Grooming the family dog or searching for crabs and winkles on the club's launching ramp, while Mum and Dad race.

evening and an excellent opportunity to boost bar and tea-bar profits for two whole days. So a really popular racing dinghy class will be able to offer open meetings every weekend, all over the country, and it's up to you to choose which ones you will attend.

Maybe Mum and Dad will never aspire to Olympic participation, but the second generation just might. Be warned: it is an expensive business; expensive in time, and in money. A teenage sailing star may find some manufacturers of boats and equipment receptive to the idea of letting him make his purchases at a discount, simply to enable their product to be seen at the right end of the racing fleet, and from here he may find more lucrative help. It all depends on his ability and enthusiasm. We do have training for selected potential megastars, run by the Royal Yachting Association with a view to selecting our Olympic sailing representatives, but our facilities are woefully weak in comparison with those of the Eastern bloc and even the sports colleges of North America.

We have been personally involved in an Olympic selection campaign, travelling all over the country, summer and winter, as well as to the Continent, so that our team could pace themselves against the cream of the world's sailors. We saw a lot of motorways, a lot of water, but had no time for sightseeing — the ratio of work on the boat ashore to time spent sailing was very high. Of course we loved every minute, but it was hard work and ran away with all our hard-earned cash.

OFF-THE-BEACH BOATS

There have been smallish, lightish fun-boats on the sailing scene for twenty or thirty years — the sort of thing in which Dad could take his exercise whilst Mum sunbathed and the kids played sandcastles. For the most part, these carried very simple masts and sails and were so shallow that the helmsman felt a terrific sensation of speed. It was like driving an open-top sports car: it did not have to go fast but it felt good.

Then came the sailboard. It was so light that one person could manhandle it on and off the car roof and it carried with it a certain macho image. It arrived on a sailing scene which was suffering from a sudden increase in cost after the oil crisis and the imposition of VAT, and it brought cheapness and, most of all, fun back into sailing.

The sailboard sounded the death knell for a lot of off-the-beach knockabouts — but not all. There is still a demand for them. After all, it isn't everyone who possesses the drip-dry attitude which is essential for the sailboard sailor. Sailboarding is not easy. It's difficult enough just standing on a board but pulling the sail and mast up out of the water and balancing them against the vagaries of the wind and waves makes the first few hours of learning a wet and humiliating business.

Fortunately for novices — and perpetual novices of which I suspect I shall always be one — there are some relatively wide, flat boards which possess reasonable stability. The younger, tougher element will soon progress to narrow-gutted designs which, like the bicycle, gain some small semblance of stability from fast forward motion. Then, for the acrobats, there are the shorter, stunt boards: the type you see in he-man posters and films, leaping off Hawaiian wavetops.

The wheel is approaching full circle. There is a new generation of off-the-beach boats which have borrowed heavily from the sailboard concept, yet are genuine two-man dinghies. Lightly constructed, they are high-tech skimming dishes which carry a simple 'wishbone' rig. The French boat-building industry is responsible for many of these new designs, and an exciting concept it is too.

YOUR FIRST BOAT

First impressions count for a great deal. The phrase 'women and children first' was never more apt than in considering the choice of boat. If Mum and the kids are given a cold, wet, frightening ride first time out they may be put off for ever. Don't be in a hurry to buy your own boat, even once you are confident that you know what you want and can afford it. It is a good idea to shop around during the winter months, when prices are generally lower and before the first spring sunshine tempts too many people to 'think boats'. Faced with a less-than-perfect boat on a day with perfect sailing weather, the temptation is to buy it, just to get afloat. Grounded in mid-summer, elbow-deep in glue, resin, screws and paint, you may not think it such a bargain.

Know what you are letting yourself in for. A wooden boat is a lovely thing but it calls for a lot of maintenance. Every inch must be rubbed down thoroughly before painting and varnishing, and between every coat. Water must not be allowed to lie in the boat, so it is essential to have a well-fitting, waterproof cover. A glassfibre boat is much more practical. A wash down with a soapy sponge and a quick check on fittings and their fastenings will probably be all she needs in the way of routine maintenance.

So far I have named only a few types of boat. There have been hundreds of different designs since the start of the dinghy sailing boom thirty or so years ago. Some were good, but found no favour. Others left a lot to be desired but became popular as a result of strenuous marketing.

But now for a few comments on some of the well-established designs which are readily available on the second-hand market, and one brand new boat which has recently taken my fancy. Racing dinghies are not covered, simply because the class of boat raced is usually dictated more by the helmsman's choice of home club. A keen racing skipper will want to race against other boats of the same potential, so he will join one of the club's established classes.

Very few wooden dinghies are built now . . . usually only the specialist racing classes can afford to support a builder of wooden boats, so prohibitive is the cost. Glassfibre has all but taken over because of its adaptability to mass-production and, from the owner's point of view, its ease of maintenance. However, there are still many second-hand wooden boats available; depending on the design, this can be an inexpensive way to start, provided you are prepared to put in some hard work.

DAYBOATS AND CAMPERS

Drascombe Lugger: 18-foot roomy day-sailer/camper with attractive tan sails. One of a range of Drascombe boats, all of which have a traditional appearance and good sailing ability.

Skipper 14: Excellent 14-foot family knock-about which is making a comeback. Her new look enables her to realise her full potential. Second-hand boats will probably be to the original, now rather basic, specification.

Skipper 17: Big sister, with cuddy for protection against the elements.

Explorer: Brand new 18-footer with long, shallow keel. Based on a traditional New England design; simple but attractively efficient rig. First rate family dayboat.

Left: The Skipper 14, a family day-sailer with cockpit seats and a large stowage bin forward of the mast.

Below: The 18 ft Explorer, a large day-sailer.

Right: The 15 ft Albacore, for racing or day-sailing.

Local one-designs: Before dinghy racing turned into a national sport, each estuary and creek had its own fleet of one-designs. Fourteen, 16 or 18 feet long as a rule, these clinker-built wooden boats were developed from local working sailboats and those still sailing today make good family boats — but they need a lot of upkeep.

GENERAL PURPOSE DINGHIES
(race, potter, row, outboard)

Wayfarer: Powerful yet stable 16-footer which will not complain under the weight of a crew of four. Enthusiastic racing fleets (she races with a crew of two, sometimes three in heavy weather). Carries a spinnaker (a big, balloon-shaped sail).

G.P. Fourteen: Robust 14-footer with racing fleets all over the country. Can be day-sailed with smaller rig. Carries a spinnaker.

Albacore: Roomy 15-footer which can be raced two- or three-up. No spinnaker. Many attractive, varnished wooden boats still available.

The Wayfarer dinghy.

Enterprise: Two-man 13-foot racing dinghy with blue sails and no spinnaker. Still to be seen day-sailing with 'cruising' rig. Perhaps not quite as stable as the others in this section, but plentiful.

Mirror: Wonderful first boat, provided you don't overcrowd it. At 11 feet she cannot be expected to be fast, but she sails very well and is stable. Cheeky red sails, spinnaker, and racing available everywhere if you want it. Available in wood only — easily built from a kit.

CHILDREN'S BOATS

Optimist: Boxy 7½-foot single-hander with enthusiastic international following. Excellent for racing against other Optimists — rather slow for handicap racing if it's the only one in the club.

Cadet: The classic start in two-man dinghies until the Mirror came along. A racing dinghy in miniature, for under-18s. Carries spinnaker and is still raced keenly.

Mirror: See general purpose section.

Topper: See single-handers.

SINGLE-HANDERS

Topper: 11 feet long, very shallow, easy to car-top (hence the name) and simple to rig. Ideal for the lighter helmsman, say, up to 10½ stone. Popular teenager's boat, plenty of racing available. Frequently used in youth training schemes.

Laser: Just under 14 feet, fast and quite a challenge in a blow. A smaller, radial-cut sail enables the lighter helmsman to cope better in heavy weather. Racing fleets all over the world.

CLOTHING

If nothing else, your new hobby will give you the chance to use up your old clothes. White flannels, reefer jackets and 'milkmen's hats' belong on the ramparts of 'Royal' yacht clubs. In a dinghy anything smarter than jeans and sweater is quite out of place. Make sure that your clothing is comfortable, hardwearing, warm, and not too tight. If you can stay dry, so much the better. You may be sitting still for long periods if the boat is easy to sail and the wind is light. It is essential to wear shoes with a soft, non-slip sole. If you have an old pair of trainers or tennis shoes, these will do for starters, though special dinghy shoes or boots are better on a regular basis. Don't sail with bare feet: it's easy to stub a toe.

To keep you dry, there are some good lightweight anoraks on your local yacht chandler's rails. Nylon which is proofed against wind and water is used a lot for special protective sailing clothing, and generally you get what you pay for. There are many weights and types of fabric available. Or you may prefer the traditional oilskin-type jacket which tends to be heavier but will probably outlast the nylon lightweights. Later on you may covet a wetsuit. Modern dinghy suits are made of fabric-lined Neoprene, thinner and more comfortable than underwater suits. In section, the Neoprene is like Aero chocolate and a wetsuit works by trapping a layer of warm water next to the body.

Then there is the thermal wear and oilskin approach, which is probably the best for family day sailing. Fibre-pile garments keep the body beautifully warm: one jacket will do the job of three or four thick sweaters. Or there is the drysuit made of waterproof fabric with rubber seals at neck, wrist and ankle — more for racing than pottering.

BUOYANCY AIDS

A good buoyancy aid is essential. A waistcoat style with plenty of closed-cell foam buoyancy in the front panels and in the collar is a sensible choice. It is the nearest thing to a full lifejacket without being cumbersome in use. Cutaway styles for water-ski-ing and dinghy racing are more comfortable but do not attempt to float the wearer on his back, with his head clear of the water.

COST

£500 for a second-hand dinghy may sound quite cheap but it may be only the tip of the iceberg if you are taking up sailing, as a family, from scratch. That £500 will buy a G.P. Fourteen, for example, which is no longer competitive. You can pick up a good second-hand Mirror for £300, but the larger Wayfarer will be nearer the £1000 mark. For a Drascombe Lugger, you'll have to reckon on about £2000.

If you are lucky, you may find that trailer and launching trolley are included in a second-hand bargain. Smaller boats like the Mirror can be roof-racked (add the price of roof-rack and securing straps), but larger ones need both trailer and trolley (add the cost of fitting a tow bar to the car and wiring for lights). A road trailer should never be used for launching the boat: water enters the wheel bearings and sooner or later the wheel falls off. A new road trailer for a medium-size dinghy will be about £200. Don't forget to insure the boat and its equipment. Our £500 dinghy will probably cost about £25 per annum. A sailing club subscription can cost between £30 and £100 for a family, depending on the club. There may be an extra boat parking fee. Clothing need not cost the earth: an inexpensive waterproof anorak could cost less than £20. Personal buoyancy is essential and must not be an area for paring the cost. A good buoyancy aid will cost about £30. So it is possible to take the family afloat sensibly and safely for £1000. By buying new and widening your horizons, it would also be possible to run up a bill of nearer £5000.

That's the capital investment for the first year. What about hidden extras? There will be petrol for the journeys to and from the boat (unless you are lucky and live close to the water). There will be the occasional drink in the club, and the occasional take-away meal on the way home because Mum forgot to turn on the automatic timer and there's a very rare leg of lamb in a still-cold oven! There will be money spent on attending club social evenings. There will be boat maintenance, probably only a few pounds each winter if you have bought carefully. There will be the occasional large item like a new sail (£150 or so). And if you do catch racing fever, there will be entry fees, travel and subsistence when competing in regattas away from home.

Whatever the cost, I hope you'll come to agree with me, and Ratty in *The Wind in the Willows*, that "there is *nothing* — absolutely nothing — half so much worth doing as simply messing about in boats".

USEFUL ADDRESSES

The Royal Yachting Association: Victoria Way, Woking, Surrey. Tel: 04862-5022. For advice on sailing clubs, helpful booklets and magazine.

PUBLICATIONS
BOOKS

Lugworm on the Loose Kenneth Duxbury (Pelham).

Lugworm Homeward Bound Kenneth Duxbury (Pelham).

Lugworm Island Hopping Kenneth Duxbury (Anthony Mott, Cornish Library Series).

Sailing and Techniques of Seamanship Wendy Fitzpatrick (Sampson Low).

MAGAZINES

Practical Boat Owner
Dinghy and Boardsailing (international)
Yachts and Yachting (fortnightly)

The 'Wayfarer' dinghy is ideal for cruising as well as racing.

Cruising under sail — creating a home afloat, making a passage and achieving a successful landfall — demands a great deal from all the family. But, as Rodney Willett says, the rewards are beyond measure.

Rodney Willett lives near Tiverton in Devon. He is married, "with a fantastic wife, a stepson and two dogs". An engineer, he has freelanced as a designer, engineering plant manufacturer's agent, and technical author since 1966. He is a regular contributor to *Yachts and Yachting* and has broadcast on BBC Radio Devon, mainly about boating.

He lived with his family on board a 40-foot ketch during the year or so it took him to write his excellent handbook *Starting Cruising* (David and Charles).

Cruising Under Sail

RODNEY WILLETT

Family cruising is more a way of life than a sport. There is the maintenance of the boat and her equipment, training, planning and preparation for cruising as well as the actual cruising itself. The demands are considerable but the rewards are beyond measure.

Families cruise to enjoy themselves. Now, the sea is a hostile environment and the family, if they are to enjoy cruising, must be well enough equipped in terms of hardware, skill and temperament to cope with every aspect of that hostile environment, so that no member of the crew suffers extremes of cold, wetness, hunger, fatigue or fear. It is the skipper's task to ensure that these conditions are prevented, a task that will exercise him — and his ingenuity — not only afloat but whenever planning or preparing to go afloat.

The hardware can be acquired; the skills can be learnt; the temperament is another thing altogether. Frankly, only those families where all the members enjoy each other's company for long periods of time and where the adults can trust each other in moments of crisis

should consider cruising. The master of a ship — husband or wife — must be second only to God. That applies whether the 'ship' is a 30-foot yacht or an enormous oil tanker. All the crew must be prepared to obey him without question at all times. In return, he must never show fear and must always give the utmost consideration to all members of the crew. If she is the second-in-command, his wife must set an example to the children by obeying her husband's commands willingly and without argument and by cheerfully coping with the inevitable discomforts and problems as and when they arise without putting the blame where it usually belongs — on the skipper!

This is deadly serious. The lives of the family are at stake and, without proper control over the crew, no skipper worth his salt would dream of putting to sea.

But enough of the demands for a moment; we shall be coming back to them in some detail later. What about the rewards?

Modern life is overcrowded and stressful. Cruising around our coasts in a sailing boat provides one of the best antidotes to stress and overcrowding that I have yet to discover. There are still plenty of hidden anchorages where one can be totally alone, where one can be close to nature and can enjoy the sense of peace and timelessness found only when one turns one's back on civilisation. We lived on board a 40-foot ketch during the year or so that it took me to write *Starting Cruising* and that time included many memorable moments when the water was like a mirror under a many-hued sunset. At such times, we would go out in the dinghy and drift with the tide as the herons flapped their lazy way back to their roosts and the waders called to each other across the still water. Somehow the sky seems so much bigger from the water and we enjoyed more sunrises and sunsets during that time than ever before.

There is an indefinable difference between visiting a place by car and arriving by boat. Perhaps it is that one's first sight of the harbour is not clouded by the suburbia and traffic that so often greet the motorist, perhaps it is that our attitude to life is different when we are afloat. Whatever the reason may be, there is a feeling of adventure linked to stepping ashore that no amount of repetition dulls.

Then there are the pleasures associated with sailing the boat; the satisfaction of making a perfect landfall, the sense of triumph at bringing the boat through some particularly foul weather and doing it safely, the feeling of one-ness with wind and wave as one uses one's skills to harness the natural forces, the pride that comes following the success of an offspring as he or she learns some new skill.

The boat offers an ideal centre for a whole host of activities, both associated with the water and otherwise. Sailing the dinghy or using it to explore creeks, fishing

and swimming are the obvious ones but there are also sub-aqua (dealt with elsewhere in this book) and nature watching, exploring ashore — many of our ports are full of fascinating history which is even more interesting to those who sail — and walking. It is often possible to join a path at some deserted point having dropped the anchor in a sheltered cove and rowed ashore in the dinghy. In short, the cruising man enjoys virtually everything that his land-based, car-driving cousin can experience — except for the frustration of the traffic jam!

MAKING A START

Having decided to take up cruising as a family, where do we start?

Obviously it all depends on whether or not either of the adults involved has any experience in boats. Let us assume that they haven't and take it from there.

One can learn a good deal from books. I have listed a few at the end of this chapter that I consider worth buying so that they are available at all times, but others can be borrowed from the local library and I would suggest that you read everything you can get your hands on. Some will be good, some not so good. We are dealing with an enormous subject and I rarely find that a book I have not read before fails to add something to my store of knowledge.

One cannot learn everything from books and I would strongly advise taking some tuition. There are a number of ways open to you. Theoretical subjects, such as navigation, are often taught during evening classes at schools and colleges. For the more practical stuff you need to go to a sailing school, or you can charter a boat with a skipper who will show you the

ropes — literally!

We all have our favourites, in every aspect of life, and my favourite sailing 'school' is based on an old Mersey ferry boat moored in the 'Bag' which is a part of Salcombe Harbour in South Devon. *Egremont*, as she is called, is the headquarters ship of the Island Cruising Club. This is a non-profit-making organisation and the members own the boats and other facilities which include a shore base in Island Street, Salcombe which is the club's postal address. The club offers tuition at all levels. You can go and stay on 'Eggy' for a week or two and learn the rudiments of sailing in the various boats that are kept in the estuary or you can sign on for a cruise along the south coast or even over the Channel on one of the larger yachts. Probably more important, you can go as a family.

'Egremont', the ex-Mersey Ferry, moored in Salcombe harbour, is the headquarters ship of the Island Cruising Club. Families can stay on 'Eggy' and receive tuition at all levels.

After your week or fortnight with the I.C.C. you should be able to go away, buy your own boat and start to gain experience which, at the end of the day, is the only way to become a seaman. Naturally you will start off making short passages in fairly sheltered waters when the weather is fair but it is surprising how quickly you can become proficient if the time afloat is used to the fullest advantage.

Far too few people carry out constant, formal, training. The Royal Navy spends most of its life doing just that so that people will know exactly what to do

whatever happens. A similar regime does not have to be over arduous and it pays hands down. Every time you take the boat off her mooring, have in mind one evolution you wish to practise or one idea you want to try out. It is an attitude of mind rather than anything else — an attitude that is not content with second-best but is constantly striving for perfection. With this approach, you will soon be a safe crew capable of coping with any emergency and, more important, capable of avoiding those situations which turn into emergencies.

Now we have acquired those basic skills we can set out on the exciting, frustrating and worrying business of buying a boat.

A heavy displacement cutter. Note the self-stowing anchor under the plank bowsprit, the inflatable dinghy on the foredeck and the lifebelt at the side of the cockpit.

THE CRUISING BOAT

This is a big subject and we shall be able to do no more than mention the bare essentials in this short piece. Inevitably one has to use a number of jargon words for convenience, so there is a list of some sailing terms at the end of the chapter which should help.

Obviously the boat has to stay the right way up even when she has a strong wind in her sails. There are two ways of ensuring that this happens; one relies mainly on the shape of the boat, the other on attaching a heavy keel. Most boats are a compromise, gaining some of their stability from hull form and some from weight.

Boats designed so that the hull form provides the essential stability can be made extremely light, especially when modern materials are used. When a certain point is reached, however, all stability is lost and the boat will roll right over. This is, of course, what happens when a dinghy capsizes. Such craft are described as being 'light displacement' boats and some folk call them 'flat plank craft'.

On the other hand, if a heavy keel of lead or iron is attached the vessel will never lose her stability. Even if such a boat were to be rolled right over, as has happened in the big seas of the southern ocean, she will still come up the right way. Such craft are described as being 'heavy displacement' or 'plank on edge'.

How is all this important? Well, your first decision will be 'do I buy light or heavy?'

From the viewpoint of ultimate safety, the heavy displacement boat would appear to be the obvious choice. If you intended to circumnavigate the globe this would be true. However, for coastal cruising it is really irrelevant. A well-designed lightweight will have more than enough stability to cope with almost any combination of wind and wave that one is likely to encounter around the UK and it is a reasonable assumption that you would be restricting your offshore work to the summer months.

The big disadvantage with carrying a heavy keel is that a good deal of the energy captured by the sails is used to push that extra weight through the water. This means heavier gear to handle larger sails if you want reasonable performance and that means more hard work for the crew. Light

displacement craft can often be trailed to the cruising ground and kept at home. This has some very important plus points: it is cheaper as you avoid mooring fees, it is a lot easier to work on the boat when she is in the garden, and you can explore many different areas that would be well outside your range if she were kept afloat. And because the gear is lighter and the sails smaller, she will be cheaper to fit out and maintain.

Unfortunately there are two big snags. Boats are a bit like horses — the bigger and heavier they are, the more placid they are. Lightweight craft will be very lively, will respond quickly to the helm and, simply because the weight of bodies on board is a high percentage of the total weight, the crew will have to act as human ballast much as they do in a dinghy. All that is very tiring and those on board have to be fit and active. The other big snag is that the worst possible thing you can do to a light displacement vessel is to overload her. This pushes her below her designed waterline, ruining her performance and tempting her crew to carry too much sail to try to regain it. This puts the gear at risk and makes her very 'wet' as the wavetops will be blown into the cockpit. So the amount of stores and other bits and pieces that you can take are limited in this type of boat. A young family who are happy to rough it a bit can get a good deal of fun out of a lightweight but they would be well advised to avoid any long passages (and by long I mean anything much over six to eight hours). Even the 'watch below' is likely to find it difficult to rest. Those who have reached more mature years will prefer the more sedate characteristics of the heavyweight with the ability to carry all the odds and ends that turn a cruising boat into a true floating home.

Personally, I would always advise buying a heavyweight for your first boat. The motion experienced in light craft can be more sick-making than the more ponderous movement found on board the heavies. The steadier motion makes such tasks as navigating and cooking infinitely easier and, as such vessels are far 'steadier on the helm', there is more time for sail handling when changing course or tacking. After a season or so afloat to gain experience the need to sail a fast and exciting boat can be gratified without the risk that, if it proves the wrong choice, the family will be put off sailing for ever. My wife, for example, finds lightweight craft make her very sea-sick and it is probable that, had her first experiences been in such a boat, they would have been her last.

Let us assume, then, that you are going to buy the biggest boat that you can handle and afford.

Generally speaking, the heaviest piece of equipment on board will be the anchor and its chain — collectively known as the 'ground tackle'. It used to be said that the size of boat that a given crew could manage was limited by the weight of the ground tackle that they could handle. Although one can now buy winches to do most of the work, this is still true.

However, it is a good rule to define the crew in such a case as 'the second strongest person aboard'. The reasoning is that the strongest just may break an arm or catch the 'flu and be stuck below decks unable to do more than issue a stream of incomprehensible and contradictory orders. In fact, the rule should apply to *all* aspects of boat handling and, if you decide that the boat is too large using this yardstick,

don't risk it — look for something smaller.

When it comes to drawing up your budget, do try to be realistic. This is far harder than it sounds. Once you have found a boat, fallen in love with her and started to imagine yourself ghosting down some lonely creek at dusk, the tiller nestling in your hand — you will find that the brain has acquired a blank spot as far as costs are concerned. You must add to the cost of purchase any repairs that are required and equipment that you need that is either not on board or needs to be replaced. As to running costs, you should have worked these out beforehand. There will be harbour and mooring fees if you intend to keep her afloat (which vary from nothing in some places to as much as £150 per metre per annum in others), insurance and routine maintenance. You will probably have to have her hauled out of the water at the end of the season, stored ashore over the winter and craned afloat in the spring. Yard costs for this vary widely and some yards will not allow you to work on the boat once she is ashore. Such yards should be avoided like the plague! I have a strange belief that boats were designed to float and, if you can find a sheltered mooring, I would advise leaving them afloat at all times. The bottom can be scrubbed off and repainted by leaning the boat against a wall or standing her on her legs unless, of course, she has twin or bilge keels (which make a good deal of sense when cruising) in which case she can take the bottom without any other support.

Although your chosen boat is within your handling capacity and your means, avoid the temptation to place a straight offer. Instead, offer to purchase 'subject to survey' and find the nearest qualified marine surveyor. For a fee of about £20 he will be willing to take a preliminary look at the boat and advise you whether she is worth having surveyed properly. This may sound like a waste of money but surveys are no longer cheap, even if they are a good deal cheaper than buying a pup. If he advises that the general condition is sound enough to warrant further inspection, tell him to carry out a full survey. You will receive a written report which will list all the defects. After reading this you can confirm your offer, reduce your offer using the surveyor's report to give you the required ammunition, or withdraw altogether, sighing with relief at your close shave.

Full surveys cost about (L × B) divided by 1.6 where L is the length overall, B is the beam (both in feet) and the answer is in pounds sterling. In addition you will have to pay for the surveyor's travelling expenses and arrange, at your cost, for the boat to be in a place where he can carry out his survey. With GRP boats, this usually means dried out on her keels or alongside a wall but wooden boats will have to be lifted out of the water, either on a slip or by crane. You will also have to meet the cost of removing any part of the boat's structure that the surveyor needs out of the way so that he can see what has been going on behind the scenes and, of course, making good afterwards. All in all, a typical charge for a 30-foot GRP boat would be about £200 and a wooden boat would require an additional £100 to cover the extra work involved.

This is a lot of money but you can end up spending a good deal more on repairs if you buy unwisely, to say nothing of the disappointment if you find that you cannot afford to use the boat as you planned because she is unsafe. In any event, you can often use the survey report to reduce the sale price and can even draw comfort if the report shows the boat to be in excellent condition — insurance companies will often reduce premiums where there is a recent survey proving that all is well.

So much for the hull; now for the things that push it through the water — the sails supported by the rigging and the engine.

With very few exceptions family cruising is carried out by very small crews — crews which are, perhaps, not totally fit and almost certainly not totally experienced. It makes a good deal of sense, therefore, to keep the rig as easy and simple as possible.

It has been claimed that the Chinese junk rig is the simplest to operate and it would be difficult to argue with that claim. However, as always seems to be the case with boats, it isn't as simple as that. Space does not permit me to enter into the for/ against argument here so I'll stick my neck out and say that the problems with junk rigs make them more suited to much larger craft than those we are considering. In any event, people on board want something to do and the more bits of string there are to pull on, subject to the whole rig being manageable by one person, the better. Again we should apply the 'second strongest' rule.

So what is the ideal compromise? If the children are small and will not be able to help much on deck, I would go for a boat with a roller reefing (as distinct from roller furling) genoa which is bigger than the only other sail — the mainsail. Once hoisted, the genoa can stay up and it can be controlled from the cockpit so that there is virtually no foredeck work when underway. I say virtually because things do go wrong with roller reefing gear and sails have been

known to split. Should either of these faults occur it will be necessary to set a normal working jib in place of the genoa and such a jib should be carried just in case. There will, of course, be work to be done by the mast — hoisting and lowering the mainsail as well as reefing it.

If there are bigger children who can become working members of the crew I would give serious consideration to a multi-sail rig with a few labour saving devices. The ketch rig with a short bowsprit and two headsails is my own favourite in this category. Because there are more sails, each is smaller and so no sail requires a great deal of strength when it is being handled. The jib, the sail set on the end of the bowsprit, should be either roller reefing or roller furling (the latter being adequate as it will be normal practice to furl this sail when the wind increases rather than to reef it). This avoids hairy work on the end of the bowsprit. It also means that the control of one of the headsails is brought back to the cockpit making either increasing or decreasing sail area up forward quick and easy. The other headsail, the staysail, can be sheeted down to a horse so that it is self-tacking. This means that, once the sheet is set up, the boat can be put about without touching it as the block on the track will slide from one side of the boat to the other. Reefing will be kept to a minimum as whole sails can be lowered instead as the wind speed increases. A well balanced ketch will sail with a variety of sail combinations; main and staysail, mizzen and jib, reefed main and jib and even, under the right conditions, just the two headsails. This multiplicity of sails gives

There is something rather special about a gaff rigged boat.

more members of the crew something to look after when they are feeling active and yet the boat can be sailed by one person quite adequately even if that means the sails aren't always setting perfectly (which rarely matters when cruising).

The rigs to avoid are the towering masthead rigs so popular with the racing fraternity. These give the boat an enormous amount of power when sailing to windward but reserves of power like this are not normally needed when cruising. The boat must have sufficient power to be able to work against moderate currents with moderate winds but the racing man's requirements to sail fast in light airs do not apply. Few cruising crews will have the strength of a racing crew and big sails can take a lot of handling. In any case, the cruising man can always turn to the engine when the wind fails.

Being a bit of a traditionalist, I love gaff rigged boats. Do they have any place in the cruising scene? I believe that they do although I accept that many would not agree with me.

The reasons against choosing gaff rig are that each gaff sail has two halliards rather than one, the gaffs themselves are fairly heavy chunks of timber and there is a complication with the backstays. On a bermudan boat, the stays that hold the mast back are rigged permanently. This cannot be so with a gaff rig and so these fixed stays are replaced by running backstays (or just 'runners'), one on each quarter, which have to be dealt with whenever the boom swings from one side of the boat to the other, the old weather runner being slackened off and the new weather runner being set up. Last of all is the question of performance. Few gaff boats will perform as well to windward as will a bermudan boat and the ones that do will have to set a topsail above the gaff.

Right, now for the advantages. The rig is not so tall and that means less top hamper. True, the gaff(s) add to the weight aloft but they will be lowered whenever there is a real blow. If you have to drop a sail in a hurry a gaff not only helps by dropping under its own weight, it helps to control the sail as it comes down. It is almost impossible for a gaff sail to get stuck in the way that a bermudan sail can. (The argument that a well maintained bermudan track will ensure that this never happens is specious. It can and does happen.) You can hoist a gaff sail regardless of wind direction without it becoming tangled in the spreaders or shrouds as will a bermudan sail if the wind is abaft the beam. You can lose a lot of sail area in a hurry without using strength by just letting go the peak halliard — the one that controls the angle of the gaff — and the gaff will drop. This is called 'scandalising' the sail, looks a bit untidy but is very efficient. Last, but not least, the lower, sturdier and less technical rig associated with gaffers is a lot easier to repair when things go wrong. A broken halliard on a gaffer is a nuisance; a broken halliard on a bermudan boat may be impossible to replace at sea. In support of my arguments are the sales of new gaff rigged boats which, after being virtually non-existent for a number of years, are now increasing. However, I would be inclined to stick to the basic simplicity I mentioned earlier if the children are very small. Not only will they be unable to assist, they can often demand attention at the worst possible moment and the parents of a very young family should look for a boat that can be handled easily by one person.

The other form of motive power available is the auxiliary engine. Purists deplore the use of such power and it is perfectly true that an experienced skipper will use the engine only on rare occasions. It is also true that surprisingly large boats can be moved using sweeps or sculled with a long oar worked over the stern. With the heavy congestion found in many of our busier ports such purism is probably misplaced and few cruise these days without some form of 'iron topsail'.

There are basically three types from which to choose: inboard petrol engines, inboard diesel engines and outboards.

Obviously the first decision is between the inboard and the outboard. To a large extent this will depend on why you want an engine. If all you need is power when working in and out of crowded anchorages and marinas, the outboard will suffice. It should be fitted with a clutch and, if possible, a reverse gear. These facilities are not offered on the smaller models but are well worth having. If on the other hand you intend to rely on the engine to get you home on time when the wind fails you, I would suggest that you think in terms of an inboard unit. To carry an outboard with sufficient power to drive you through a heavy ground swell or against wind and tide calls for a heavier unit than most sailing folk would wish to see hung on their transom.

Having said that, there is a good deal to be said for fitting an outboard bracket to the boat if you have a small unit designed for use on the tender. It will not be able to stay aboard the tender when you are towing it at sea and so will have to be stowed somewhere and a lifting bracket which keeps it well above the waterline is as good a place as any. Lower the bracket and you can use the outboard as an emergency power source. Even a very small engine will push along quite a big boat so long as the water is calm.

Petrol or diesel? To my way of thinking there is no contest. Diesel wins on all counts. Petrol is highly inflammable and the less of it you carry the better. Secondly, the electrics associated with petrol engines are very prone to failure in the salty, wet atmosphere in which marine engines live. If a petrol engine is fitted to the boat of your choice and you cannot afford to replace it, it is essential that you cosset it as you would a baby. The petrol must be switched off at the tank at all times unless the engine is in use and any sign of a leak must be repaired at once.

It must be admitted that diesel smells abominable and, being a searching agent, gets everywhere unless you are very careful. Diesel engines tend to vibrate more than petrol engines and some folk find this irritating. However, smells and vibrations never killed anyone, explosions have!

Whatever engine you carry, you must have aboard a copy of the instruction manual together with any spares and tools that you might need. Obviously you should make yourself as familiar as possible with your engine before you go to sea and it must be admitted that this is another plus factor for petrol engines; as they are very similar to car engines many people know a good deal about them already.

BELOW DECKS

Before we leave the boat we should take a quick look below decks. There is no such thing as an ideal layout for the accommodation. Fitting everything that is required into a small and oddly shaped hull is a

This modern ketch rigged boat has a central cockpit and a small after-cabin.

difficult task and there are as many answers as there are designers. However, what is important to you — and only you know what that is — may not have been as important to the designer. If none of your family ever picks up a book unless they have to, you won't want bookshelves. If reading is the main activity when there is nothing else to do you will think very differently. So, decide what you are looking for and compare it with what the boat has to offer. This area below decks will be your home for the period you are on holiday. It matters.

If it is obvious that the designer thinks very differently from you, his boat will never work for you.

What do I consider important? Well, in the first place, it is vital that everyone has his or her own bunk, that it is comfortable to lie on, easy to sit up in (for reading, etc.), easy to get into but secure once you've made it (which may mean lee boards to stop you from falling out when the boat heels). There's only one way to answer all those questions: get in and try 'em out! Go on, ignore the odd looks that the owner is giving you. Now, if you can so arrange things that you don't have to make up the sleeping berths before you turn in, that's a tremendous plus. Most folk put the children up in the fore-cabin and they sleep in

'Sherrakin', with her large roller reefing genoa and relatively small mainsail, has an easily worked rig and boats of this type and size make excellent family cruising boats.

the saloon, using any quarter berths that there may be for the adults when at sea. Now, I feel that this is not always the best way to organise matters. Later we shall be talking about making night passages so that youngsters can be below during what is, to them, a potentially boring part of the holiday. The part of the boat with least motion being the mid-ships area, it is then sensible for the youngsters to be in the quarter berths. Although there is the risk of waking them when you go below to navigate or make a cup of coffee, it eliminates the risk of a frightened child in the fore-cabin calling for a parent who, thanks to the noises on deck, cannot hear it. In port the adults can use the fore-cabin where they will be less disturbed than if trying to sleep aft and, if they find being forward too uncomfortable at sea, they can use the saloon berths when under way.

The main problem, if you have two children, is that few boats are fitted with two quarter berths. However, you might be able to consider one of the growing breed of craft fitted with a small, two-berth stern cabin and hand that over to the children. This is, in my view, the ideal situation.

Apart from the sleeping berths the most important place below decks is the galley. Can you stand or sit comfortably and reach everything when you're cooking? Is there adequate storage for food, crockery and cooking utensils? Where will you stand the dirty washing-up and the clean crocks as they dry? Where will you stand the plates when you're dishing up hot grub? You will have to perform all the usual functions and perform them at sea when the boat is heeling to the wind and pitching in a seaway. It's a bit much to expect the owner to let you cook a meal, eat it and then clear up again afterwards but try to work out how everything would be done (the owner may be able to help by explaining how his crew manage).

Where will you stow the wet oilskins? There is almost nothing worse than having to share living space with dripping clothes and the nearer to the companionway the oilies live, the better.

These and a hundred other questions should flit through your mind as you inspect your proposed purchase but, human nature being what it is, the odds are that you will remember a host of important matters just after you arrive back home. Try to write out a list of your particular requirements before you go and also to make as many dimensioned sketches of the boat, both on deck and below, as you can. These will help you to answer those questions that you forgot to ask when on board.

The real test comes when you first stand on the boat after your cheque has been cleared and it's too late. Now you will begin to see all the snags (we always do) and begin to wonder whether you've been a bit hasty. If it's any consolation, hardly anybody buys the right boat the first time round and most of us are still trying to find it when age and decrepitude finally anchor us firmly ashore. You can read all you like but it is only when you first actually live aboard a boat that you find out what really matters to you and begin to acquire an 'eye' for the sort of accommodation that suits you and your family. However, humans are very adaptable and can enjoy themselves hugely even when things aren't quite perfect.

PEOPLE

Cruising is not really about boats — it's about people; people on holiday, people enjoying themselves, people sharing moments of magical calm and moments of boisterous uncertainty.

The skipper has a vital role to play if the holiday is to be a happy one and, although it is a role that he may well share with his wife, at the end of the day he must take the responsibility. Obviously safety is of paramount importance. The loss of a life or of the boat may be unthinkable but it is something that must be thought about.

Safety calls for a crew willing and able to take a high degree of discipline; happiness calls for as much freedom as possible. The skipper of the family cruising boat has to resolve this dilemma. The happiest families afloat are those where all matters relating to the boat are handled along strict naval lines and where everything else is pretty lax and subject to a good deal of democratic discussion which includes the youngest articulate children; those too young to be able to talk relying on the benevolence of their parents' dictatorship. That is a pretty glib answer; certainly it is a lot easier to talk about it than it is to achieve it.

In my book *Starting Cruising* I wrote the following. '. . . when things go wrong, as they will, and he (the father and skipper) starts to blame everyone else, as happens, he should stop for a moment and consider that either he is failing as a skipper and is giving orders badly, or he has failed as an instructor and the crew do not understand him, or he has failed as a father and the crew do not want to understand him.' I believe that this passage sums up the demands placed on the father and skipper and I repeat that the demands are considerable but the rewards beyond measure. How do we set about achieving this Utopian state?

As already suggested, a very good start for those with no boating experience whatever would be a week or two at some school or club such as the I.C.C. Even that, of course, leaves a tremendous amount still to be learned and the basics will need to be practised until everything comes as near to being second nature as makes no difference.

Actually, one has two separate subjects to learn — seamanship and living together as a family in a confined space. You can learn a great deal about living together and

'Speedwell' is one of the Island Cruising Club's boats which can be used by novice families sailing with an experienced skipper.

about working together by having a short holiday on a canal or river. Neither my wife nor my step-son (he was nearly ten when we married) had any 'previous experience' and we found that a narrow boat made the ideal nursery school. With no worries as to tides or gales, lee shores or collisions at sea, they were soon handling the warps as we worked the boat in and out of the locks and it wasn't long before they were steering, gradually gaining confidence as they went along. After a few days we began to work as a team (one of the hallmarks of a 'crew' as opposed to a 'family group').

I learned too. I learned that the great

temptation to do everything myself had to be overcome. It is terribly difficult to just stand by and watch as someone makes a complete mess of a very simple task. However, snatching a warp from a small boy as he fumbles about trying to tie a bowline is the quickest way to destroy his confidence and remove any desire that he may have had to learn. So long as the basic rule about safety is not involved, it is far better to let people learn from their own mistakes.

To suggest that we learnt a lot about boat handling would be wrong — there was neither the time nor the opportunity. What we did learn was how to tackle learning — they learnt to trust my orders and I learnt how to explain what was needed beforehand. We also learnt a lot about living in a small space, which was just as well. A few weeks later we turned our backs on the land and moved on to our 40-foot ketch.

From there on it is really a question of taking things gently and training, training, training. Naturally one chooses a cruising area which includes a fair amount of sheltered water. Places such as the River Fal with its wide expanses of protected water and the Harwich area with its rivers are eminently suitable. If it is possible to make this first cruise early or late so as to miss the height of the season, so much the better. For your first trial run you want to avoid crowds if you can.

Devote the first three or four days to pure training. That sounds terribly boring but you will be trying out a lot of new things and that should provide plenty of interest as well as ensuring that you all turn in pleasantly tired each night. This is not the place to give a detailed training schedule and, in any event, this will depend on a number of factors, not least the ages of the children. Suffice to say that you should be more than competent at anchoring and mooring both under power and under sail, setting sail, reefing, steering a compass course and steering by the wind, working out the expected depth of water at any given place and other basic navigational skills including fixing the position of the boat using compass bearings and setting a course to allow for tidal streams. It will also include a lot of slow working so that you can take the boat into crowded anchorages and the like without worrying too much. Off the boat, you will have learnt how to handle the dinghy (under oars and, if you are carrying one, outboard engine) and so on.

These few days will give you a chance to learn how the boat behaves under a wide range of conditions as well as training the crew so that they know how they should behave. It will do more than that. Subconsciously you will be learning how to move about the boat safely. You will know where to put your feet and where the grab handles are without having to fumble to find them. This is valuable for everyone but specially for children as you may find that some of the steps are too high for them (particularly when climbing out of the cockpit) or that hand holds are too far apart. It may be necessary to make a few additions when this happens. You can hurt yourself quite badly by missing a grab handle or taking a false step when in a seaway, and the more you have moved about the boat, both on deck and below, in sheltered waters first, the less the risk when you go outside.

Children become bored very quickly and these training sessions should be broken up into a number of different occupations.

Even when something obviously needs a lot more work done on it, it is better to leave it and come back to it again later than to let it become a bogey. Sessions spent in the dinghy or even helping in the preparation of food can be interspersed among the more serious stuff to everyone's advantage.

Cruising provides the perfect opportunity for a bit of role reversal. Many families move aboard and follow almost exactly the same routine as they do at home; mother does all the cooking while father looks after the boat. There is nothing that dictates that only a man can steer, hand and reef (the time-honoured requirements of the Able Seaman). Indeed, there is a lot to be said for ensuring that all who are old enough are given ample opportunity to perfect as many skills as they can grasp — including navigation, taking compass bearings and passage planning, subjects usually managed by the skipper alone. The day may well come when it is extremely fortunate that someone else can hold those reins for a while!

Meanwhile, one can hardly blame the wife who, after a season acting as galley slave and nursemaid, insists that the next holiday be spent in an hotel! Mothering, of course, cannot be delegated in quite the same way, especially when the children are young, which brings us to our next subject.

CHILDREN

A question which crops up fairly often is 'how easy is it to cruise with children?' The true answer, of course, is that it all depends. However, in general terms children take very well to cruising when they are very young (say under six) and when they are old enough to be able to take an active part in running the boat. The last will vary as far as age is concerned; some children of eight or nine are very keen and very competent whilst others may be 15 or 16 before they gain sufficient interest and some, frankly, are never interested.

Babies present virtually no problems once the logistics have been solved. They need somewhere comfortable and secure in which to sleep, and a normal carrycot lashed on to a bunk or on to the cabin sole is ideal. Food presents no problems as the quantities involved are tiny and most will be tinned. Disposable nappies are probably essential although some people prefer to use the ordinary ones and solve the laundry problems. Few babies are worried by sea-sickness and many find the motion simply soporific. A baby bouncer is helpful when in port; it can be rigged from the boom in the cockpit. Another useful device is a canvas hammock chair, but avoid the plastic ones as they are a bit hard and can give the baby a nasty knock in a seaway. The canvas types with the metal frames can be mounted on a wooden base which can be fixed down quite easily.

The real fun begins when baby begins to crawl. At this stage it is essential that netting is rigged right around the deck so that there is absolutely no risk of baby going over the side. At home it is usual practice to start moving things up out of reach as the youngsters become mobile. This can be difficult in a boat and is usually impossible in the galley which is danger area number one below decks. If the layout below lends itself to some form of gate — best made of netting — which restricts the toddler to the safer parts of the cabin, this should be rigged. Making a boat safe below can be a problem which will exercise the brain of the parents for many a winter's evening!

The crunch comes when taking babies and toddlers ashore in the dinghy. Very small babies can be carried in one of the body slings which hold them securely and leave both hands free. When they are too large for those, a harness with two lines attached plus a life jacket provide the safest solution to the problem. An adult on board (or ashore) holds one line, the adult in the dinghy holds the other. The youngster is virtually swung from one to the other until it is old enough to help itself. Handing an unattached child over the rail is not a good idea. I mention life jackets with some trepidation. The theory is obviously good but the problem is to find one which both fits a youngster

Safety netting is an essential precaution when young children are aboard. It is also useful if you take your dog to sea.

and which then holds the youngster the right way up should it be used in earnest. The first can be tested on dry land; the other cannot and I would hesitate to suggest that a 'wet test' be carried out even though that is the only way to be sure. As I understand the situation it is something to do with the fact that the centre of gravity of a small child is higher than that of an adult. Whatever the reason, I know of a number of instances when children have actually been turned upside down by their life jackets and ended up with their heads under water. Under no circumstances should they be relied upon — hence the two lines on to the harness so that both adults can support the child if anything should happen.

Incidentally, children like playing with switches. It can be annoying to find the batteries have run flat because something has been switched on. Either fit a master switch which is key operated or bring all switches to a central box with a child-proof cover. Local control can be effected by

Children can soon learn to be responsible for handling the dinghy.

switches on appliances in series with those in the control box.

Very young children will be kept below when under way and it makes a good deal of sense to make any long passage over night. As soon as they are old enough to be on deck when at sea, they must be trained so that they automatically wear their harnesses and safety lines at all times. The only way you can achieve this is to wear *yours* too! Incidentally, most children's safety lines will be fitted with standard clips for attaching them to strong points on the boat. These will be too tough for little fingers. Since the children will never be on deck in really boisterous conditions, augmenting these with something that they can manage is acceptable and will help to train them to clip-on without being told.

Try to avoid the word 'don't' at this stage. You are laying the foundation stones and if they feel that being aboard is hedged in with hundreds of restrictions they will be less likely to be happy members of the crew when they grow older. You want them to think about sailing as fun rather than a bore.

As the child grows, it becomes important that he has some part of the boat that is private. The bunk and a shelf alongside plus a handy locker will be sufficient so long as they contain nothing but the bits and pieces the child wants around him. If a curtain can be rigged to make his area truly private, so much the better.

He will now be in a standard bunk and this must be both comfortable and secure. There are ways of fitting lee clothes (bits of canvas that stop the child falling out even when the boat heels) and these are essential. He will also need a lot of entertainment.

The foreshore with its mud or sand and its rocky pools and seaweed alive with crabs and other goodies makes an ideal playground when the boat is in port. Swimming and fishing might well be on the menu but the weather is not always kind and the stores must include some of the children's favourite games. The parents must be happy to play endless games of ludo (or whatever) whilst praying for the sun to shine. Since there is not much space, the games chosen should be those that offer the maximum entertainment value for the minimum of bulk. Cards are one obvious choice. Parents whose offspring enjoy reading are truly blessed but even when this is not the case, it is sensible to carry reference works so that children can look up interesting facts about the things they will see. The Observer series is ideal to start with as the range covers Birds, Wild Flowers, Butterflies, Trees, Ships, Weather, Sea Fishes, Flags, and one very important one on the Sea and Seashore.

Even when standard fishing is pointless children can occupy themselves for hours catching crabs using no more than a bit of bacon rind tied on the end of a piece of string.

As soon as the children are big enough, they should be taught to row the dinghy. Soon afterwards they can be made responsible for rowing everyone ashore and for looking after the dinghy and keeping it clean and tidy. Inflatables are often used these days as they save having to tow the tender but these will rarely appeal to youngsters in the same way and it's worth the extra problems for them to have 'a boat of their own'. If this can be rigged with a simple sail they may even be able to take part in some of the local regattas that take place in many of the ports around the coast and, as they grow older, can carry out all the winter maintenance on the dinghy, rubbing it down and repainting it ready for the next season. Most boats have the deck space to carry a canoe or a sailboard. These can add to the children's enjoyment enormously and I know of one family whose children often set off in their two-man canoe complete with a tent and a few provisions to spend a night camping up a river when conditions are right. At what age one can allow this degree of freedom will depend largely on how well the children have been taught to care for themselves in a watery environment.

Children aboard are always a worry, can be an absolute pain in the neck, can ruin any holiday. They can also be great fun and can add enormously to the cruise by becoming extremely valuable members of the crew. The day may even come when you can no longer cope *without* them!

PETS

I have known people take all sorts of pets with them — dogs, cats, a tortoise, budgerigars and even once a lamb! First of all it cannot be stressed too strongly that no pets should be taken if you intend to 'go foreign'. The anti-rabies regulations are rightly very strict and we have them to thank for the present rabies-free situation. You will not be allowed to bring your pet back into the country unless you are prepared for it to stay the required six months in quarantine.

Dogs present few problems apart from the difficulty associated with taking them ashore as required. All dogs can swim but some precautions may have to be taken to stop them falling overboard, as a swimming dog in a seaway is almost impossible to find. Netting as used for children is

sufficient. You can train a dog to use some handy part of the deck which can be washed off, which avoids the trips ashore, but it's not easy. Having spent so much time training them that they keep the 'home' clean you may find it is just not worth the effort. In any event, they will need the exercise.

Do not try to cruise with any dog that has not been well trained and is obedient. Apart from the fact that an unruly dog will ensure you become the least popular boat in port, it can cause chaos on deck when things start happening in a hurry and must obey the order to go below (the usual command being 'bed'!). One big advantage is that a dog can be left to guard the boat in your absence.

Cats are easier if they have been trained to use a litter box. Some cats find the vibration of an engine unbearable and, if this is the case, you cannot take them with you. Indeed, any animal may find life afloat too difficult in which case it is cruel to insist that they accompany you on board. The other problem with cats is that, since they cannot be trained, they have to be contained on occasion; your cat will be a most unwelcome visitor if you allow it to wander freely on to other people's boats.

Give thought to how you are going to get your pet from the dinghy to the deck. You can buy, or make, a suitable harness which will help you lift a dog aboard but I have found that a stout, wide collar is all that is really needed as dogs' necks are very strong.

You will inevitably end up with a wet, muddy and smelly pet. We have found that the only answer is to rig some form of canvas protection in the cockpit and have at least two old rugs so that the dogs can dry off before they come below.

CRUISE CAMPING

It may well be that the funds are not available for the purchase and maintenance of a cruising boat. A great deal of fun can be had with a suitable large dinghy and basic camping gear.

There are two ways of tackling cruise-camping. One way is to use the boat as a means of transport only, camping ashore; the other is to camp aboard the boat using a boat tent supported by the boom. Dinghies such as the Wayfarer are ideal if you are camping on land, and the Drascombe boats, which come in various sizes, fulfil the requirements for camping on board. These boats have a number of water-tight lockers in which the gear can be kept dry, can carry heavy weights without becoming sluggish and are unsinkable. Even a family with two small children can enjoy a holiday of this sort in one of the larger Drascombes and, since such boats will be on trailers, one can explore places like Chichester Harbour regardless of where one lives.

TO SUM IT ALL UP

Cruising offers the family the chance to acquire an enormous range of skills from ropework to helmsmanship, from carpentry to sailmaking, from navigation to weather prediction. It teaches children to become more self-reliant, to back their own judgement and to carry responsibility. It also teaches them to work as a part of a team. Many families that have taken up cruising have found that the whole of family life has benefited. Children have a greater real respect for their parents having seen them coping at sea, and parents have, perforce, a clearer understanding of their children's characters, abilities and limitations.

The scope of various sports and other activities open to the 'outdoor family' when cruising is, as we have seen, very wide and so it would be wrong to consider the actual cruising as the be-all and end-all. Apart from anything else, there is scope to enjoy the more competitive side of life by taking part in regattas which will almost certainly include races for out-and-out cruising boats.

Above all, perhaps, the boat-based holiday can be spent far away from the rush and noise of modern life, close to nature and the natural forces. Not only does such an environment recharge batteries exhausted by civilisation's demands, it offers new values and a new perspective which can make those demands easier to bear.

SOME SAILING TERMS

Backstays (runners): The wires leading aft from the mast to prevent it from bending forward.

Ballast: Weight carried low down to counter-balance the 'heeling effect' of the wind in the sails.

Bermudan: A rig with no gaff but triangular sails only.

Block: A pulley.

Boom: The spar to which the foot (lower edge) of a sail is attached.

Bowsprit: A spar projecting horizontally from the bow in front of the ship.

Companionway: The entry from the cockpit to the cabin.

Furling: Gathering up and securing a sail.

Gaff: The spar to which the upper edge of a quadrilateral sail is attached.

Genoa: A large triangular headsail.

GRP: Glass fibre construction.

(To) Hand: To furl a sail.

Halliards: The ropes used to hoist a sail or flag.

Headsail: A triangular sail set forward (ahead of) the fore- or main-mast.

Horse: A rail or wire running across the deck on which a sheet travels.

Jib: The foremost headsail.

Ketch: A two-masted vessel in which the mizzen-mast (the after or rear one) is shorter than the main-mast and stepped forward (ahead of) the sternpost.

Leeward: The side opposite to that on which the wind is blowing.

Mizzen: The after (rear) mast in a Ketch or Yawl — shorter than the main-mast.

Quarters: The sides of a boat, behind the midships area.

Reefing: Shortening sail as wind strength increases.

Scull: To move a boat using one oar over the stern.

Sheet: A rope by means of which a sail is trimmed (adjusted) to the correct angle.

Shrouds: Wires giving sideways support to a mast or bowsprit.

Spreader: A strut on a mast to spread the rigging.

Staysail: A triangular sail set on a wire or 'stay'.

Sweep: A big oar.

Tacking: Zig-zagging a ship to make progress into the wind.

Tender: The dinghy.

Transom: A type of flat stern.

Warps: Ropes by which a vessel is secured or moved along.

Weather (or windward): The side of a boat on which the wind is blowing.

PUBLICATIONS
BOOKS

Since some authors suit folk better than others, in general I would suggest that you have a look through the books in your nearest library and then buy the ones that you find most helpful. The sections to look in are 623.8 which deals with technical matters such as care of hulls, engines and sails, 629.045 specifically about navigation, 797.1 for books on how to sail and sailing technique, and 910.41 covering the biographies and autobiographies of sailors. Having said that, three books that you might like to have on your bookshelves are:

This is Sailing by Richard Creagh-Osborne. This assumes that you know nothing and are starting at the very beginning. Full of clear and colourful illustrations it is easy to follow and covers all the basics. Published by Fontana in a soft cover at £6.95.

Starting Cruising by Rodney Willett. It is very bad form to suggest that you buy this book but I wrote it specifically for people who had the basic knowledge offered by Richard Creagh-Osborne and who then wished to take a cruising holiday with the emphasis on the word holiday. Had there been another book available with that approach, I would not have written it. Published by David and Charles at £9.50.

The Macmillan and Silk Cut Nautical Almanac. As far as I know, no one else has ever suggested this book for beginners. Although mainly concerned with making coastal passages around the UK, about a third is devoted to all sorts of information from selecting the right rope for a given task (and then how to splice and knot it), through basic navigation to the 'Rule of the Road'. Having learnt the bits you need to know, you can then browse through the 'Harbour, Coastal and Tidal Information' and start to explore the coast from your armchair, dreaming the dreams that all sailors dream. Published by Macmillan. The 1984 issue is £12.95.

MAGAZINES

The editors recommend the following magazines, all available from newsagents:

Practical Boat Owner, Yachting Monthly, Yachting World, Yachts and Yachting.

An evening on the river.

Perhaps you may feel that canoeing is only for the young and agile, and not for families? Once that may have been true but not today. At Fladbury, on the Worcestershire Avon, David Train has begun an exciting new approach to the activity, based on a belief that canoeing is about 'being on the water not in it'! He has pioneered teaching methods for placid water canoeing that include using very stable, open-cockpit kayaks — no more early sessions in swimming pools practising capsize drill. 'The Fladbury Way' has now been officially adopted by the British Canoe Union as the standard method for teaching placid water canoeing. Safe and easy, it can be enjoyed by every member of the family and opens up new prospects both for touring and racing. There is now a National Coaching Scheme and courses are being arranged countrywide.

David Train began canoeing with his wife Eileen and three sons, Stephen, Andrew and Michael, on the canals of the West Midlands. In 1972 the family moved to Fladbury and the local rector asked David to show a few youngsters how to build canoes. Their club flourished to such an extent that in 1977 they won the British Team Championship. Five members of the club are now in the national Olympic Squad. These include David's three sons who between them have held every British Record in racing and have won every National Title for both sprint racing and marathon. Although very interested in top-level paddling, David is equally pleased that his revolutionary teaching methods for placid water have brought canoeing within the reach of all. Besides creating the new Placid Water Coaching School, David is Chairman of the Sprint Racing Committee, the Olympic Squad Coach for Canadian paddling and the BCU (British Canoe Union) National Coach for racing. His wife Eileen enjoys 'a gentle paddle on the Avon on a summer's evening' but she too has competed in team events for the club in both marathon and sprint. The first book, *Getting Started*, in his series *Canoeing the Fladbury Way*, has recently been published. Details are given at the end of the chapter.

Canoeing

DAVID TRAIN

Canoeing is a marvellous activity for the family. Every member can take part, it is relatively cheap to get started, the running costs are small and it can be combined with a host of other activities.

For us, the Train family, it all began when a friend gave us a kit for a canvas and lath kayak. The boys, Stephen, Andrew and Michael, were then aged four, two-and-a-half, and one year. That was 18 years ago. Now, in 1984, the family are preparing to compete, together with friends from their club, in the Olympic Games. We have enjoyed 18 exciting years of family canoeing which have brought us from our first trip on a canal near Walsall to Los Angeles in 1984.

At first we just took our kayak to our local canal to try it out; then we bought another double-seater kayak and were able to go on small trips together. For a few years we enjoyed picnic trips on Sunday afternoons and sometimes took the kayaks with us on holiday to use as play-boats on the edge of a lake. In 1970 we moved to Bedford, joined a canoe club and found out about a whole range of canoeing

activities — slalom, white water, sea canoeing, marathon, and sprint racing. We became interested in racing. In 1972 we moved to Fladbury.

Fladbury is a beautiful village in the heart of Worcestershire. It lies on the placid river Avon between Evesham and Pershore. It has a population of under one thousand, an ancient church, two mill houses and two pubs. It was the ideal place for us to start our own canoe and kayak club; our teaching methods and the types of kayaks and canoes we used led to the club growing quickly and soon becoming very successful. Out of this emerged the 'Fladbury Way' of canoeing. As a family, we were concerned that all the members should find canoeing both safe and enjoyable.

THE FLADBURY WAY

Mention the word canoeing to almost anyone in Britain and their immediate image will be of a young man or woman strapped into a kayak, wearing a crash helmet and wetsuit, performing turns and rolls on rapidly moving rivers. For historical

Left: The conventional image of canoeing on fast moving water, in kayaks with close fitting cockpits.

Above: A group under instruction at Plas y Brenin Outdoor Centre, Wales.

reasons almost all of the formalised training for canoeing in Britain is about paddling on rough water. In consequence small-cockpit manoeuvreable boats are used, in which a great deal of attention has to be given to capsize and rescue technique, rolling and struggling to keep in a straight line. For those who enjoy this alpine-type sport it is fine, but there are many more who would never attempt to canoe because of this image.

This emphasis on flowing water technique has meant that everyone taught canoeing started in kayaks with close-fitting cockpits. In the event of a capsize in such a craft it is unsafe to try and get out until the kayak is upside down. So capsize drill must be taught very early in

training. This in many cases means capsize practice in the local baths before going on to the cold river or canal. Most clubs, schools, and training centres introduce canoeing this way, starting with a session in the swimming baths. They then lead on to touring or competition on moving water.

So if you are interested in rough water and advanced sea canoeing then I would advise you to join one of these clubs. There are courses throughout the country and the British Canoe Union (the BCU, governing body of the sport in Britain) will supply the name of your nearest club and advise on courses. Clubs have access to water, they know the local conditions and they provide a social environment.

But there is an alternative based on the approach to canoeing we teach at Fladbury. The 'Fladbury Way' is now the British way, having been officially adopted by the BCU for teaching placid water canoeing. It is a form of canoeing that can be enjoyed by every member of the family, opening up exciting new prospects for touring and racing. There is a new Placid Water BCU Coaching Scheme and courses are springing up all over the country.

At Fladbury there are no sessions in the swimming baths, capsize drill is not practised in the early stages, everyone starts in an open-cockpit, wide-beam kayak or canoe, and no one wears crash hats or wetsuits. We feel that canoeing is about being on the water, not in it! One of our objectives is to teach people to explore safely the many miles of placid rivers and canals in this country in the right kind of kayaks and canoes. With the teaching methods we have developed we find it is possible to teach anyone to canoe and enjoy themselves.

It is true that for a short time when we first started at Fladbury we did use the small-cockpit type kayak. We are fortunate in having a weir in the village and had we continued to develop in that way we would have become a slalom-based club. However, it became clear very early on that although some teenage boys quite liked capsize drill, there were many more people who would take up canoeing if they were not asked to capsize. We had other family-type touring and stable racing boats and we started to use them. From that evolved the Fladbury Way of teaching kayak.

We then became interested in Canadian canoe paddling, and from our kayak experience developed a series of canoes of varying levels of stability so that again we are able to teach anyone how to canoe without having to practise capsize drill — the first stage touring Canadian is an ideal boat for the family paddler with very young children.

Our activities can be compared with walking and running. Some use their kayak or canoe for the 'evening stroll' or family picnic. Some use it for 'jogging' or keeping fit. Most members progress into simple fun-racing in the club and then into external marathon races — our 'cross country' event. Our 'track' event is sprint racing — the Olympic event.

CANOES AND KAYAKS

Canoeing is used generally to describe the sport of both canoeing and kayaking.

The most common craft in Britain is the kayak and unfortunately it is the boat that most people call a canoe. It is the craft where the paddler is sitting down and using a double-bladed paddle. It is derived from the Eskimo kayak which was a hunting, sea-going boat.

The canoe is the boat of the North American Indian, the sort of boat used on recreation lakes with a wide beam, turned-up ends and completely open deck. It is normally paddled with a single blade but there is no reason why a double blade can't be used if it is preferred. In racing a single blade must be used for canoe and a double-ended blade for kayak.

At Fladbury we use a range of boats to suit all kinds of ability in both canoe and kayak. Most of our boats can be used for touring, fun-racing, sprint and marathon racing. The kayak may be used for estuary and sea canoeing in reasonable conditions, but not for advanced sea canoeing when the smaller cockpit is needed. The canoe is not used on the sea because the open deck may easily be swamped by waves.

In racing you will hear people talk of K1 and C1. A K1 is a single-seater kayak, a C1 is a single canoe. For fast touring, fun and marathon racing we use K1s and C1s and

the double K2 and C2. In addition to this, for sprint racing we use the four-seater K4 and the four-man canoe, the C4.

Before you buy a canoe or kayak try both types of craft if possible. The Canadian touring canoe is a great boat to have. It can be used for teaching the skills of both canoe and kayak, for fun-racing, or for a picnic with the family. It is a craft which will always be useful and give a lifetime of pleasure no matter what other type of canoeing activity you follow.

KAYAKS AND CANOES FOR PLACID WATER CANOEING

It is important that our sort of boat should travel easily — in straight lines, not circles — so we use kayaks of a special design. All

Canoeing the Fladbury Way. The first-stage Canadian makes an ideal family boat.

our kayaks tend to be long and thin. The length means that they cut easily through the water and this, combined with a long flat keel, makes them easy to paddle in a straight line. But we do have a range of varying widths and hence stabilities, so that the fifty-plus touring canoeist can feel as much at home in perhaps a little wider boat as the top class competing athlete can in his narrower one.

All our kayaks have open cockpits so that the knees are not trapped under the deck. This enables the paddler to sit comfortably in his kayak without getting stiff legs or cramp. With an open cockpit, getting in and out of the boat is easy, and in the unlikely event of a capsize you will not have to follow any special drill underwater to escape. In fact, as you are wearing a buoyancy aid, you may not even get your hair wet!

THE KAYAKS

Touring Kayak Single: This is a stable kayak 14 feet long and with a 24-inch beam. It need not be fitted with a rudder. It is a cheap and simple boat, ideal for school use.

Fast Touring Kayak Single: This kayak is 17 feet long with a 20—23-inch beam and can certainly be used for racing as well as touring. It is the backbone of our club training programme since it is the ideal training boat for all ages, abilities and aspirations. It can be used for estuary and lake canoeing. Because of its length it is fitted with a rudder.

Stable Racing Kayak Single: This kayak is 17 feet long with a 20-inch beam, and has the same shape on the deck line as the modern racing kayak. However, its underwater and waterline shape gives it much more stability than the racing kayak.

Racing Kayak Single: This is the modern Olympic class kayak, 17 feet long and with a 20-inch beam. There are many designs with slight variations to suit paddlers of different weights. Each has a characteristic 'feel' when propelled at full speed by a top paddler. When viewed from above there is a strange widening in the rear deck. This is because international regulations specify a minimum width for racing kayaks and designers place this widest point out of the way of the paddler. The kayaks are much narrower than 20 inches on the waterline. Youngsters soon learn to handle these kayaks, but for adults it takes time, so if you are a beginner it is wise to stay with the more stable boats.

Crew Boats: At all levels of stability we have doubles and for racing the four-man K4. But our introduction to kayak skills is carried out in a single-seater.

WHICH KAYAK TO START WITH?

If possible, attend a club before making a choice. At a club following the Fladbury principles you will have no problem — you will start in the first level kayak (the first in my list) and you will be advised when to move on to the next. But what should you do if you have to teach yourself? Of course, it does depend on whether you are a complete beginner, whether you are young or old, man or woman, tall or short. Your guiding rule should be to choose a kayak in which you feel stable. You may be tempted to buy a narrower boat because it goes faster — don't. The speed of a kayak is a combination of the paddler and his craft. Most people can paddle in the stage 2 kayak and, with care, that is the best choice, although I would advise, if at all possible, you try to get some practice in the stage 1 kayak first.

Prices for kayaks and canoes vary from about £50 second hand to hundreds of pounds for the latest design.

THE KAYAK PADDLE

To cover the needs of every type of canoeist there is a wide choice of paddles — wooden, plastic, flat and curved blades, fibreglass or alloy shafts. For placid water curved and asymmetric blades are a must. The paddle is balanced and does not flutter. Buy the best paddles you can afford as they make an enormous difference to the paddler. They cost between £10 and £40. Whether you have wooden, alloy, fibreglass or carbon-fibre shafts is a matter of personal choice. Wood and fibreglass have more spring and are not cold in the hands for winter training. Most people find them adequate. Very strong and fit paddlers may prefer alloy and carbon shafts which are stiffer. Although adults should buy the best possible paddles, it might be wise to buy cheaper sets or kits for youngsters, who will need a number of sets while they are growing. However, always insist on curved and asymmetric blades.

Paddle Feather: All kayak blades used for placid water canoeing are feathered at slightly less than 90°.

SPRAYDECKS

A spraydeck is a cover which fits around the cockpit of the kayak, covering up your legs. In the early stages of teaching we do not use them, as if they are too tight the paddler may find difficulty in getting out of his canoe in the event of a capsize. This is particularly true in the case of young children — something to consider if you are teaching yourself.

RUDDER

A rudder is not needed on kayaks up to 15 feet long, but over this length it is necessary. Once the very basic strokes are mastered, a kayak with a rudder is much easier to paddle whatever its length. The rudder is operated with the feet by moving a tiller bar. Wires pass along the kayak and are connected to the rudder wheel at the stern. The kayak is turned by moving the tiller bar, right to go right, left to go left.

There are two types of rudder — understern and overstern. The understern is used for deep water. The overstern is designed to lift over anything it touches and so is used in shallow or rocky water.

THE CANADIAN CANOES

The same principles are followed in teaching the Canadian canoe. All newcomers start in a wide boat and then progress, if they wish, to a narrower, stable and faster craft. But there is one main difference: the Canadian canoe is much easier to paddle as a double; it is indeed a crew boat, ideal for the family.

A number of different paddling positions may be used in this canoe. The three basic ones are sitting, kneeling on both knees with the posterior resting against the seat, and the high kneeling or racing position. If a kneeling position is used then always kneel on some sort of pad. Closed cell plastic foam is a good material for this.

Most Canadian canoes can be used by one, two, three or more people. It is more important to think about the canoe's load-carrying capacity and manufacturers generally indicate the maximum safe load for their canoes. As with kayaks, there is a range of four canoes which fit the needs of most paddlers, and either of the first two are stable enough for the beginner.

The Touring Canadian: Generally these are between 14 and 18 feet in length and have a 30—36-inch beam. They are great canoes for youngsters to learn to play in and the best craft for the family. They are ideal for going for a picnic, studying wildlife, photography or general pottering.

The Fast Touring Canadian: They can be used for touring, fitness training or racing. They are fairly stable craft which are ideal for school use. Adults taking up the sport can soon master the craft and begin to feel the pleasure of movement. The lengths vary from 14 feet for a single to 16 to 18 feet for doubles; beam 30 inches and below.

The Stable Racing Canoe: These sleeker but more unstable craft are good for marathon racing and may be used to introduce paddlers to the higher kneeling positions used for racing. Lengths are 14 feet and 17 feet for singles and up to 21 feet for doubles.

The Racing Canoe: As with the kayaks, these are the modern Olympic class canoes, 17 feet long but with a 30-inch beam. With their extra wide beam taken well back they are strange looking craft and extremely difficult to handle in side winds.

CANOE PADDLES

As with kayaks, there is a wide-ranging choice of canoe paddles. It's a little easier to choose because almost all canoe blades are flat and the shapes don't vary much. Most top paddlers use wooden paddles. For growing youngsters who must keep changing the length, alloy-shafted plastic paddles are suitable.

CANOEING ACTIVITIES FOR PLACID WATER

The range of activities for placid water canoeing is wide. First, if possible, attend a course to learn the basic skills. You will be able to practise these pottering or touring. You can go further and canoe for fitness and perhaps by then enjoy racing.

THE COACHING SCHEME

There is now a National Coaching Scheme for teaching people to canoe on placid water. The number of clubs offering courses is growing and you can get an information sheet giving the names of those in your area (details at the end of the chapter). The BCU also supplies a list of approved centres for canoeing holidays.

The coaching system takes you in four stages from basic paddling through to handling open-cockpit kayaks and canoes on open and moving water. Certificates and badges are available for each stage. In addition there are tests for achieving a range of distances in the racing and marathon canoes and kayaks.

KEEPING FIT AND COMPETITIVE RACING

I said earlier in this chapter that our sort of canoeing activity can be compared with walking and running. The previous section was our equivalent of walking or a country ramble. For those who wish to 'jog' the transition is delightfully simple. There are fun races and tourist trials and then racing with the Open Racing Scheme. This is our 'cross country' event and there are over one hundred raced throughout Britain, organised by local clubs under the rules of the Marathon Racing Section of the BCU.

The first stage in racing could be a club time trial, handicap race or an achieving marathon. These events are open to all, and provide a very gentle introduction to racing — more to be seen as fun races. The time trials are run as part of the National Coaching Scheme. Certificates and badges are awarded for distances of 6.5, 13, 9.5, and 26 miles when paddled under a set time.

Many clubs run regular handicap races. These are usually over a distance of four to five miles. The idea is that the slowest start first, the fastest last, and if the handicap is correct they will all cross the finishing line together. This is a very important part of

Placid water canoeing on Lynnau Mymbyr, Capel Curig, North Wales.

the club activity. It is an event that all members of the club can take part in with a real objective. The absolute beginner is racing against the Olympic Squad athlete. At National level we are now trying to create a system where across the country each person will know their handicap — rather like golf. They will then be able to take part in any of the club races with the correct handicap.

The first-ever achieving marathon, and the event that started the sport in Britain, is the Devizes to Westminster. This takes place at Easter each year. The course is 125 miles long and has 76 portages, where

Canoeists on the Thames during the 'Thamesday' festivities, September 1980.

the canoes or kayaks are carried around the locks. Although nowadays the race is won in about sixteen hours, there are many people who go out and complete the course in either one, two, three or four days. Like running a marathon, it is something that is great when you have done it!

Other less arduous events are the Westel Tourist Trials and the Stratford—Fladbury —Tewkesbury Stage Marathon. The Westel event which takes place on the Basingstoke Canal is a real family affair and all sorts of craft are used. The participants — they are not seen as competitors — decide what standard to aim for over a series of distances. The Stratford—Fladbury—Tewkesbury Stage Marathon is designed for the serious racer and family tourist and all those in between. It's in two stages of about twenty-one miles with a camp and barbecue on the Saturday evening. It is a race for single kayaks and double canoes and it reflects the Fladbury approach — 'something for everyone' from the top class racing paddler to the family tourist.

Most of our families join in Marathon Racing with the Open Racing Scheme. Although called Marathon Racing the distances start at about five miles. There are nine divisions and everyone races together. The winner of a division is promoted to the next division. Marathon Canoe and Kayak racing is a fast-growing sport with a great deal of variety. Races are held on canals, rivers, lakes and the sea. Part of the enjoyment is to win points for the club championship. The races are divided into the sports regions of Britain and the leading three clubs from each region compete each year in a final for the Hasler Trophy. This is the most important trophy in Marathon Racing and was presented to commemorate the raid by marines on Bordeaux Harbour shipping in 1942 (portrayed in the film 'Cockleshell Heroes'). At Fladbury many of our parents have taken up racing to keep fit and have contributed greatly to our team success.

If Marathon is our 'cross country' event our 'track' event is Sprint Racing. This is the Olympic event for canoeing and kayaking. Distances raced are 500 metres and 1000 metres, and for World Championships 10 000 metres. The centre of Sprint Racing in Britain is at the National Watersports Centre at Holme Pierrepont, Nottingham. Here, six weekends a year between April and September, paddlers of all ages and levels of ability compete in single and crew boats. It is a wonderful sport and provides continuous activity for both the paddler and spectator. The newcomer arriving at the centre may well find it daunting at first, surrounded by international paddlers and officials. Don't be put off — there are many friends there willing to give advice and you will soon become part of the scene. Sprint Racing is being developed at other centres and within the next four years should be available in most sports regions.

TOURING

There are over two thousand miles of navigable water in Britain suitable for pleasure craft — there are many more suitable for canoes. Once you have covered the basic skills you should be capable of enjoying these waterways. Remember the points made on safety (see below) and access if you do it yourself. Beware if you are paddling on waters which you do not know well and always remember that placid rivers can become dangerous and fast flowing in flood conditions. If you have just started canoeing stick to the canals and rivers when they are flowing slowly.

WHERE TO CANOE

Almost any stretch of sheltered water is suitable for placid water canoeing. There may be problems with fishing interests — in common with other water users — but these are relatively minor. A deep locked river of two or three miles is ideal. Canals also provide excellent canoeing and so do small lakes. Larger lakes and estuaries demand more specialised skills to cope with waves and wind and are best avoided by beginners unless accompanied by an experienced instructor. A good guide to the suitability of a river is the presence of a rowing club.

In order to canoe on most rivers and canals you will need to pay a licence fee (clubs often have a block licence). The BCU publishes a leaflet on access which includes a list of addresses from which licences can be obtained. It is very important to remember that you must find out the exact legal position and what fees may be payable before you canoe on any waterway.

SAFETY

Swimming. Obviously, with the closed-cockpit slalom boat, people must be confident both in the water and under it. For placid water canoeing it is much better if people can swim, but we don't overstress the need. We have members who have canoed for many years, have never capsized and would hate even putting their heads under water! We don't think this need stop them canoeing — quite the reverse — providing they always wear a lifejacket or approved buoyancy aid. However, we would encourage everyone to become a good swimmer if possible.

Lifejackets and Buoyancy Aids. A lifejacket is designed to keep a person in a safe position even if he is unconscious; a buoyancy aid will not. But as lifejackets are rather bulky for placid water canoeing, most people wear buoyancy aids. *It really is vital that every member of the family should wear a lifejacket or approved buoyancy aid when canoeing.* Make certain you get the correct size, especially for small children. It is easy to slip out of an oversized aid and if a youngster does capsize he may become alarmed if his aid floats up around his head.

Never go in a closed cockpit kayak without first attending a BCU course.

Remember that the Fladbury system of teaching is for flat and slow-moving water. If you intend to canoe on fast-flowing, rough water, open lakes or the sea, then you must attend a BCU course designed for that purpose. Most clubs teach rough water canoeing and the BCU will supply the name of your nearest club and advise on courses.

The BCU is now training instructors in placid water canoeing. If there is instruction available, then go on a course. It will save you time in the long run and you will be taught basic safety for you and your family.

Never wear wellington boots or heavy clothing in a canoe.

Keep away from weirs of all types unless accompanied by an experienced instructor.

In the unlikely event of a capsize, leave the boat upside down to form an air trap. Keep hold of the boat and swim to the side. Remember to keep hold of your paddle.

Keep out of the way of pleasure boats. Many are handled by inexperienced people. Pass on the right if at all possible; otherwise keep close to the bank.

Keep clear of fishermen's lines.

Go out with others whenever possible. There is safety in numbers.

CLOTHING

For placid water canoeing you require nothing special. Whether touring or racing, you have no intention of falling into the water so you have no need of a wetsuit. These restrict movement, are unpleasant to paddle in and impossible to use when racing. However, you do need to adapt your clothing to cope with the different weather conditions prevalent in Britain and to suit your own type of canoeing. On a cold day you will obviously have to dress more warmly if out for a gentle paddle as opposed to a training session in a racing boat.

It is important to protect yourself against the wind, both in winter and summer. On a windless day even in winter you will become quite warm paddling hard on a river like the Avon, and thermal underwear along with a vest will be sufficient. At the same temperature with a wind blowing you will need an anorak too.

For general purposes, canoeing clothes should be comfortable and not too bulky. Except in really cold weather an old pair of trousers with a shirt or woollen jumper (with a waterproof on top of that if necessary) would be adequate. In summer, shorts and tee-shirt are quite enough. I prefer to have a woollen garment next to the skin. For windy, cold days you will need a waterproof anorak. The lined anoraks are ideal for canoeing as they feel warm and do not cling when wet inside with condensation. On the water, the kayak paddler's legs may be protected by a spraydeck or waterproof trousers. The ones with zips in the legs are best as they are easy to get on and off. Canoe paddlers need to protect their legs as well, and in cold conditions should wear waterproof trousers. Normal shorts are not long enough in the leg for comfort and many canoeists prefer cycle shorts or cut-down tracksuits. It is not a good idea to wear cut-down jeans because the hard seams can cause severe cuts.

If you are covering long distances in any conditions be prepared with your anorak to hand for when you get cold and tired. Plimsolls and training shoes are best for touring and general purpose canoeing. If you are racing it will depend on whether you are taking part in sprint events or marathons where there are portages. Many sprint racers canoe with bare feet but for portages it is best to wear training shoes with a good grip as they are almost always muddy, wet and slippery.

In summer a sun-hat is often useful and in winter, when a great deal of heat is lost from the head, it is a good idea to wear a woollen hat.

TRANSPORT

At some stage you will need to transport your boat. A ladder-type car roof-rack is ideal, especially for canoes. For kayaks a 'V'-bar is often used. There are traffic regulations governing the amount of overhang that is allowed at the front and back of the car. Pad the rudder (in the case of a kayak) and put a brightly-coloured rag or a triangle at the rear. When travelling, ensure that the boats are secured at the front and rear as well as on the rack.

NOW TO GET STARTED!

I hope that having read this chapter, you will be bitten by the bug and take up canoeing. For the Fladbury families like us it has become a lifetime passion. We canoe ourselves, we watch our youngsters develop, and we follow with pride and interest those who have travelled the world representing Britain. I hope you and your family will be joining us on the canals and placid water rivers. Perhaps we shall see you at one of the many Fladbury events. And, who knows, maybe a member of your family, after reading this, will set off on the course which will lead him to the Olympic Games in the year 2000!

USEFUL ADDRESSES

British Canoe Union: Flexel House, 45-47 High Street, Addlestone, Weybridge, Surrey KT15 1JV. Tel: 0932 41341. The British Canoe Union is the governing body of the sport in Britain and it looks after the interests of all of us at national, regional, and local levels. I have referred in the text to the information leaflets on many aspects of canoeing which it distributes. If you become a qualified instructor or enter competitions, you must be a member.

Two organisations which welcome the tourist are:

The Canoe-Camping Club: Merrydown House, Off Reading Road, Chineham, Near Basingstoke, Hampshire RG24 0LU.

The Canadian Canoe Association of Great Britain: Secretary, Leslie M. Rowe, Queen Elizabeth Training College, Leatherhead, Surrey.

PUBLICATIONS

BOOKS

The BCU Canoeing Handbook. This is the most complete and up-to-date work covering the whole spectrum of canoeing. It includes an excellent bibliography. Just one word of caution: when reading this book remember that most of the authors will be talking about kayaking in closed-cockpit slalom-type kayaks, the skills needed and the rules which apply to them, so interpret with care. Chapter 14 is about the Fladbury Way of teaching.

The BCU Guide to the Waterways of the British Isles. This is a detailed guide to the rivers and canals in Britain.

The Racing and Marathon Yearbook. This is published annually. It contains all the latest rules and fixtures and is available from the BCU Sprint and Marathon Committees.

The following are all published in the series *Canoeing the Fladbury Way*. Number 1 is available now and the others will all be available by the end of 1984.

1. *Getting Started*. This is an introduction to placid water canoeing showing the skills needed in canoe and kayak. Available from the BCU, some shops, or myself (see address below), £1.95 (please add 45p for p & p).

2. *Moving On*. How to use placid water boats on moving and open water.

3. *Into Racing*. The first steps in competition canoeing including the racing awards.

4. *At the Top*. Written for those interested in marathon and sprint racing.

THE FLADBURY INFORMATION SHEET

An information sheet is available from the author which lists the latest details of canoes, kayaks, and equipment suitable for placid water canoeing. Also included are details of courses and clubs which teach the Fladbury Way of canoeing. To obtain the Fladbury Information Sheet, send s.a.e. (A5 size) to: Canoeing the Fladbury Way, Glen Villa, Fladbury, Pershore, Worcestershire.

MAGAZINES

It is a great help to be able to keep up to date with the latest developments. If you join the BCU you will get regular copies of its magazine *Focus*. Other magazines you will enjoy are:

Canoeing published by Ocean Publications, 34 Buckingham Palace Road, London SW1W 0RE.

Canoeist available from 13 Wellington Crescent, Baughurst, Basingstoke, Hampshire RG26 5PF.

The Train family all set for the Olympics, 1984.

Take your family cruising on some of the 2400 miles of canals and rivers that make up Britain's inland waterways and you will discover a different country! Canals, says John Gagg, generally hide from towns. They vary widely in their appeal, from the spectacular Monmouthshire and Brecon canal, which clings to the mountainside above the Usk valley, to the Birmingham Canal Navigations — an incredible near-100-mile network in the Midlands. In this simply-written, informal introduction John Gagg reveals a wisdom born of many years experience of our fascinating waterways.

Former teacher, trainer of teachers, and schools adviser, John Gagg has written several educational books now in wide use both in Britain and overseas. For many years he has studied and cruised the whole of our inland canal and river systems. He has taken nearly twenty thousand photographs, written numerous articles and given regular radio talks.

Through these activities, and on his own boat, he has introduced many families and young people to the waterways. He also lectures frequently and is a Council member of the Inland Waterways Association. This voluntary national body has campaigned with great success since 1946 for the use and revival of waterways for both commerce and leisure. John Gagg's books about waterways and the countryside include: *Canals in Camera 1* (Ian Allan); *Canals in Camera 2* (Ian Allan); *5000 Miles, 3000 Locks* (Arthur Barker); *The Canaller's Bedside Book* (David and Charles); *A Canal and Waterways Armchair Book* (David and Charles); *Canals* (Observer's Book series). His 'Looking at Inland Waterways' series includes: *Locks, Tunnels, Narrow Canals, Broad Canals, 250 Waterways Landmarks, Canals in a Nutshell* (obtainable from the author, see end of chapter). His books for children include: *Rivers in Britain, Boats and Boating, Boats and Ships, The Countryside, Maps and Symbols* (all Blackwell's Learning Library).

Cruising Inland Waterways

JOHN GAGG

Inland waterways offer an obvious family interest, whether you walk their towpaths, drive to some of their highlights, or — best of all — boat on them. They are usually well away from the noise of traffic and resorts, and full of unusual interest and activity.

You can fish in them, too — a quiet day in the fresh air for young or old, not needing much energy. But there's no doubt that it's floating along waterways that gives you the real flavour, whether by canoe, day-boat, sailing dinghy, or more likely a form of cruising boat you can live on during a holiday. Anyone may use these, and they can be hired with every mod. con. at many places. Large numbers of families, after trying such a holiday, go on to own a boat of their own.

The two main questions parents generally ask are, "How safe is it for children?", and "Won't they be bored?" Safety is, of course, vital near water at any time, so simple lifejackets should be worn by children on boats unless they can swim well. And a few safety rules are necessary for the younger ones on the boat, particularly at locks. Many thousands of families take all this happily in their stride. As for boredom . . . well, I have never heard of a bored child afloat on an inland waterway. There's so much to do, see and explore, and on canals especially the variety is endless. The days never seem long enough.

WHAT IS AN INLAND WATERWAY?

There are, of course, many lakes to boat on and fish in, but the inland waterways that I shall be talking about are the watery roads — canals and rivers — that link up to form a countrywide network, plus a few which are separate from this system. Most of them are in England, but there are some in Wales, and some separated ones in Scotland. Altogether there are about 2400 miles of waterways with about 2100 of these in the linked network. This includes some rivers controlled by locks, but not tidal lengths of rivers except in a few cases where these are regularly used by inland boats as part of the network. There about about 1400 locks in use on these waterways.

You may wonder why I say 'about' so

many miles and locks. This is because all the time there are enthusiasts restoring derelict canals. Since the Inland Waterways Association was founded in 1946 to save more and more waterways from falling into ruin, very many miles have been brought back into use by voluntary bodies. And this is still happening on the Kennet & Avon Canal, the Rochdale Canal, the Montgomery, the Huddersfield, the Pocklington, the Basingstoke, the Wey & Arun, and several others. You may end up with your family joining in this exciting (but muddy) work. These navigable waterways are of different types and the differences are worth knowing, as they affect your cruising or walking.

NARROW CANALS

The word 'narrow' really applies to the locks, rather than the canals themselves, though these canals are on the whole not as wide as others. The vital point, though, is that their locks are only 7 feet wide, which means that wider boats can't get far! The locks are usually about 70 feet long, however, and that's why the old commercial boats looked so long and thin. The correct name for them was *narrow boats*, or *longboats*, and enthusiasts are sarcastic if they hear them called barges (a *barge* is 14 feet wide or more).

These canals are, in many people's minds, the most attractive of all. They meander along, often amid trees, but also — especially in the Black Country — making their hidden and fascinating watery way through built-up areas. Most narrow canals are in the Midlands and West, and some have many locks where they climb towards the Birmingham area plateau. Almost all inland waterway boats are built

to fit the locks of these narrow canals. Some of the bridges, too, are only 7 feet wide, as well as some aqueducts. So taking a boat on these waterways does call for careful steering.

BROAD CANALS

'Broad' again refers to the locks. But of course the canals themselves are usually wider and deeper than the narrow ones. Many broad canals have locks 14 feet wide, which will take two narrow boats side-by-side if necessary, or just one 14-foot wide barge. Surprisingly, some broad canals — especially in the north — have locks shorter than the 70-foot length of narrow locks. All very confusing, especially if you try to take a 70-foot by 7-foot narrow boat through (for example) the 62-foot by 14-foot locks of the magnificent Leeds & Liverpool Canal!

There are commercial canals with wider and longer locks, particularly in Yorkshire, where you may be intrigued to meet large barges and even 'trains' of floating containers. They're quite used to pleasure-boats however. On the Gloucester & Sharpness Ship Canal, indeed, you'll meet small ships squeezing through the many swing-bridges. Even larger ones use the Manchester Ship Canal, but pleasure-boats are not too welcome there.

RIVERS

The whole waterway network is really based on rivers, with the many man-made canals linking them. So with a canal-cruiser you can enjoy rivers, too. The Thames and the rivers of the Broads have long been used by pleasure-boats, and angling is considerably better in rivers.

Rivers, however, need greater care than canals, since they can flow quite swiftly and are wider. Thus boats need anchors in case of engine failure, and you do need to make firm rules for children. At river locks there will be a weir nearby — a sort of waterfall to lower the river-level — and it is important to keep away from these. The bigger rivers such as the Trent and Severn call for particular respect. But in summer, unless there has been heavy rain, cruising on all rivers is very pleasant.

And there are a few tidal river-lengths (that is, with no locks before the sea) which are used by experienced inland boaters as links in the waterway system.

A pair of 'hotel-boats' on the Macclesfield Canal. Beautifully kept and decorated (notice the traditional roses and castles), these boats are perfect for a relaxed family holiday.

WHAT SORT OF BOAT?

Look at any waterway, and the great differences between the boats make them far more individual things than cars. Quite apart from the many types available, people seem to let themselves go in for painting and decorating their boats and adding bits and pieces, even to flower-boxes on the roof.

Sailing dinghies appear on lakes, reservoirs and the bigger rivers. Live-on sailing yachts move on lakes and the Broads mostly, though they are also seen on wider rivers. Canoes are everywhere, some even carrying camping gear for long journeys. Runabouts with outboard motors, and inflatable boats, are rare on canals but more likely on rivers. Speedboats are not usually allowed on inland rivers and canals (where there is normally a speed limit — 4 mph on most canals). Which brings me to the many kinds of live-on motor-boat which are ideal for a family cruise.

Sixteen-foot cruisers are a bit cramped for more than two people. Seventy-footers fit most canal locks — just (except in the north as mentioned earlier), and provide lots of room but cost lots of money. Roughly, the choice is between the smaller GRP (fibreglass) boats usually called cruisers, and the more traditional narrow boats, often built of steel.

There are bigger GRP boats on rivers, probably suitable for sea-going, and too wide for narrow canal locks. The great majority of boats for hire nowadays, away from the Broads and Thames, are canal-style narrow boats, which can travel even the narrow canals. But most families, when buying a boat, start with a small GRP cruiser.

CRUISERS

These are usually from 16 to 35 feet long; 25-footers are common. With this length you can have two cabins: one for the children to sleep in, and one convertible

A family cruising through the heart of Birmingham. The bicycle is often useful for pedalling to locks or for shopping sorties.

from saloon/galley in daytime to a double or two single beds at night. There'll be a small separate toilet compartment, storage under bunks, and so on, and of course a cockpit to drive from.

Cooking is by bottled gas, maybe with a small oven. A gas fridge is possible too. Water is either directly from containers, or more likely from tap(s) worked by a pump from either portable containers or built-in tanks. There'll be a sink and perhaps a separate wash basin. You can fill up with water from taps on the bank at fairly regular intervals. If you have an inboard engine it's even possible to have a water-heating system connected to it, so that you have hot and cold running water.

Lavatories may be modern chemical ones, using disposal points along the way. Or there are simple flushing types — emptied by pump-outs at boatyards — though these are more common on the bigger boats. Electric lighting is available too, either from the engine-driven generator or from a battery which you need to recharge ashore. So, all in all, even the smaller boats are quite civilised places for a family to live for a holiday cruise.

LARGER BOATS

With a bigger boat you obviously have more space to play with. Those for hire may sleep 10 or 12 people, though they sometimes have to slumber sardine-like in bunked cabins. It's best, if you can, to hire one which offers more berths than you need. Four people hiring a six-berth will have room to breathe (and keep things, wash, move about, cook, eat). Think also about where the separate cabins are, for children going to bed earlier.

With these boats running from around 30 feet to 70 feet long (you need practice to handle the big ones), there'll be h. and c., fridge, shower, big cooker, electric pump-out lavatory with holding-tank, full electric light, and perhaps central heating. There'll be wardrobes, drawers and other ample storage. And of course, with hired boats, there'll be all the equipment for cooking, eating, and sleeping.

Almost certainly there'll be a biggish cockpit at the back from where you steer the boat, and a quiet sitting-out one in front. (Some cruisers, by the way, are steered from the middle, and there are even boats steered like a car with a wheel at the front.)

Think, also, about wet clothes. Four or five people, well-dressed for rain, become a bit of an embarrassment swarming into the boat for a meal or shelter. When you get around to planning your own boat, you will probably have a wet-hanging-cupboard just inside the door. In any case, have a no-go area where no outside footwear or rainwear are allowed (spread newspaper there, perhaps). Some boats are carpeted, but I'm not keen on this, as grit and wet come aboard all the time and get in the pile. Better loose rugs, put down on a cleaned floor at night.

ENGINES

Once you get beyond a canoe or a dinghy, you have to decide about engines. Smaller boats, and even some biggish cruisers, have outboard engines clamped on the stern. The smaller outboards can be taken home for safety.

Bigger boats have their engines inside. Superior types have a magnificent engine room, but most have their engine under the stern cockpit floor. Some of these drive an outdrive, rather like the bottom half of an outboard. Both outboards and outdrives have the advantage of tipping up so that you can get at the propeller when things get caught in it.

Most inboard engines, though, drive a propeller on a shaft through the end of the boat. You have to keep the 'stern gland' on this shaft packed with grease to keep the water out. All engines, of course, need regular care and attention especially in cold and wet weather.

There are diesel engines in many bigger boats, but smaller boats generally have petrol engines, and the outboards mostly use a petrol-oil two-stroke mixture. Diesel engines are safer than petrol ones; there is less risk of fire and they seem more reliable. Some people don't like the noise or the fuel-smell of a diesel but neither of these should be a bother if the engine and tank are properly fitted and insulated. And — an interesting point for the budget — diesel fuel is tax-free if taken on at the waterside and so it is much cheaper than petrol.

GETTING HOLD OF A BOAT

You can buy all sorts of boats, all over the waterway system. Boatyards, boatbuilders, and individual sellers advertise in the boating magazines — especially *Waterways World* and *Canal and Riverboat* for inland boats. But, as I said earlier, you can hire boats in many places and it is better, unless you have already become 'hooked' by a trip with friends, to try a hiring holiday before thinking of buying a boat.

For hiring, the magazines give you many addresses on canals, rivers and lakes everywhere, but go and have a look at some boats if you can, asking in advance when this is convenient. Some firms take a lot of trouble to let people see their boats.

As usual, you get what you pay for. There are cheap tatty hire boats and much dearer luxury vessels. There are not so many really poor ones nowadays so you can expect a fair degree of comfort even in the less expensive boats.

Good firms teach you how to drive and how to work locks. They will also be quick to come to your aid if you break down.

Hire-boats usually provide the gear for cooking, eating and sleeping, and all you need to take are towels and personal items — maybe tea-towels — and of course food. There will be a detailed list of what is provided in the brochure. Many firms will even arrange for a grocery order to be put aboard for you. Pets, by the way, are sometimes permitted under certain conditions — dogs, like children, love boating. And you will find many boats are equipped with radio and even TV.

So probably the best way to begin is to pick a few likely firms and write and ask for their brochures.

Just a word, if you do decide to buy a boat. You need a boat licence on nearly all inland waterways, so it is wise to check up on this. Almost all canals, and many rivers, are covered by one licence from the British Waterways Board, but there are still several waterways for which you need to obtain separate licences.

DRIVING A BOAT

Although there are no driving tests and you do not need any driving licence to use the waterways, it is as well to read up the elements of boat control before your first trip. Remember that boats — unlike cars — float about with wind and current and when you make a turn they seem to slide over sideways away from the turn. This affects a number of manoeuvres.

The only way to stop a boat, apart from hitting something, is to put the propeller in reverse (you only have forward and reverse), but this takes a long time to produce results, since the boat keeps gliding forward under its own weight. So you have to reverse in good time, and speed up the engine fiercely, in order to slow down and/or stop effectively.

If, as with smaller boats, you steer with a wheel, you turn it in the same way as a car. Unfortunately for car drivers, however, most bigger boats have a tiller — an arm at the back to be moved left or right — and if you want to steer the boat to the *left*, you push the tiller to the *right*, and vice versa. This becomes obvious as soon as you move off, but the danger is that you may forget in emergencies and think you're in the car. Even experienced boaters have been known to do this, and as a long boat is slow to respond you may not realise you have done the wrong thing straight away. This slowness of response is a bit tricky and takes some getting used to. Watch the very front of the boat and see when it begins to swing. Then bring the tiller back, or the boat will swing too much. Watch also the sideways slide mentioned above. If you're steering to the left, for example, make sure there is room for the back end to move a bit over to the right as it swings. All this, on a long boat steered from the back, can be quite alarming at first, for you seem so far removed from the front end!

Illogically, I've left starting off till now because it's affected by what I said above, that is, you can't drive away from the bank as if in a car, because the stern swings in and hits the bank. So you must get your crew to push the bows off first. The boat is then pointing away from the bank, so you can drive out at that angle without any swing as your crew leap back aboard!

When it comes to mooring, again, you can't pull up and draw in as with a car. Bring the bows slowly in at an angle, going into reverse in good time. The crew must jump off the bows holding the end of the mooring rope as soon as they are close enough, leaving some loose coils on the boat (or it will pull them back). On canals especially they will also need to take a mooring-pin and hammer, for there are rarely any posts or rings to tie up to. Then, by putting the tiller towards the bank, you may be able to bring the stern in with a short engine burst, after which (you hope!) you just step nonchalantly off with the stern rope. Learning to throw a rope without dropping it in the water, however, is a matter of practice — the secret is to coil it properly first.

There is one other vital thing about driving. As you cruise along the waterway, it is best to keep away from the banks, especially on narrow canals. However, when you meet another boat, *move over to the right to pass*, for on the waterways we always drive on the right, not the left.

WORKING THROUGH LOCKS

I think the most interesting part of waterway cruising is going through locks. Children especially find it exciting. It is only fair to remind you, though, that there are safety problems. Not only is it far more dangerous to fall in a lock than to fall in the waterway elsewhere, but the lock mechanism can also cause accidents: trap fingers, even break bones. So do take great care at locks, and have clear rules for the children.

WHAT IS A LOCK?

A lock is a sort of 'water-box' to lower or raise boats from one level to another. Locks on rivers are built either to by-pass a mill-stream, or to enable one length of river to be dammed and thus made deep enough for boats. There is a lock by the dam (which makes a weir), to lower boats to the next deepened length.

On canals, locks make it possible to climb up slopes and over hills. Water has to be level, so a canal is a lot of level pounds with a lock between each level and the next. The steeper the slope, the more locks, with shorter pounds in between them. So, put simply, you take your boat from one level into a lock, raise or lower the water-level in the lock, and take the boat out at the next water-level. We talk about filling or emptying a lock, but of course it is not actually emptied altogether; it is merely lowered to the corresponding level of the next pound.

LOOKING AT A LOCK

Although they vary a great deal, most locks have the same basic features. At each end there is a door or doors to keep the water in or out. There may be only one, or a pair meeting at an angle in the middle. On some rivers there is a metal guillotine gate at one end instead, which moves upwards to open. Ordinary gates are usually swung open by pushing on a balance beam sticking out over the land. Keep on the side of the beam away from the lock.

At each end, too, there are openings to let water in and out, though you can't see them. They may be little tunnels underground, or holes in the gates. They are closed by covers called paddles or sluices, and these are opened and shut by paddle-gear which you operate yourself. This either has a variety of cogs, or it works hydraulically, and there is a spindle on which you put a windlass to turn the gear. Some gear has a windlass already fixed to it, and there are other forms of mechanism on some canals. But they all open and close water-openings somehow.

Locks may also have bollards to tie to (except when lowering a boat), ladders to climb in and out, and steps down the towpath slope at the lower end. They may also have a nameplate, and children like to collect lock-names such as Bumblehole, Giggety, Oddy, The Delph, Ell Meadow, and The Bratch.

Often there is a footbridge at the bottom end outside the gates. It may have a slot through its middle, for the towropes when horses were used. There are some intriguing designs about. Usually, though, you cross the lock on narrow footplanks fastened to the gates, making sure you hold the handrail.

CLIMBING UPHILL

Now let's imagine coming to a lock which is going to raise you uphill a bit, say six feet or so higher. In front of you are the tall-looking gates, which will be closed unless another boat is just coming out. You moor the boat, and your crew takes a windlass to the gates. If the lock is full (at its high level) he winds open the paddles to let the water out — provided there isn't a boat from the other direction about to use the lock. Watch that the water coming

Right (above): Operating the paddle-gear at a lock.
Below: The canal at Hatton in Warwickshire has a flight of 21 locks. They are called 'The Golden Steps to Heaven'.

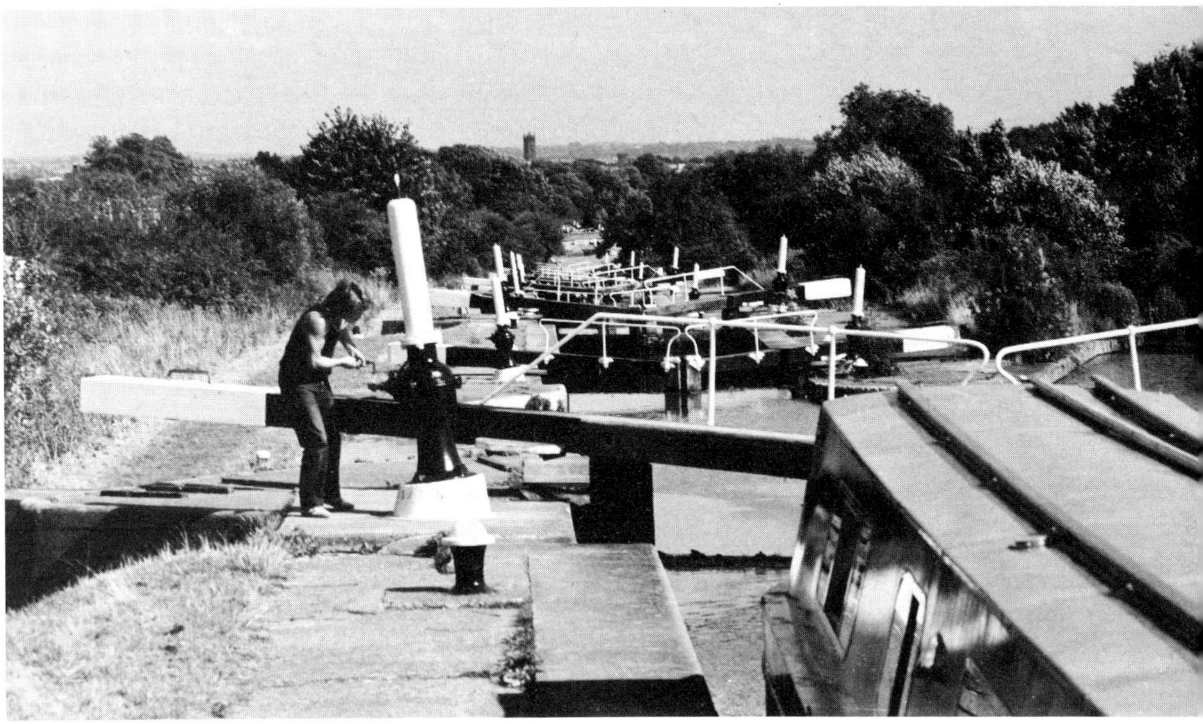

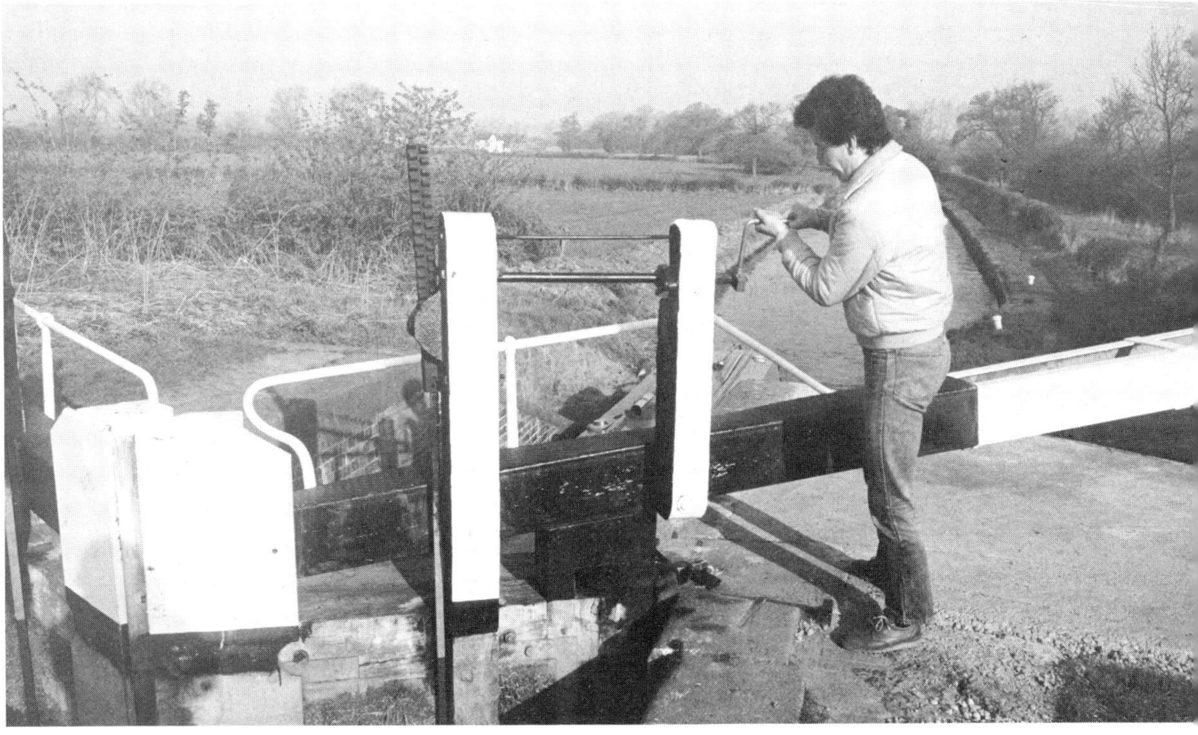

out doesn't wash your boat about. The crew should carefully put the ratchet (or some similar catch) on the paddle-gear, and then take off the windlass for safety.

It isn't possible to open the gates until the water has dropped to your level. When they are open, take the boat in. After a while you will be able to drive it in, which saves time and awkward pulling on ropes, as well as not keeping others waiting. Once in, close the gates and wind down the paddles. Don't let them drop, as this may break them.

Making sure the boat is tied, or held tightly, slowly open the paddles at the top end. If they're opened quickly the water pulls the boat forward. And again, when they are fully open, put on the safety-catch and take off the windlass. Keep the boat clear of the gates to be on the safe side as it rises.

When the boat is up to the next level, the far gates can be opened and out you go. Close the gates, wind down the paddles, pick up the windlass, and you're on your way to the next lock.

It sounds easy, but it is surprising how many things can be forgotten when you are a beginner, or when others are waiting, or when you are surrounded by *gongoozlers* (people who gather round on canals and watch you). For example, some people forget to lower the first lot of paddles, and find that the lock won't fill up. Or worse, they don't wind them right down, so that it isn't obvious that they are slightly open still. Try to have your own drill sorted out, and a checker at work as well.

GOING DOWNHILL

This is more or less the same sequence of actions as climbing up, but a bit easier,

since the boat isn't pushed or pulled by the water as it lowers in the lock. On the other hand, don't tie it up or it may hang from the ropes. And don't leave it too far back either, or it may be sinking down on the cill which supports the bottom of the gates behind it.

Whether locking up or down, always watch the boat, for there may often be odd protrusions or bulges waiting to catch it.

VARIATIONS

You may recall that most canal boats just fit nicely sideways in narrow locks, so this helps when using them. But in broad locks these boats can swing sideways quite alarmingly, especially when locking upwards. So unless you are lucky enough to have another boat to sit alongside, make sure your boat is securely held to one side by its ropes. One tip, when locking up, is to open the paddle on the same side as the boat; the incoming water then tends to hold the boat against the wall.

Another tip: there's no need to open both gates at the end of a broad lock to let an ordinary boat in. Just open one — it saves a lot of work.

Here and there on canals you will meet staircases of locks. These are where the land slopes so steeply that there is no room for canal pounds between locks. There may be two or as many as five locks cheek-by-jowl (eight on the Caledonian Canal). You have to watch that the water from a full lock isn't emptied into a full one below it, as it may flood over the sides if there is no overflow. In staircases of narrow locks, too, you must not enter if there is already a boat coming the other way, for of course you can't pass. The busiest staircases usually have instructions displayed, and even a lock-keeper to help.

On the bigger canals and rivers, especially where there are barges operating, the locks are often worked electrically by a keeper in a high cabin, and have traffic-lights to guide you.

CRUISING ALONG

Let's look now at some of the problems a boater may meet, cruising along a waterway. I will write later of other things to look out for, but this section is for anyone actually handling a boat. I have already talked about the driving of the boat, and getting it through locks, so now you are ambling gently along. You are doing about 3 mph, making no waves by the bank (that's a crime!), and keeping near the middle except when meeting another boat, when you ease over — not too far — to the right. What are you likely to come across that calls for special care?

BRIDGES

The first item, almost certainly, will be a bridge. They're all right on rivers, but on narrow canals the 'bridge-holes' are narrow too. You can only just squeeze through some, hence the sloping cabin sides of most boats. A few bridges are treacherously low on the side away from the towpath. And as sure as eggs the bridge will be on a bend and another boat will suddenly appear coming the other way. Blow your horn, anyway, but don't assume anyone will hear it. So slow down and be wary, and watch the wind doesn't blow you out of line.

If you can spare the time, look at the beauty of some of our canal bridges. They come in all sorts of pleasant shapes depending on the original canal company, from the red-brick ones of the Oxford Canal to the mighty grey stone bridges of the Pennines.

MOVABLE BRIDGES

Another matter entirely, these. The Leeds & Liverpool Canal has around fifty-seven which *swing sideways*; the Oxford and Llangollen Canals have different types which *tip up* at an angle, and there is even one in Huddersfield which moves upwards bodily. Indeed, there's a bridge *full of canal water* which swings sideways over the Manchester Ship Canal to let ships pass by!

There are electrified bridges on commercial canals, but elsewhere you have to operate the movable bridges yourself. The swinging ones are not so bad, though sometimes awkward because of grit in the bearings, use by cattle, or damage by heavy lorries. But at least they can't drop on your boat. It is the tip-up drawbridges that need the most care — and sometimes a bit of brute force. One rule above all: don't let casual passers-by open them for you, unless you are quite certain they are in full control, and unlikely to lower them prematurely as you pass under.

TUNNELS

Probably the most disconcerting things on canals — there are none on rivers, of course — are the tunnels. We cannot any longer go through the 3¼-mile Standedge Tunnel in the Pennines, but there are several others well over a mile long still in use. A number lately have had to be repaired extensively, and some of the old brickwork, grimed with smoke, chemicals, minerals and water-leaks, has been replaced. One repaired

Above: The magnificent bridges across the River Ouse at York.

Below: A lift-bridge on the Monmouthshire and Brecon canal.

Right: The mighty Pontcysyllte Aqueduct in North Wales.

tunnel now has a concrete tube for a long distance, but at least it is usable again.

Some tunnels are only wide enough for one-way passage, and a tunnel-keeper, or notices, will control this. In most of them, though, boats can just manage to ease past each other. You have a headlamp (check it in advance), and an oncoming one may dazzle you, since they don't dip. You need to slow right down to pass the other boat, and may well brush the side. It's all very eerie!

In long tunnels you cannot always see the other end at first if the day is dull or misty. Then it shows as a pinpoint, growing ever so slowly larger. Perhaps it's a relief to emerge at last into daylight again, but navigating a long tunnel is an experience to remember.

AQUEDUCTS

On an aqueduct you may be high above the ground — 120 feet up in one case — viewing the road, railway, river or even another canal far beneath you. Some aqueducts are quite wide, but the longer ones may be too narrow to pass another boat, so make sure there isn't one already on it. There is one like this near Stratford, but the mightiest is the famous Pontcysyllte in Wales, a spectacular sight and quite an experience.

GOING AGROUND

This can happen, especially on narrow canals, usually on mud at the canal side, and the important thing is not to get your 'back end' too far on. This propeller end is deeper than the bows, and of course more liable to damage. So before trying to use the propeller again, take the long pole (called a shaft) that every boat should have, and push the back end off. Keep yourself safely in the cockpit in case the shaft slips. Then you may be able to reverse off.

Whichever end is aground, don't have too many crew go there, or it will sink lower with their weight. If possible, some-one may go ashore and push, but if a shaft is used for this take care it does not go through a window!

Sometimes just rocking the boat helps to get it off the mud, and only rarely do you need to ask another boat for a pull.

THINGS TO LOOK OUT FOR

Whether you use a boat or your own feet, waterways offer an enormous variety of things to see. Schools in particular realise how very interested children become, and they take parties to look at waterways, to waterway museums, and even for a week or two on camping boats. Large numbers of families find the same pleasure, so here is a list of some other features worth looking out for.

Boats. Besides the great variety of boats used for pleasure, there are still commercial boats to be found, especially on the wider canals and rivers. Barges carry all sorts of heavy goods on Yorkshire's canals — for example, coal, sand, oil, grain — and on a few waterways you will actually meet small ships. Look out also for gaily-decorated narrow boats selling coal on some narrow canals. They have patterns using roses and castles in bright paint which are copied by many pleasure boats.

Pubs. There used to be many boatmen's inns for rest and refreshment, and quite a few still remain, usually by road bridges. They will have 'watery' names — *Navigation, Boat, Wharf, Barge, Anchor,* and so on — and often the bars are filled with canal designs and pictures as well as boaty bric-a-brac.

Cottages. Some of the old canal cottages still stand, though many of the lock-keepers' houses were too remote, and have gone. But look out for those remaining, with strikingly different shapes on different canals. There are also bridge-keepers' cottages on some waterways where the bridges have to be swung or lifted for ships or barges.

Other buildings. A few old warehouses still remain. You may also find the remains of stables where the boat-horses were kept, and toll-houses where boatmen paid their fees to enter a different canal. Old wharves and basins have often been turned into modern boatyards and hire-bases, and the present waterway authorities have their own maintenance organisations to do repairs to canals, build new lock gates, supply dredgers, and so on.

Mileposts and other posts. Many canals and rivers had mileposts along them. Some are more like road mileposts, but on the Trent & Mersey Canal and the Shropshire Union Canal in particular they have very distinctive shapes.

There are also boundary posts to be found, giving perhaps the canal's initials and showing the edge of the land owned by the canal company. Metal posts are often seen on bridge corners to stop the old towropes from wearing away the bricks (and the metal has deep grooves in it). There are posts at set distances from locks, and sometimes signposts at junctions, too.

Numbers. Canal bridges are almost always numbered. In fact, this is the best way to know where you are, from the waterway guide. Some have names on them as well. The plates vary — those on the Staffs. & Worcs. Canal are especially attractive.

There are sometimes numbers on locks, particularly where there are many in a flight, and in the Birmingham Canal Navigations the lock-cottages and other buildings are numbered also.

Notices. Like the railways, the waterways had many notices which may seem amusing these days. The museum at Stoke Bruerne has several examples, and you will find them at locks and bridges in many places still. One bars 'extraordinary traffic';

INLAND WATERWAYS OF ENGLAND AND WALES

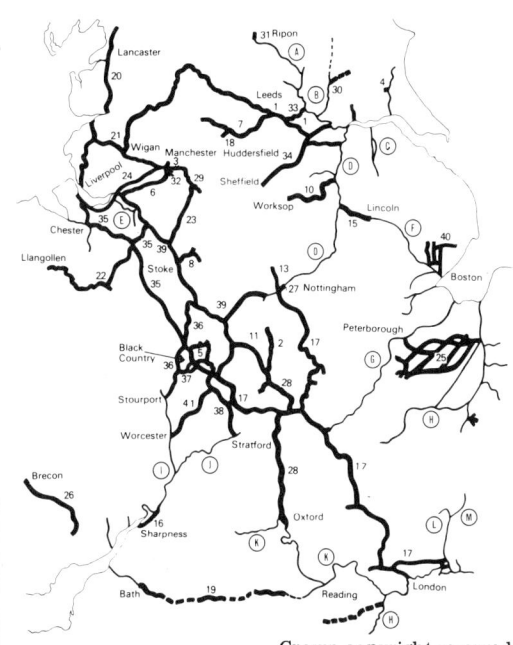

Crown copyright reserved

RIVERS

(A) River Ouse

(B) River Derwent

(C) River Ancholme

(D) River Trent

(E) River Weaver

(F) River Witham

(G) River Nene

(H) River Great Ouse

(I) River Severn

(J) River Avon

(K) River Thames

(L) River Lee

(M) River Stort

(N) River Wey

	CANALS	Miles	Locks
1	Aire & Calder Navigation	41½	17
2	Ashby-de-la-Zouch Canal	21¾	0
3	Ashton Canal	6¼	18
4	Beverley Beck	¾	1
5	Birmingham Canal Navigation	106¼	139
6	Bridgewater Canal	39¾	1
7	Calder & Hebble Navigation	21½	37
8	Caldon Canal	20¼	17
9	Caledonian Canal	60	27
10	Chesterfield Canal	26	16
11	Coventry Canal	38	13
12	Crinan Canal	9	13
13	Erewash Canal	11¾	15
14	Exeter Ship Canal	5	1
15	Fossdyke Canal	11¼	1
16	Gloucester & Sharpness Ship Canal	16	1
17	Grand Union Canal (all sections)	250	275
18	Huddersfield Broad Canal	3¼	9
19	*Kennet & Avon Navigation	86½	104
20	Lancaster Canal	45¼	6
21	Leeds & Liverpool Canal	141¼	104
22	Llangollen Canal	46	21
23	Macclesfield Canal	27½	13
24	Manchester Ship Canal	36	5
25	Middle Level Navigation (and Old Bedford River)	91¾	7
26	Monmouthshire & Brecon Canal	33¼	6
27	Nottingham Canal (and Beeston Cut)	5	3
28	Oxford Canal	77	44
29	Peak Forest Canal	14½	16
30	*Pocklington Canal	9½	9
31	Ripon Canal	1¼	1
32	Rochdale Canal	1¼	9
33	Selby Canal (with R. Aire)	11¾	4
34	Sheffield & S. Yorks Navigation (and New Junction)	48½	29
35	Shropshire Union Canal (and Middlewich Branch)	76½	50
36	Staffordshire & Worcestershire Canal	46¼	45
37	Stourbridge Canal	5¼	20
38	Stratford-upon-Avon Canal	24½	55
39	Trent & Mersey Canal	93½	76
40	Witham Navigable Drains (approx)	87	2
41	Worcester & Birmingham Canal	30	58

* parts of these canals are not yet restored.
(Locks to tidal waters are not included unless in normal inland use)

another says that stones must not be tipped near the canal, and another says that lift-bridges must not be dropped by boatmen.

Items at locks. Besides the working parts of locks described earlier, look out for kebs — long rakes used to remove debris or weed from around the gates. Bollards have been mentioned for tying up boats, and sometimes stop-planks will be seen. These can be slotted down across the canal outside a lock to act as a dam. Water can then be pumped away on one side to allow repairs to be made. Stop-planks are also used at narrow bridges to dam off lengths of canal.

Birds, flowers, insects, animals. Needless to say, wild life flourishes by waterways. Many families, afloat or afoot, go bird-watching along towpaths, or take picture-books to identify the abundant flowers, from water-lilies to every imaginable kind of land-flowers, too.

Spring is delightful by the water. Dragon-flies hover on their shimmering wings; kingfishers flash blue; everywhere you see moorhens, ducks and coots, and sometimes herons and swans. Water-voles scuttle away as you pass but rabbits seem tamer by water. Even a fox is not such a rare sight.

SOME WATERWAYS

It is impossible here to describe all the various waterways, so I would refer you to the books listed later. But perhaps I can glance at a few canals and rivers in different areas to give you the flavour.

Worcester and Birmingham Canal. If you fancy lots of locks, and scenery varying from the heart of Birmingham through pure countryside to a cathedral city, try this one. It has 58 locks altogether, though there is a level 14 miles from Birmingham before the locks start, then the first 42 in only five miles! The locks work easily, and it's pleasant exercise from the Black Country down to the Severn. There are five tunnels, one a very long one.

Llangollen Canal. This is a popular canal, sometimes crowded. The locks are spread out, and there are some photogenic lift-bridges. There are also three tunnels and two striking aqueducts, including the famous Pontcysyllte. It is rural all the way, ending in the foothills of the Welsh mountains.

River Thames. Very different from the canals and perhaps too sophisticated (and busy) for some people. The river is well looked after, all the locks are operated by keepers, and often surrounded by flowers. Some very superior boats will be encountered and of course there are famous towns and cities such as Windsor, Henley and Oxford.

Aire & Calder Navigation. This is the place to meet barges at work, and trains of 'Tom Puddings' — floating boxes taking coal to Goole. It is wide and deep, and the locks are all worked for you electrically. They have traffic-lights, and seem huge compared with most canal locks. You can even cruise into the port of Goole. Experienced canallers may use the ship-lock there into the tidal Yorkshire Ouse, and cruise up to York.

Monmouthshire & Brecon Canal. This one is isolated from the network — a delightful 33 miles with only six locks. It clings to the mountainsides above the Usk valley, with magnificent views and masses of flowers in spring.

Trent & Mersey Canal. Ninety-three miles with 76 locks, this canal offers everything. There are very rural and some industrial lengths, the famous Harecastle tunnel (and other odd ones), and some striking groups of locks. It starts from the Trent but no longer actually joins the Mersey. It even has the remarkable Anderton lift to take your boat down to the River Weaver.

River Nene. Perhaps for connoisseurs, this runs for 65 miles from Northampton to Peterborough, and almost all its 37 locks have great metal guillotine gates at their bottom ends. It keeps its flood-meadows away from towns and villages, so mostly you see just cattle and sheep. There is always a village or town nearby, though, with church towers in plenty to count as you cruise along.

Right: The Monmouthshire and Brecon canal which runs along the hillsides over-looking the Usk valley.
Below: The popular Llangollen canal.

Kennet & Avon Navigation. You may be moved to join in the full restoration of this waterway, via the Kennet & Avon Canal Trust. Eighty-six miles and 104 locks from Reading to Bristol, it is part River Kennet, part River Avon, with a canal link between them. Large parts are now restored to use after dereliction, but not all. There is still a staggering flight of locks at Devizes to be restored and there are some fine aqueducts and old water-pumps working again. There are trip-boats on most navigable lengths.

Birmingham Canal Navigation. An incredible, near-100-mile network in the Midlands. Although in a vast industrial area, the canals are strangely remote at times, and it is easy to become devoted to them. Many locks lead up to this area from different directions, but there are then long stretches on the level.

Leeds & Liverpool Canal. A majestic canal over the Pennines, with solid locks and bridges, and vast moorland views. The paddle-gear at the locks is especially interesting. Although seeming to pass through several industrial towns at its Yorkshire and Lancashire ends, it is often hidden from them. A canal to remember.

River Avon (Warwickshire). This river has been restored to use quite recently, giving a lovely and not-too-difficult cruise from Tewkesbury on the Severn to above Stratford. Not easy to find moorings, and you need two different licences, but Evesham and Pershore are towns in rich fruit-growing country.

The Broads. These are rivers and lakes with a long history of pleasure-boating. They are in Suffolk and Norfolk, and not connected to the main waterway system, and the boats and facilities are more sophisticated. The waters are more crowded, too, but there are some very pleasant areas to explore.

Calder & Hebble Navigation. This is a distant waterway for many canal-users, but worth seeking out. It runs from Wakefield into the heart of the Pennines at Sowerby Bridge, where the hills tower above. There are many towns around but, as so often, the waterway usually hides from them, except at the pleasant basins at Brighouse. There are interesting locks, and part of the route is the River Calder itself.

'Cheshire Ring'. This unofficial name is given to a round cruise on part of the Trent & Mersey, the Macclesfield Canal, the Lower Peak Forest Canal, the Ashton Canal, a short length of the Rochdale Canal, and the Bridgewater Canal. It ranges from the centre of Manchester to remote Cheshire, and includes some canal lengths only restored to use after vigorous action by waterway enthusiasts, against much original opposition.

HIRING A BOAT

There are hire-bases all over the country. Many advertise in the magazines (listed in Magazines), and the *Inland Waterways Guide* (listed in Books) gives comprehensive lists.

SHORT BOAT TRIPS

All over the waterways boats offer trips for an hour or more on canals and rivers, often in interesting converted commercial narrow boats. Lists of most of these can be obtained from the British Waterways Board.

CANAL SOCIETIES

Many canals have their own local society. Ask anyone boating on your own canal for the secretary's address. Even derelict canals almost always have an active society or trust dedicated to restoring them.

MUSEUMS

The Waterways Museum. The official British Waterways Board one, dealing with the majority of our canals and some rivers. An ideal family outing, with intriguing material. Address: Stoke Bruerne, Nr. Towcester, Northants. NN12 7SE.

The Boat Museum, Ellesmere Port. Not only has a growing number of remarkable indoor exhibits, but also a floating collection of historic inland boats of all shapes and sizes. Address: Dockyard Road, Ellesmere Port, S. Wirral L65 4EF.

Canal Exhibition Centre, Llangollen. Interesting small exhibition on The Wharf, Llangollen, Clwyd.

Black Country Museum at Dudley, alongside a canal, has much canal material and activities, as well as other exhibits of Black Country life and industry, including old shops, a pub, a working tram, and so on. Address: Tipton Road, Dudley, W. Midlands DY1 4SQ.

There are also other exhibitions including waterway material, for example, at Shardlow (Derby) Exeter, Ironbridge (Telford), and Nottingham.

USEFUL ADDRESSES

British Waterways Board. As already mentioned, the Board controls almost the whole canal system and some rivers. It provides the licences for these, and has much information and waterway material on offer. Write to the Information Office, British Waterways Board, Melbury House, London NW1 6JX.

Inland Waterways Association. This nationwide voluntary body (a charity) has campaigned to save and restore canals for about 40 years. It has been largely responsible for the continued existence of many of them, and their rescue from dereliction. Well worth supporting. Membership brings a magazine, local meetings, and the opportunity to meet others concerned with waterways. Both family and junior membership are available. Address: 114 Regents Park Road, London NW1 8UQ.

PUBLICATIONS

BOOKS

These may not always be found in bookshops, but they can all — together with many more — be obtained from the Inland Waterways Association (Sales), 114 Regents Park Road, London NW1 8UQ. Send s.a.e. for latest list.

Ordnance Survey Guides to the Waterways (Nicholsons). There are three of these — North, Central and South — covering most waterways (but not the Broads) in very full detail, at 2½ inches to the mile, except in Yorkshire. Every bridge, lock, village, and so on, shown, with much description.

Waterways World Guides. Issued for the more popular individual waterways, with very useful details of what to see and what you need.

Stanfords Inland Cruising Map. Shows the whole waterway system of England and Wales, on one large folding sheet (out of print at the moment).

Observer's Book of Canals (Gagg). A recent book in the well-known pocket series of potted information, dealing with every aspect of our waterways. Many photographs, including colour.

Looking at Inland Waterways series (Gagg). Six inexpensive (50p) booklets on different waterway aspects, with many illustrations: *Tunnels, Locks, Narrow Canals, Broad Canals, Waterway Landmarks, Canals in a Nutshell.* Obtainable from the author, Shootacre House, Princes Risborough, Buckinghamshire HP17 9NN. All six £3 post free.

Story of Canals (Ladybird). Children's book in this well-known series.

Inland Waterways Guide. A useful compendium issued annually, with brief details of waterways and the addresses of over 400 hire firms.

Shell Book of Inland Waterways (McKnight). A magnificent volume covering all our waterways with much detailed description.

Canals are My Life and *Canals are My Home* (Bryce). Two fascinating books on a couple who sold their home to live on a canal boat.

History. If you feel moved to delve into the history of waterways, there are many books available, especially a series by Charles Hadfield. All are listed in the IWA leaflet mentioned above.

MAGAZINES

Two magazines deal entirely with inland waterways: *Waterways World* (Kottingham House, Dale Street, Burton on Trent DE14 3TD), and *Canal & Riverboat* (37 Church Street, Lenton, Nottingham NG7 2FH). The British Waterways Board also has a small magazine available to the public (see address below).

Increasing numbers of families are now exploring the magical world beneath the seas. As Horace Dobbs says, the discovery of this world is possible for anyone, young and old. There are no limits to what he terms this 'underwater fairyland' with its colourful plants and creatures, and romantic history. Getting started presents no problems. All you need is a snorkel, mask and fins, and the expert guidance you will find in this chapter.

Dr Horace Dobbs is one of Britain's leading pioneer amateur underwater explorers and cameramen. He is a fellow of the Royal Society of Medicine. In 1974, after a successful career which spanned nuclear chemistry, veterinary surgery and human medicine, his life took a new turn after an encounter with Donald, a wild dolphin. He decided to devote all his time to underwater exploration and photography and especially to the study of dolphins. This led to the launch of International Dolphin Watch in 1978, of which he is the Honorary Director.

Horace Dobbs has obtained the highest qualifications for diving in the British Sub-Aqua Club — that of First Class Diver. As the club's first Films and Photographic Officer, he has been responsible for the setting up of the world's first major library of underwater films. Today he leads expeditions to many parts of the world and is well known for his film lecture presentations. He frequently contributes to radio and television programmes.

Married, with two children, he lives in Humberside.

Horace Dobbs is the author of several books, including *Camera Underwater* (Focal Press), *Underwater Swimming* (Collins), *Snorkelling and Skindiving — an Introduction* (Oxford Illustrated Press), *Dolphin Spotter's Handbook* (with R.J. Harrison, D.A. McBrearty, and E. Orr) (International Dolphin Watch publications), *Follow a Wild Dolphin* (Souvenir Press), and *Save the Dolphins* (Souvenir Press).

Sub-Aqua

HORACE DOBBS

The sun was shining. The sea around us was brilliant blue. Melanie — my 12-year-old daughter — and I drifted down like two feathers into an underwater fairyland. Tiny brightly-coloured fish flashed as they darted to and fro. The sand on the seabed was dappled with ever-changing patterns of light reflected from the waves above us. We were slowly swimming together when a different flash of light on the coarse sand caught our eyes. We exhaled slightly and sank down to look closer at what appeared to be a small piece of copper buried in the sand. We dug our hands into the sand and pulled it out. It nestled in the palm of my hand. I fanned away the coarse sand and there before our eyes was a solid gold ring, embossed with mysterious symbols. We examined it closely and Melanie slipped it on her finger. It fitted perfectly.

That happened when Melanie was a schoolgirl. Now she is married, yet she still wears the ring and nobody can tell us the significance of the markings. So we still don't know if it is very old or modern.

The event I have just described took place on a family diving holiday, and if you are interested in coincidences and astrology you may make something of the fact that we found the gold ring off a tiny Mediterranean island called Gemini on the day that the very first American Gemini rocket went into space — and Melanie's birth sign happens to be Gemini.

It was a very happy holiday that none of us will forget — not just because of finding the treasured ring but because of the many other adventures the entire family had together. The excitement really started when we heaved the heavy pack of the inflatable boat on to the roof-rack of the car and stowed the aqualung cylinders in the boot.

With the car very heavily laden we crossed the English Channel, drove across France and climbed slowly through the Alps. One spectacular view after another unfolded for us. However, as we descended I was sharply made aware of just how much weight we had in the car because the brakes ceased to work through overheating. Fortunately I was able to glide into a side road and stop without damaging the car or its occupants.

When the wheels had cooled down we continued our journey and the next day we were greeted with our first sight of the brilliant clear blue sea of the Mediterranean. As we crossed on the ferry to the island of Elba the excitement mounted, especially when we were close inshore, because the water was unbelievably clear. We could see the rocks plunging down into mysterious pale blue depths — with just a hint of green.

My two children had spent the winter months training in a swimming pool in the heart of Yorkshire. Now they were on the brink of their first proper underwater adventure. As we approached the island I told them that the Mediterranean was the cradle of diving and underwater exploration because it was here that the pioneers first discovered this recreational pastime which quickly spread around the world.

HOW IT BEGAN

It really all started when an American called Guy Gilpatric discovered that by wearing a pair of goggles when he swam underwater he could see into the undersea world as clearly as if he was looking through the side of a gigantic aquarium.

He also discovered that the fishes he saw were unafraid of him. So arming himself with a spear he set out to secure his supper. Such was the success of his early undersea hunting activities that he soon gathered round him a gang of fellows whom he described as 'my little band of serious sinkers'. The sport of 'goggling', as it was called, was born.

Gilpatric wrote a book called *The Complete Goggler* in which he described in a very amusing manner the antics he got up to (or should I say got down to) to impale the unsuspecting denizens of the deep.

When it was published underwater hunting for fish spread like wildfire.

In his inimitable style Gilpatric took the title of his book from Isaac Walton's book *The Compleat Angler* which was written in the 17th century and remained the standard work on the subject of sport fishing for over a century. However, Gilpatric's book, although a classic of its kind, was not to enjoy such longevity. For the pastime he had helped to found developed so quickly that the equipment and techniques he described were out of date within a few years of publication.

The simple spear that Gilpatric used was soon supplanted by powerful spearguns. Such was the efficiency of the new weapons that fish populations were decimated in many popular diving areas of clear water. In the heady early days the underwater hunters treated the wildlife of the underwater world like those who took guns into the African continent at the end of the 19th century. It was not until many species of wildlife were threatened with extinction that people realised that the slaughter could not go on for ever. The word conservation came into popular use when it was realised that if people went on shooting what they liked (above and below water) they would destroy the very thing that gave them pleasure.

Fortunately, it was also discovered that shooting with a camera can be just as exciting as shooting with a gun. So most of the families that now set off to explore the wonders of the underwater world arm themselves with photographic equipment. They bring back pictures not corpses with which to relive their memories. And they

Filming a grouper fish off the Bahamas.

leave the undersea world waiting to be enjoyed to the full by the ever-increasing number of people who enjoy healthy exercise either as individuals or in groups.

So if you and your family fancy taking the plunge, how should you go about it?

GETTING STARTED

You start very simply by learning to swim underwater with fins, mask and snorkel.

Of these three items the mask is the most important — without that there would be no point in going down because you won't see anything very distinctly, even with your eyes open.

Human eyes evolved to function above water, not beneath it, and it is essential for them to be in direct contact with air to see properly. The watertight goggles

worn by Guy Gilpatric provided air in contact with his eyes and the glass fronts provided windows for him to look through into the watery world beyond. Goggles unfortunately have a severe shortcoming due to the increase in pressure that occurs as the goggle-diver descends. This pushes the goggles harder and harder on to the face and is called 'the squeeze'. Severe cases of the squeeze cause bruising. Indeed, in his book Gilpatric makes reference to recognising a fellow goggler by his two black eyes. As this may lead to suspicions of a family at war rather than a family peacefully exploring the underwater world together, I am pleased to tell you that the problem does not arise when the goggles are replaced by a facemask that encloses the nose, allowing the pressure inside the mask to equal the outside pressure. This is achieved simply by exhaling slightly through the nose into the mask.

WHAT TO BUY

When selecting any diving equipment it is worth going to a specialist shop. This applies especially when purchasing a facemask because it is essential to select one that is comfortable and leak-tight. A good diving shop will have a wide selection to choose from and the shop assistant will be able to advise on the best one to suit the contours of your own particular face. A good test is to put the mask in position, but do *not* put the strap over your head. Then inhale gently through your nose. If the mask feels comfortable and does not

Left: A family learning how to use aqualungs in a swimming pool.

Right: Melanie Dobbs exploring the underwater world with snorkel, mask and flippers.

drop off when you give a little suction through your nose it should not leak underwater.

The underwater world is fascinating to peer into through a facemask when floating on the sea. When you do this for the first time you quickly discover that with your nose inside the mask and your mouth submerged you cannot breathe unless you lift your head clear of the water. The early gogglers also discovered this irksome need to keep breaking off from their undersea viewing. One person got round the problem by putting one end of a short length of garden hose in his mouth and holding the other end clear of the water. This simple solution to the problem was soon commercially developed and the first snorkel tubes came on sale. Modern snorkel tubes have changed little from those first

models which had a rubber mouthpiece. The mouthpiece had two spiggots which were gripped between the front teeth and kept the tube in place. A rubber flange which was inserted between the lips and the gums provided a waterproof seal.

All kinds of gadgets were devised to keep the water out of the tube when the diver descended. But they all had their shortcomings and nowadays no self-respecting snorkeller uses them. He uses an open-ended tube and simply blows out the water when he surfaces. 'Clearing the tube', as this has become known, soon becomes an automatic response and is accomplished by a short, sharp blow. However, it is much easier to clear a tube if it is not corrugated and is fairly narrow in diameter (without restricting breathing). When selecting a snorkel tube, then, go for

one that is comfortable in your mouth and is simple in design. The tube can either be pushed between the side of the facemask and the head strap or attached to the strap with a rubber securing band.

When you lie on the surface of the water with the front of your face submerged the tube will project above your head and you can breathe in and out in comfort until you want to descend.

Everybody, nowadays, is familiar with the final items of basic equipment worn by a snorkeller. This is the pair of fins needed to give that extra propulsive power to send the diver smoothly on his way.

When selecting fins, once again go for comfort. Those with a full shoe fitting are preferable to those with only heel straps. But whatever you do, don't buy a pair that is too tight, because after a short time they will be painful to wear. The blades of the fins should be flexible but not floppy.

So if you are setting off on holiday to a location where the water is clear then my advice is for each member of the family to have his own set of basic equipment, that is, fins, mask and snorkel.

LEARNING TO SNORKEL DIVE

Learning to snorkel dive is neither difficult nor dangerous if certain fairly obvious safeguards are observed. Indeed, it is equivalent to learning to ride a bicycle. You don't go out on to the main road until you are competent. Likewise with learning to snorkel you stay in safe, clear, shallow water until you have mastered the techniques.

One of the things you will discover when you try it out for the first time is that the facemask has a tendency to mist up. This is often caused by wax which slowly exudes from new rubber. I therefore advise that the inside of a new mask should be washed with soapy water and well rinsed before it is used. Thereafter, spitting into the mask and spreading a very thin layer of saliva over the inside glass surface will usually keep it clear.

Don't despair if you don't pick up the art of snorkelling immediately. It sometimes takes quite a bit of practice before you feel really comfortable breathing through the snorkel on the surface with your mouth submerged. Even more practice may be required to clear the mask of water. This should not be done by removing your mask. Instead, gently press the top of the mask against your forehead and exhale sharply through your nose with your head in an upright position. Any water in the mask then runs to the bottom and is expelled by the air pressure. As you become more confident you will find you can do this when you are well submerged.

If you can do the crawl stroke in swimming you should have no difficulty learning to use the fins. If you can't do the crawl then you will probably be tempted to use your legs with the same motion as that you use to pedal a bicycle. Such a movement is pretty useless for propelling you through the water as you will soon discover when you use the correct method, in which the legs are alternately moved up and down with the knees slightly bent. Splashing on the surface also wastes a lot of energy as well as frightening the fish. So keep your fins submerged — even when cruising along the surface. You will soon develop your own style and will feel which type of leg movement propels you most efficiently through the water.

When you can comfortably snorkel on the surface it is time to start diving. Duck diving is best carried out when swimming forward. Bring your arms sharply down and at the same time bring your knees towards your chest. Then immediately stretch your legs, raising your feet above the surface.

This should send you gliding smoothly into the depths with the minimum of disturbance. Thrashing with your fins half out of the water sends the fish scurrying for cover as well as looking ungainly. So practise until you can make a nice clean entry.

Once underwater you can fin headfirst down with your hands at your sides. As you descend the water pressure will increase and this pressure will be felt by your ears unless you equalise the pressure on both sides of your eardrums. Sometimes this happens spontaneously and you feel your ears click. If it doesn't equalisation can be achieved by pinching the nose through the facemask (most masks are designed so that you can do this) and gently blowing as if blowing into a handkerchief. If your ears do not clear and they become painful *do not descend any further* as this may lead to the eardrum rupturing (or perforating as it is sometimes called).

What happens when you clear your ears is that air passes through narrow passages at the back of your throat (the eustachian tubes) into the inner ear thereby balancing the pressure on both sides of your eardrums. Some people's eustachian tubes dilate very easily and they have no trouble clearing their ears. Others, the author included, are unable to clear their ears rapidly even after lots of practice. This is because the structure of their eustachian tubes is such that they do not open up to allow the rapid passage of air. Nasal decongestants can ease the problem if accumulated mucus is further reducing the passage

of air along the tubes. However, there is no real solution and divers with slow clearing ears must resign themselves to the situation and accept the fact that they will never be able to hurtle swiftly into the depths. I have perforated an eardrum as a result of descending too quickly. Fortunately it healed up quickly with no detectable aftereffects. Since then I have made patience override my natural desire to go chasing after my friends who can plummet speedily into the depths without any problem.

I believe that when nature built our bodies she built in a lot of safety devices and we disregard them at our peril. Thus if I had heeded the pain in my ears I would not have burst an eardrum. The same applies when holding your breath underwater. There comes a time when you feel that you must breathe in. When this happens it is a sign that the level of carbon dioxide in your blood is reaching a high level. If you do not take any notice of it you may black out underwater — which could obviously have fatal consequences.

Naturally, when you are snorkelling underwater you are bound to want to see how deep you can go and how long you can stay there. My advice is enjoy yourselves but use your common sense. And if your family is like mine there will be friendly rivalry between the members to see who can go the deepest and stay down the longest. But remember — nature's warning signals have a purpose.

AQUALUNG (SCUBA) DIVING

The undersea environment has been dubbed the world of inner space. For a very modest investment in basic snorkelling equipment it is possible for the entire family to invade that space and enjoy the wonders it has to unfold. If you get hooked as I did you are going to find the need to keep returning to the surface to get a breath of air rather irritating, especially when you have discovered something very interesting or beautiful at the far limit of your capabilities as a snorkel diver. And if you have a spirit of adventure you will want to go deeper and stay down longer. For those with this spirit the next logical step is to consider aqualung diving.

I have already said that learning to snorkel dive is like learning to ride a bicycle. Provided you are sensible you can learn to do it yourself via your mistakes and not too much harm should come to you. Learning to dive with an aqualung is like learning to drive a car. Like a car, an aqualung can be a lethal weapon. So it is essential to have a proper course of instruction from an experienced diver — preferably one who is also a qualified instructor.

There is no legal requirement in most countries for a diver to have the equivalent of a driving licence before he goes diving in the sea. However, most diving establishments insist on some form of certificate of competence before they will hire out equipment and it is obviously sensible to take an approved course of instruction and attain a diving qualification at the end of it. The governing body for the sport of diving in Britain is the British Sub-Aqua Club, with branches throughout Britain and in many other parts of the world. This organisation is respected for the high standards of safety and instruction it has established. All those who join the British Sub-Aqua Club (or Beesac as it is often affectionately referred to) receive a very comprehensive diving manual and a monthly magazine. The Sub-Aqua Association caters for independent clubs, most of which pursue qualification courses similar to those laid down by the British Sub-Aqua Club.

Learning to dive with a club involves practical lessons in a swimming pool and compulsory lectures. The time taken to reach a level of competence at which the newly fledged diver can go safely into the sea varies with the aptitude of the individual and the resources available. An average time for this via a diving club is about six months for a good swimmer. There is also a minimum age (usually 15 years) for aqualung training.

Although learning to dive throughout the winter months by weekly attendance at a friendly diving club where instruction is by unpaid personnel is a very pleasant way of learning the basic skills, not everyone has the time to do so. The alternative is to go to a diving school where intensive courses are offered. As some schools are located by the sea it is possible to combine a diving course with a holiday.

Aqualung diving is often referred to as scuba-diving — particularly in the USA. They both mean the same, the word 'scuba' being derived from the first letters of the words 'self-contained underwater breathing apparatus'. The apparatus supplies the diver with his own supply of air — never oxygen.

THE AQUALUNG

The aqualung consists of a cylinder (sometimes called a tank or a bottle) of compressed air which is fitted with a demand valve. The demand valve, or regulator as it is also called, enables you to breathe air from the very high pressure inside the cylinder at exactly the same pressure as your surroundings. As you descend in the sea the pressure increases and the pressure of the air delivered to the mouthpiece increases accordingly. Thus it is as easy to breathe when you are 100 ft down as it is on the surface.

The aqualung is strapped to the diver's back with a quick-release harness. Although the tank and valve are heavy on land, their weight in water is minimal and varies from one model to another. Indeed, some aqua-lungs are positively buoyant, that is, they can float.

One thing that often surprises a person wearing an aqualung for the first time is that he or she does not immediately sink. With lungs full of air the human body floats. As the aqualung provides the means of filling the lungs and itself adds little if any weight to the submerged diver, the overall effect is that he or she bobs up to the surface unless deliberately swimming downwards with the fins above the head. To overcome this the diver uses a weight-belt with lead weights which are adjustable to personal needs.

The diver should adjust his weights so that he attains a state known as *neutral buoyancy*, that is, he is just suspended in the water. When he inhales he rises and

Putting on an aqualung at the bottom of a swimming pool.

when he exhales he sinks.

In order to understand the problems he will face underwater and why rigid safety laws must be adhered to, a diver must know something about the basic anatomy of the human respiratory system and the effects of pressure on gases. These will be detailed in his diving manual and will be included in his lectures on the theory of diving.

THE FIRST RULE

One cardinal rule when wearing an aqualung is *never ascend whilst holding your breath*. To do so could cause injury or death, even in a swimming pool. It is most likely to happen to a beginner who fills his lungs full of air on the bottom, panics and then rushes for the surface with his mouth tightly shut. The air trapped in the lungs expands as the pressure is reduced on the way up. If the lungs cannot expand to take up the increased volume of the trapped air they rupture. Any air bubbles that pass into the bloodstream can block blood vessels, thereby causing oxygen deficiencies which in turn cause paralysis. Such an occurrence is called an embolism.

The extent and nature of injury (in

A family explore the sea together.

addition to the ruptured lungs) will depend on the severity of the embolism. Nobody should get an embolism because prevention is so easy. All you have to do is remember to breathe out on the way up during a rapid ascent. During a normal ascent the problem should not arise if a natural breathing rhythm is maintained.

GETTING FAMILIAR WITH THE EQUIPMENT

Most people learn the basic skills of diving in a swimming pool or special training tank. During this time they will learn how to ditch their equipment and swim back to the surface.

They will also learn how to retrieve the equipment by putting all of the gear on the bottom and then swimming down to it. The first thing to do on a retrieve dive is to switch on the air supply and breathe from the aqualung. Next the facemask should be put on and cleared of water. When he has finally fitted all of the equipment the diver can return to the surface.

Such an exercise compels the diver to become familiar with the equipment. This will obviously enable him to cope better with any problems or adjustments that have to be made whilst diving in open water.

LIFEJACKETS

Before venturing into open water the diver will need some additional items of equipment which are not necessary in a pool. These include a watch, depth gauge, compass, and knife. The majority of dive organisers also insist on a lifejacket that has been specially designed for divers and functions in such a way that an unconscious diver will float with his mouth and nose clear of the surface when the jacket is inflated. The type most popular with British divers has adjustable buoyancy. Air is fed into the lifejacket in a controlled manner either via a direct feed from the aqualung or via a separate high-pressure air cylinder attached to the air-bag. There is also a valve which enables a diver to bleed air from the bag and thereby adjust his buoyancy underwater. The air in feed bottles can also be used for respiration in an emergency. And part of the training of most divers nowadays includes practising breathing from the lifejacket.

KEEPING WARM

One hazard which is often not rated as seriously as it should be, perhaps because it is not so obvious and dramatic as the others, is the cold. It is now widely recognised that old people can die from the cold in winter as a result of their bodies cooling and giving rise to a condition termed and giving rise to a condition termed *hypothermia*. Young persons are much better able to resist the cold. Even so, it can be a killer — usually indirectly because a person suffering from hypothermia is often unaware that he or she is losing strength and dexterity. Thus a diver weak with cold may find it difficult to remove his knife from its scabbard, or to form a seal with his lips if he suddenly needs to inflate his lifejacket orally.

There is a great deal of truth in the saying 'a warm diver is a happy diver'. To stay comfortable in most waters — except the warmest tropical seas — some protection against the cold is required.

Wetsuits are most commonly used and the thickness of the suit and the extent of bodily cover it affords varies with circumstances. It also varies with the individual. A thin person requires more insulation than a fat person!

All diving suits are restrictive, and a two-piece wetsuit has the advantage that only the jacket need be worn in semi-warm conditions.

A wetsuit should be comfortable, with good seals round all of the openings. These do not have to be watertight because, as the name implies, the diver actually gets wet when he is wearing it. But the gaps should not gape so that water can move freely in and out. Zips on the legs and arms make it much easier to get out of a close-fitting suit. A full wetsuit with hood, boots and sometimes gloves is needed for the cold waters around the British Isles. An alternative is a drysuit in which the diver is hermetically sealed. Experienced divers are increasingly turning to drysuits as more models become available. It is generally accepted that they are warmer and more comfortable. However, there are disadvantages, such as a great loss of insulation if they are accidentally torn. They also require greater skill in use. So my advice for beginners is to start with a wetsuit and then perhaps graduate to a drysuit when they have had some diving experience and have discussed the pros and cons with an experienced diver who has used both types.

CANALS, LAKES AND RIVERS

An aqualung diver's certificate is a passport to the waters of the world. So let's see where our family of divers can head for after they have completed their pool training and done their open-water qualifying dives.

As approximately four-fifths of the earth's surface is covered with water there is no shortage of places for them to explore together. These range from gently drifting down the local canal to gliding into a sunken World War II warship deep in the Pacific Ocean. Both of these two extreme locations can offer hours of enjoyment. Indeed, it is just such a diversity of opportunities that has maintained my interest in diving for nearly three decades.

So let's start in Britain and then consider diving further afield.

I was quite serious when I said you could start by looking in the local canal. A friend of mine who lives close to a stretch of disused canal has become an expert on the fauna and flora in the water and along the canal bank. I have spent many happy hours in his company peering into the green water. We have seen shoals of perch with dorsal fins erect sparkling in sunlight, watched toads mating, seen eels slithering sinuously into the weeds. We have even tickled young pike into a state of stupor and had them nestling in the palms of our hands — all in less than five feet of water. Together, with our underwater eyes, we have watched the changes that take place in the canal through all the four seasons.

It is virtually impossible to swim in a shallow canal without stirring up sediment from the bottom and dislodging it from the weeds. Underwater visibility is quickly reduced, especially by clumsy divers. So the secret of nature watching in such confined places is to proceed very slowly and with the minimum of disturbance.

There is invariably some flow of water in canals — even if they appear at first sight to be static. So one way of keeping the annoying effects of disturbance to a minimum is to swim upstream. This way the sediment is carried back past the divers who are always heading into the clearest water.

When exploring confined inland waters give consideration to the others who may also be enjoying the amenity — the fishermen and the boating community. In an ideal world we should all be able to enjoy our respective recreations without interfering with one another. But the ever-increasing demand for water space in an age when leisure time is also increasing can lead to conflict of interests.

I have found out by experience that some fishermen become very irate if they think the fish are being disturbed by anyone — not just divers. So if there are fishermen in the area in which I am going to dive I usually make a point of speaking to them before I go into the water. I tell them about the plants and animals under the surface and how unafraid fishes are of a quiet observer like myself. In this way I try to allay their fears and avoid an angry confrontation later.

A number of my friends like collecting old bottles and they spend many happy hours grubbing around on the bottoms of rivers searching for rare specimens. They are ever hopeful they will make a really valuable find. If you are a bottle collector it is worth looking at places that have been popular picnic spots over the ages. It is not only the modern generation who toss away their empty drinks containers when they have finished the contents.

In addition to being littered with modern junk, rivers can be a rich source of interesting and sometimes valuable objects. The river bed around old bridges can be particularly rewarding to investigate. The silt on a river bed is constantly on the move. Objects are continuously covered up and uncovered. Thus a good time to dive is shortly after a river has settled down following a storm, when the fast-flowing water may have swept a new area clear of sediment.

An experienced river diver will tell you that the best time to dive is at dusk with a torch. The beam from the torch throws the tell-tale silt-covered lumps on the river bed into sharper relief.

When diving in rivers, boats are a hazard that must be taken into account. A float, called a 'blob buoy', bearing a flag and towed by a diver should indicate to an informed boatman that there is a diver nearby. However, it is no guarantee of safety from a whizzing propeller. So listen carefully before you surface. And if there is the slightest possibility that a boat is nearby, stay on the bottom until the danger has passed.

DIVING WITH DOLPHINS AND FRIENDLY FISH

One dive is still vividly imprinted on my memory. The event took place some years ago in Port Saint Mary on the Isle of Man. I was kitted up with full aqualung diving equipment and sitting on the seabed about five metres down. My son Ashley, who was 13 at the time, was snorkelling over my head. I looked up and saw his black silhouette pass across the setting sun which appeared to glow as an orange disc on the surface. Then a large submarine shape rushed past me in the water and disappeared. It was a friendly wild dolphin called Donald who was attracted to divers and often played with us. A very short time later a plume of bubbles emerged in the water alongside Ashley. Out of the foam emerged Donald — whose estimated weight was about 250 kg. Donald had leapt clean out of the water and plummeted back in very close to my son. Fearful that the dolphin might injure Ashley I rushed to the surface

Sketching Donald, the friendly wild dolphin.

to tell him to get into the safety boat we had moored nearby. But before I could tell Ashley what to do I saw the boy rise out of the water. He was sitting on the head of the wild dolphin. Then to my utter amazement he sped away from me riding on the dolphin. It was like a modern version of one of the ancient boy-on-a-dolphin legends.

I didn't know at the time that the incident was to change my life. The full story is told in my book *Follow a Wild Dolphin* and its sequel *Save the Dolphins*, both of which were published by Souvenir Press.

One of the significant events to take place after our encounters with Donald off the British coast was that I was commissioned to photograph and film a friendly wild dolphin who was delighting the divers off the remote island of San Salvador in the

Bahamas. However, by the time Ashley and I arrived in the incredibly clear and warm tropical Bahamian waters, Sandy, as the friendly wild dolphin was called, had left. He was never seen again. However, Ashley and I were compensated by some dives with a large Nassau grouper we named Lord Marmaduke, who became extremely friendly. I must admit that we encouraged the friendship by offering the grouper food.

When we discovered that Lord Marmaduke had a passion for sausages we could guarantee his appearance on a dive as soon as we entered his territory on the reef. For Lord Marmaduke was able to detect the presence of sausage even when he was hidden in his lair deep in the coral. After we had spent a few minutes wafting a sausage in the water he would appear and head straight for us. If the sausage was not relinquished immediately he would bite our fingers. He would then set about devouring any other sausages we took in with us. It was no use trying to hide them in the pockets of our lifejackets because he would quickly scent they were there and then proceed to attack our lifejackets until the contents were released. As he was a very large and powerful fish with an apparent complete lack of a sense of humour, it was never long before we had surrendered every edible item to him and he had consumed it. His appetite for sausages seemed insatiable. Indeed, his antics to procure food were the source of a great deal of amusement to the other divers who accompanied us from the diving centre at Riding Rock Inn.

Closer to home, the much smaller territorial fish called wrasse that live in breakwaters at Port Erin on the Isle of Man have also discovered that the presence of humans can be providential as well as dangerous. A diver who swims in the area may find that the wrasse are unexpectedly tame. This has come about because divers from the Marine Biological Station often feed the fish when swimming out from the shore on their scientific projects. Now the beautifully coloured wrasses will intercept any underwater swimmers who enter their respective territories in the hope that the clumsy two-finned mammals from outer space will bring with them some morsels of food.

However, the charming friendliness of the fish at Port Erin pales into insignificance compared with the response to divers of the sergeant-major fish in the 'Coral Gardens' in Eilat in the Red Sea. Because they are visited by divers almost every day throughout the year some fish rush forward and inspect every diver who goes in the water. The fish very quickly establish if he is carrying food. If the answer is positive the word goes out and the diver will find himself at the centre of an almost solid ball of fish who will rush in and snatch the food from his fingers.

In the Caravan Hotel, which caters mainly for divers, the manager expects half the bread he puts on the table in the morning to disappear into plastic bags for the fish.

Some marine biologists and environmentalists have been critical of the practice of fish feeding, saying that the divers are creating an unnatural situation and the fish are becoming accustomed to food they would not normally eat. While fully understanding their arguments I do not support the view that fish feeding should be stopped. I think to do so is pushing the idealism of conservation too far. In my opinion, possible adverse effects are outweighed by the development of rare harmonious

Swimming with fish in the Red Sea.

relationships between man and fish. From the fishes' point of view it must be a desirable reversal of roles from the usual one in which the fish ends its days by feeding man — accompanied by chips and sprinkled with vinegar!

Most novice divers are so entranced by their first overall impressions of the underwater world that they fail to notice many of the individual species that go to make up the complex patterns of marine and freshwater life. Learning to observe and identify the sometimes bewildering variety of species can provide amateur naturalists with endless hours of interest and enjoyment long after the dive is over.

HISTORY UNDER THE SEA

Some people spend hours in libraries tracing the stories of ships that have foundered. By carefully assessing all the records they decide where the ship or ships sank. An expedition is then mounted to search for the remains of the vessel and — perhaps more importantly — its cargo. But this is not the only way by which major finds of historic interest have been made.

There have been many instances where a diver, idly swimming over the seabed, has noticed something unusual on the bottom. Close examination has revealed it to be a cannon covered in encrustation. This in turn has led to the discovery of an entire wreck dispersed over a large area.

Christ of the Abyss. This statue is in the centre of the John Pennekamp Coral Reef State Park in the Florida Keys.

Such was the case with the finding of the Spanish galleon *Trinidad Velencera* off the west coast of Ireland, discovered quite by chance by a diver from the Derry Sub-Aqua Club.

When the possible significance of the find was realised the club contacted the archaeologist Colin Martin. Colin visited the site and helped the divers organise a plan for the recovery and conservation of the wreck. Firstly, however, the underwater site had to be accurately surveyed. This enabled a map to be drawn indicating the position of the cannons and other artefacts that were visible on the seabed.

From the position of the anchors and other objects Colin Martin deduced how the ship, one of the Armada vessels attempting to get back to Spain, had come to grief.

The divers who found the wreck and their families then all joined together to mount a very careful underwater archaeological dig. It took place over several years because diving was confined to the summer months when an airlift could be safely positioned on the site. An airlift is like a huge underwater vacuum cleaner. It is used to suck up sand. One fascinating item after another was revealed when the sand which had covered them for centuries was carefully removed. At this stage many of the artefacts were in an extremely fragile condition. A wooden plate, for instance, had the consistency of soggy cardboard. It was very carefully packed in a box of sand on the seabed before it was lifted to the surface for the long process of preservation.

The excavation could not be rushed because if too many objects had been recovered they would have disintegrated before they could be properly dealt with.

As one item after another was lifted and painstakingly preserved the group were able to put together a picture of life on board a galleon. In addition to studying history they were also making history; for this group were one of the first to prove that amateur divers could behave in a very responsible manner if they discovered a wreck of historic importance. Great credit must be given to the archaeologist Colin Martin who fired the enthusiasm of the divers and their families to do the work properly and at the same time persuaded them to refrain from simply pillaging the wreck for any treasure it might contain. And, as so often happens, the divers regarded the pieces of history they were unlocking as more significant than any silver or gold they might have found.

You don't have to discover an ancient wreck to find history under the sea. Much more modern wrecks can be equally fascinating. In 1981 I led an expedition to what is now generally accepted as the best site for modern wreck diving in the world. It is a place called Truk Lagoon in the West Pacific Ocean. The Lagoon lies within the flooded rim (about fifty miles in diameter) of a long-extinct volcano. It provided a haven for Japanese ships in the Second World War and has been described as 'the Gibraltar of the Pacific'. However, in 1944, in a massive raid called 'Operation Hailstone', the Americans attacked and sank a large number of the vessels at anchor in the Lagoon. Because of the remoteness of the location the sunken ships were left undisturbed for three decades. During that time coral started to grow on the wrecks and those that were close to the surface were transformed from rusting iron hulks into coral gardens of exquisite beauty.

Some of the wrecks that lay in deep water were only partly encrusted with coral. Inside everything remained as it was on that fateful day in 1944 when hundreds of sailors went down with their ships. Now each wreck is a time capsule. Slowly sediment has settled on most of the inside surfaces. When a diver swims inside it swirls up in thick clouds that can reduce visibility to nil in a few seconds. In some wrecks the cargo holds are open. I can recall drifting down through the open hatches of one such vessel into a hold full of aircraft and other military items, all completely free of silt and in a remarkable state of preservation. Indeed, I sat in the cockpit of a fighter of the type used by the kamikaze pilots on their suicide missions. Much to my surprise when I moved the joystick the elevator and ailerons still moved. The hold of another vessel was littered with shells and boxes of ammunition. In yet another wreck we found porcelain bowls and other crockery decorated with pictures depicting Mount Fuji, together with wine glasses and cut glass decanters. As we handled the various artefacts we thought about the men who were the last to handle them. They were young Japanese naval officers who were caught like flies in a web of war from which they never escaped. Now the wrecks in the placid waters of Truk Lagoon serve as salutary reminders of the folly and waste of war.

A SPORT FOR ALL

Truk Lagoon has become a magnet for divers of all nationalities and all ages seeking adventure beneath the sea. I suppose it is about as far away from a disused English canal as you can get — in terms of both distance and the cost per dive. But that is undoubtedly one of the attractions of diving. It is a recreation that can be enjoyed by families of very modest means. However, for those who can afford to travel further afield there are exotic locations around the world which offer completely different experiences.

Diving can be graded to suit almost any individual — regardless of age or physical fitness. In the Florida Keys, for instance, it is possible to go out on a dive boat with a platform on the stern at water level; getting into the calm, clear, shallow and warm water is no more demanding than stepping into a swimming pool. Thus old people and youngsters who are physically

Top: A scorpion fish photographed during the Leopard Reef expedition off Kenya. A puffer fish, off the Bahamas.

not very strong can enjoy the romance of swimming beneath the sea in an underwater fairyland full of coral and beautiful fish. When accompanied by a competent instructor they can dive with complete safety. One-day diving excursions are well organised for visiting holidaymakers, many of whom safely make their first and only dive under these idyllic conditions.

For the more adventurous, who are well trained and qualified, there are boat-based tours that are planned months in advance. These can range from a two-week luxury diving cruise in the Galapagos Islands to a six-week expedition to explore the cold and often rough waters around Iceland.

When sport diving started it was generally regarded as an activity that could only be taken up by the fit and young. This was especially so in Britain where most diving was confined to the relatively cold waters around our coast. Attitudes changed when many families went abroad for their holidays and realised that the joy of underwater swimming need not be such an exclusive activity after all.

Over the years the age range of people taking up diving has continuously widened. Many men and women in their sixties are now learning to dive. Provided they plan their adventures under the sea to stay comfortably within the limits of their physical capabilities there is no reason why they should not dive with their grandchildren.

So you see, underwater swimming really is a recreation that can be enjoyed by all members of the family. The picture of a family group drifting amongst the corals, accompanied by shoals of brilliantly coloured fish in a clear blue sea would have been regarded as total fantasy at the time Jules Verne wrote *20,000 Leagues Under the Sea*.

Now it has become reality.

USEFUL ADDRESSES

The British Sub-Aqua Club: 16 Upper Woburn Place, London WC1H 0QW. Tel: 01-387 9302. This is the governing body for the sport of underwater swimming with over 1,000 branches worldwide.

National Snorkellers' Club: 16 Upper Woburn Place, London WC1H 0QW. Tel: 01-387 9302; has branches throughout the UK and overseas. It caters for youngsters but does not include aqualung diving as one of its official activities.

DIVING SCHOOLS

The BSAC has granted official recognition to a number of diving schools where private tuition is available. BSAC-recognised diving schools have to meet high standards and are subject to periodic inspection by the Club. A list of schools is available from the BSAC, address as above.

The London Underwater Centre: P.O. Box 345, London W14 9QW. Tel: 01-385 5307. A diving school used by several television personalities. Its director, Reg Vallintine, is Chairman of the BSAC Recognised Schools Association.

Sub-Aqua Association: 22/24 Buckingham Palace Road, London SW1. Tel: 01-828 4551. The Sub-Aqua Association is an association of independent diving clubs — mainly in the UK but with overseas members as well.

Marine Conservation Society: 40 Grays Inn Road, London WC1X 8LR. Tel: 01-405 0224. Consists mainly of divers who are actively engaged in underwater projects to increase our knowledge of the marine environment. It also embraces aspects of conservation outside the UK.

The British Society of Underwater Photographers: Secretary, Jan Lennett, 122 Rannock Road, London W6. Concerned with all aspects of underwater photography and filming and holds regular meetings in London. Beginners are welcome.

Twickers World: 22 Church Street, Twickenham TW1 3NW. Tel: 01-892 7606. A specialist holiday organisation that caters for activity holidays to exotic destinations including diving expeditions — escorted by the author — to such places as the Galapagos Islands.

Twickenham Travel: 84 Hampton Road, Twickenham TW2 5QS. Tel: 01-898 8361. A holiday organisation that pioneered diving holidays to the Red Sea.

Plymouth Oceans Project: Fort Bovisand, Plymouth PL9 0AB. Tel: 0752 42570. A centre for many diving activities with organised courses on subjects such as archaeology, explosives, photography and marine biology. Diving excursions and holidays on board the MV *British Diver* are also available.

PUBLICATIONS

MAGAZINES

Diver: Eaton Publications, 40 Grays Inn Road, London WC1X 8LR. Tel: 01-405 0224. The official journal of the British Sub-Aqua Club, published monthly.

Subaqua Scene: Ocean Publications Ltd., 34 Buckingham Palace Road, London SW1W 0RE. Tel: 01-828 4551. The official magazine of the Sub-Aqua Association. It is published monthly.

Both magazines contain articles on a host of underwater activities — from the development of the latest diving equipment to details of exotic holidays. They also include information on forthcoming events such as the Festival of Underwater Sport which takes place at the Crystal Palace National Sports Centre in April each year.

(his earlier courses were run on Exmoor), and his interest in survival began when he joined a Survival Equipment Research organisation in Bristol as a volunteer worker. On leaving college he joined 23 SAS Regt. (V) in the Midlands, which widened his survival and expedition experience considerably. His interest in exploration led to his election as a fellow of the Royal Geographical Society in 1977.

Stephen's colleague at W.E.S.T. is Paulette Agnew, a mountaineer and skier, brought up in the remoter parts of Cumbria and Scotland. She read biochemistry at university and is particularly interested in the physiology of survival. Recently she spent three months teaching bushcraft skills at a mountain training camp in the USA.

To enjoy the challenge of any kind of outdoor activity — especially with the responsibility of a family — it is important to have the right attitude of mind. Self-confidence is the key to this. Stephen Doughty runs courses in survival and bushcraft which enable everyone to experience the satisfaction of returning to "a simplified, natural way of life", and by responding to the challenges of such a life — under expert tuition — develop the self-confidence needed to cope with emergency situations wherever they may occur. The only qualifications required are an open mind, a fair degree of physical fitness and to be aged over seventeen.

Stephen Doughty runs his Wilderness Expedition and Survival Training Centre (W.E.S.T.) from Gatesgarth Bothy, Buttermere, near Cockermouth, in one of the most beautiful parts of Cumbria. He was born and brought up in the West Country

Bushcraft and Survival

STEPHEN DOUGHTY

Why the sudden interest in survival training in recent years? We are after all less likely to have to survive in the modern world — cushioned as it is by technology and social institutions over which we have little direct control. I think that the growing interest being shown in wilderness survival training is in part a need for physical challenge and also a reflection of our desire to turn towards something we have perhaps some command over. It is an over-used cliché but most of us at some time have a longing to return at least fleetingly to a simplified natural way of life. Survival training is one way of achieving this.

I tell students when they arrive at my school that contrary to popular belief their bodies are very well adapted to living in the wilds. Our alimentary canals may take some adjusting to unrefined foods, but it is only a matter of time before this takes place. However, our minds have to be completely retrained to cope with primitive outdoor living under what can often be very demanding conditions. The heart of the matter lies in attaining a necessary frame of mind needed not only to survive in the wilds, but also in today's society. Survival is about an attitude of mind. However, although such training may be comprehensive in terms of techniques taught, it can never anticipate all emergencies. What survival training should do is to inspire a confidence that never wavers and an attitude of mind that is never surprised or dismayed whatever the turn of events. For survival it is essential to hold the conviction that every hazard will be overcome. Self-confidence is the key to this. The confidence gained by living in wild primitive conditions will spread over into our civilised lives and enable us to cope with the increasing mental pressures of urban living.

Many of the people who come to W.E.S.T. do so because they are followers of outdoor pursuit sports, and they are looking for training that will equip them to cope with an unplanned hazardous event. The majority of them are, if you dig deep enough, looking for something more fundamental than this. They are looking for survival training in the broadest sense of the word, the training of the mind and the self-

confidence that goes with it. I have found that people learn to be survivors most effectively by being taught bushcraft skills, which is not quite as obvious as it might at first appear. Having said that, bush living is not all misery and wet cold nights. If done properly it is a very enjoyable alternative to 'normal' camping, leaving behind the new technology stoves and tent materials to rely on simple equipment and one's ability to improvise. It is a stimulating and creative way to become part of the natural scene without feeling that one is an imposition on the landscape.

Bush living can be an enjoyable alternative to camping.

HOW DOES BUSHCRAFT FIT IN WITH SURVIVAL TRAINING?

I suppose that most of the people who come on our courses have the idea that we are actually going to teach them how to survive. Well, I am sorry to have to disappoint them and you — *you* are the only person who can teach yourself to survive! This ability is, as I have already said, an attitude of mind. It must therefore come from within. We cannot alter your approach towards solving your problems; you must do the changing yourself. Well, to be fair, this is not altogether the case. What we can do is teach you the basic skills to enable you to cope physically with a wilderness emergency. On their own these skills are useless without the self-confidence and adaptability that must go into combating the problems of such a misadventure. Bushcraft, whilst teaching you useful skills and procedures, is an excellent medium for learning how to cope with survival situations in any walk of life. It does not matter whether you are surviving in the wilds, the commercial world, industry, classroom or even at home; the same self-confident attitude of mind is required to win through.

The limited material resources taken into the wilds by the bushman, and the fact that he is looking for his supply of shelter, fuel and perhaps food from nature, gives him the edge over others. The bushman has to be observant. He cannot afford to miss anything that might be useful to him, from fishing pools to baler twine on a fence. In passing he will see much more of the wildlife, its ways and habits becoming second nature to him. He has to be flexible and adaptable to cope with changing conditions. He also needs a quick analytical mind to plan a course of action, just in case he cannot rely on outside help or technology. A bushman is a practical person who is able to use basic tools and primitive resources. If he is in a group then a fundamental awareness of those with him and how they tick is of paramount importance.

I am not saying that you have to be a superman or that bushcraft is the only way to learn these skills. What I am saying is that through the medium of bushcraft you can start to develop these skills without even realising it. This will lead to the realisation of your own strengths and weaknesses and with it comes the self-assurance which makes you a survivor.

BASIC EQUIPMENT

The pursuit of outdoor activities has become very gear-orientated. We have to 'be seen' with the latest gear and we think that we need a lot of it. This is simply another reflection of our modern materialistic society. Bushcraft as a pursuit is the antidote to this trend. The equipment is simple, inexpensive and you do not need much of it. Indeed you can make most of it yourself. I have made knives, stoves, basha sheets (see below) and many other objects from materials that other people have discarded. Somehow this home-made equipment always gives more pleasure and better service than shop-bought items.

Let us look at what is needed to get started. Our first priority is shelter. A simple 'basha sheet' of PU-coated nylon 7 ft 6 ins long by 5 ft wide with eyelets round the edge is all we need to provide the roof. A similar sheet, slightly smaller, for the ground is placed over a bed of bracken. The roof is supported by nylon cord (para cord in the trade) from improvised poles or a convenient tree or bush. The total weight is about 3½ lbs, the cost £7.50 if you buy the sheeting yourself and sew a hem round the edge, or £14 if you go to a supplier.

Next we need a weatherproof firelighting kit which consists of a flint and steel plus a capsule of volatile 'tinder', total cost approximately £2.50. There is no such thing as a waterproof match, despite the fact that they are sold as such. Other firelighting kits are usually either too complex or fail on contact with wind, water or tired, fumbling human beings.

A good all-round knife is a must. I advise my students, when looking for the all-in-one tool, to buy a diver's knife. At about £15 they offer the best value for money. You will expect your knife to cut small timber, dress game, make tinder and dig Dakota Hole fire pits at the very least,

so buy the best that you can afford. Do not forget that you will have to sharpen your knife constantly in the field so take a small oil stone and file with you.

A waterbottle, mess tin, mug and spoon should cost no more than £10. I would recommend the genuine army pattern ones for quality, lightness and durability. Many is the time that a mess tin or mug has been used on a W.E.S.T. course as a shovel or improvised fire carrier!

A first-aid kit is a must. Ours at W.E.S.T. are all very simple and include Condy's Crystals (potassium permanganate) used for water purification, as an antiseptic and also, with a few grains of sugar added, as

A simple basha sheet provides adequate shelter, the roof supported by nylon cord.

emergency fire tinder. My own first-aid kit is packed into a tobacco tin and has all I need for a two-week trip into remote country. The same size of tin is also used to carry fishing line, No. 10 and 12 hooks, weights, some matches, a candle, fire tinder and some spare batteries for my torch.

People in general tend to take into the hills a large heavy two-cell torch which will illuminate half a mountainside. All you need is a small penlight to read a map or see you over rough ground in those shadowy wooded valleys. There is plenty of natural

light available for you to see at night if only you can be patient and let your eyes adjust to the dark. This they will never do if dazzled by a torch. I also carry some form of pyrotechnic to signal for help if needed. My walking clothes, wind- and waterproof shell and sleeping bag, are very much the same as used by the traditional backpacker (see Christine Roche's chapter on backpacking). However, I always choose dark colours — greens, browns or sometimes dark blues — to blend in with the wilderness. I want to feel part of it, and not look like some sort of Belisha beacon and scare off all the wildlife.

You need not even go to the expense of

The kit supplied at the beginning of the W.E.S.T. weekend course. This includes rucksack, sleeping bag, socks, woolly pullover, basha poles, bivi-bag, first-aid kit, firelighting kit, mug, torch, water bottle, para cord, Hexi stove and fuel blocks, fishing kit, spoon, mess tin, knife, axe, trowel, notebook, maps, compass, and whistle.

a rucksack. On W.E.S.T. courses people are taught to wrap up their belongings in their basha sheets and sling the whole assembly around their necks. You can even float your bundle across a water obstacle if needs be. Weights of up to 80 lbs have been transported by this method.

A simple map and compass should always be carried in the wilds together with a watch and notebook. With a little instruction people on our courses head off on quite long journeys using natural signs such as wind-blown plants and the position of the sun with the aid of a sun compass. We also teach them how to make their own maps for return journeys in the event of having lost their OS map.

A spare pair of socks and a woolly-pully complete your kit. Some simple rations, with some spare sugars and carbohydrates 'for emergency use only' makes you into a self-contained unit ready to travel anywhere in the temperate zone in all but the worst of weathers and terrain. The final kit weight with rations should be no more than 20 lbs for a week-long trip. The total cost of this 'specialist' survival kit is no more than £40, the real bonus being, of course, that you carry very little man-made equipment to form a barrier between you and your wilderness experience.

BASIC SKILLS

We in Britain live in what is euphemistically called a temperate climatic zone. The joke is that we have weather, not a climate. The study of weather patterns and cloud formations is covered in some detail on our courses because the weather has such a profound effect on outdoor activities in the UK. Therefore, it goes without saying, some means of protection from the weather is very important.

SHELTER

Shelters can be made entirely from natural materials. But a log framework roofed with turf or bracken takes literally all day to construct. Not the sort of shelter you would build for a short-term stay, but ideal for a permanent site especially for the family group when time is worth investing. So how do we make a shelter in 30 minutes, almost anywhere and in any conditions, with the minimum of equipment? Simple. We use a basha sheet which is set up in a variety of ingenious ways to produce a weathertight shelter. It is almost true to say that there are as many different ways of constructing a basha as there are sites and bushmen. So long as you follow the basic rules about where to build your shelter, learn a few simple knots and have that peculiar form of lateral thinking common to all bushmen, you will not go far wrong.

Make certain that the site is intrinsically safe: no rockfalls or tree branches about to descend on you, no possibility of a flash flood or that you are on a human or animal bush highway. There should be a good supply of fuel for your fire and a source of fresh water not further than a kilometre away. If you can, try and site your shelter away from the prevailing wind and facing the early morning sun.

For the daywalker or mountaineer, benighted unintentionally, the polythene bivi-bag shelter can be a lifesaver. Just find a sheltered spot to sit down on with a comfortable back-rest and foot-jam. This keeps as much of your warm body off the cold ground as possible. Do not lie down as this defeats the object of the exercise. Place the bivi-bag over your head with a small hole cut in the corner to create your own mini-tent and microclimate. Although you will suffer from condensation problems the wind will be kept off, thus giving you a chance to maintain body heat. Do not use the newer 120-gauge bivi-bags (freezer bag thickness) but buy the standard 500-gauge bag (fertilizer bag thickness) as this is an important safety factor. The new Gore-Tex bivi-bags are very good as they breathe, thus preventing the formation of condensation. They are expensive but well worth the investment as they can be used in conjunction with a sleeping bag in normal conditions. Everybody on a W.E.S.T. course uses a polythene bivi-bag; there are some interesting comments afterwards.

Let us consider in greater detail why shelter is so important. Wet alone will not harm you. You can remain damp for days without ill effect. Cold on its own will not hurt you, provided you are not exhausted and are well fed. I have worked in the arctic in temperatures of −15°C to −20°C in my shirt sleeves without discomfort. If the wind is warm it will not harm you. However, the combination of cold, wind and wet kills you very quickly. Take the example of a summer's walk up a 3000-ft mountain in Wales. A still air temperature at the bottom of 20°C is not an uncommon summer temperature, nor can it be said to be anything but pleasant. However, the gain in height will lose you 1°C per 300 ft, resulting in a summit still air temperature of 10°C. Now consider the additional effect of a moderate 20-mph wind and the not-uncommon light soaking from a shower suffered on the way up. We have just added in the Wind Chill Factor and in this case it produced an actual air temperature of 0°C, literally freezing cold. It must be obvious, then, why it is so vital that you get out of the weather and under some form of shelter.

FIRE

Fire is important to the bushman for a variety of reasons. There is hardly a survival

Paulette Agnew finds shelter on the mountainside in a polythene bivi-bag.

or bushcraft subject that does not involve fire or heat in some way. The ability to make a fire is vitally important as it can mean the difference between life and death.

You should always carry a firelighting kit with you and enough kindling sticks for the next three fires. My firelighting kit consists of a flint and steel and a lighter fuel spirit capsule. Small dry kindling sticks are found on the tree, not on the ground. No one prunes wild trees so there is always plenty of dry, dead wood hanging up in the tree waiting to be harvested. Even in the wettest of weather this wood will be relatively dry.

Green wood, with the exception of ash, does not burn well and it smokes profusely. The taking of green wood from a living tree is not good for conservation either. There is no need to build a large fire. A base of 2 ft by 3 ft is a very large fire in survival terms. Half that size is all you require. Large fires are too hot to cook on, too hot to get close to for warmth and take up too

Building a pyramid of fine twigs. The secret of easy firelighting is preparation.

much energy in wood collection.

The secret of easy firelighting is preparation. Before lighting your fire always collect all your tinder and firewood. Seven armfuls of hardwood logs will keep a suitable fire going for twelve hours. The following is the method we teach at W.E.S.T. for lighting fires. Build a pyramid of fine twigs at the centre with larger and thicker sticks progressing in layers towards the outside. Light the kindling in the centre with your flint and steel. In wet and windy conditions put a layer of wet leaves over the pyramid to act as a lid to keep the heat in the centre of the young fire. The pyramid shape gives a good updraught to bring the fire to a stage where you can start putting on the larger logs quickly.

Fires like plenty of air spaces in between the burning sticks and they do not like to be constantly tampered with. When using the wet-leaves-assisted method, I generally send the students off to do some other task for a few minutes to prevent them poking the fire out when all they can see is smoke and no flame. They are always amazed to return to a blazing fire.

Always be careful to avoid spreading fire. Do not light fires in areas with dry peaty soil, a ground cover of heather or long grass, or in dense scrubland. I cannot over-emphasise how important it is to control your fire. Never light a fire in places where you have not got the consent of the landowner.

On our courses we teach students to build Dakota Hole fires. These are windproof and unobtrusive. They also build platform fires for cooking game. Firecraft is a skill that you can always add to and improve upon. Let's face it, everyone is a pyromaniac to some extent!

WATER

Water is of paramount importance to support life. The human body is made up of 60% water and this level must be maintained if we are to continue to function. At an ambient temperature of 60°F we need four pints of water a day to keep our water intake and output in balance. This includes water in food eaten. In higher temperatures intakes of two gallons or more may be required and the need for water is just as important at sub-zero temperatures, especially if you have been sweating heavily in warm clothing. Without water death is certain in a little over a week, in a temperate climate.

It goes without saying how important it is to be able to find and if necessary purify water. In most of the wild areas of Britain finding fresh water is not a problem. On the whole the water found in our mountain streams is better for you than tap water, but don't forget to check upstream for isolated habitation and the odd dead sheep. The skills of finding and purifying water should be understood by all bushmen.

There are many indicators pointing to sources of water. Animal life and tracks, vegetation in valleys, spring-lines on scarp slopes, the convergence of three or more dry valleys and of course human habitation either used or derelict. Once the water has been found it may well have to be purified. Impurities in the water take three forms: mechanical, biological and mineral/chemical. They may be natural impurities or man-made.

The mechanical form is quite obvious — sand, grit and general solid muck. In concentrated form, as in glacial meltwater which is loaded with rock flour, you can start to suffer from stomach ulcers if you drink mechanically polluted water for more than ten days. Biological impurities can take the form of dead animals, animal dung which collects at water holes, human sewage and also rotting vegetation. The chemical/mineral impurities can take the form of excess natural iron or copper dissolved in the water or the pollution from remote mines and wood pulp plants. In lowland areas excess fertilizer that is washed off the fields into the ground water can be the most common form of chemical pollution.

The purification processes are an interesting study. Distillation is by far and away the most useful as it removes all the impurities in the polluted water, and improvised bush stills are fun to make. They enable you to reprocess human waste water or seawater if you are in a really desperate situation. You should never drink salt water as the salts upset the concentrations of water in the body and it takes a greater volume of water than the amount of salt water drunk to remove those salts in the water. By drinking salt water you are speeding up the dehydration process, not slowing it down.

If your problem is limited to mechanical impurities then a simple filter made from fire charcoal held in a bag of tee-shirt material will take out all but the finest particles. Biological impurities are removed by boiling for 15 minutes.

Commercial filters and purification systems do exist and can be purchased at low cost from survival equipment suppliers. They can be efficient and should be considered when you know that you are going into an area where water purification is going to be a day-to-day problem.

FOOD

Food is body fuel and without it activity and physical efficiency are reduced. In survival terms we can split the issue into two areas of interest. First, short term energy foods and second, the longer term sustaining and maintenance foods.

Many people who come on our courses are surprised to find that the last thing they should ever consider doing, when benighted on their favourite lakeland mountain, is to put out animal traps for a breakfast feast. You might consider setting traps in a similar situation in some remote part of, say, Scandinavia, but then only after it had become apparent that you were going to be there for some time. You would set a trap today to catch a meal in four or five days' time. It takes this long for traps to settle down and become accepted by the animal community. You also have to take into account the fact that it takes 12 snares to yield one rabbit, a sobering thought. I might add that the use of snares is cruel and so they should only be used in a true survival situation. On our courses we encourage our students to catch fish either with lines or by tickling. Most catch at least one fish. Do, however, make certain that your stream or lake is well stocked. This is done by careful observation.

The meals that trapping produces are protein-rich. As a survival food, protein is at the bottom of your list of priorities. It is a building material for worn out body cells and produces relatively little energy for your body to work on. The fat content of game is very low, as is that of wild rabbit. Having said that, fats are a good survival food as they produce a lot of energy for their weight. Eskimos eat pounds of fatty food to keep warm. Fats are the form in

Fish are a good source of protein, easily caught with lines or by tickling.

which the body stores surplus food but it takes some time to convert the fat back into useful energy, so don't think that you can take your emergency rations with you in excess body weight! It takes the body some time to digest fats and proteins and convert them into useful materials. This digestive process also needs more water to work than the breakdown of sugars and carbohydrates. In a survival situation the amount of water available may also be a problem as we have already discussed, so there is no point in making the problem worse by eating the wrong foods. I hope that you can now see why the acquisition of protein and fats from the wild is a long term project and not really relevant to a

UK survival situation.

The carbohydrates and sugars that we do need to give us energy can be acquired from plant life. The advantage of plants is that they do not run away. The disadvantage is the difficulty of knowing which ones make a safe meal. There are a few ground rules to help us along. I accept that there are some well known exceptions to these rules, but in general they hold true. Do not eat any part of a plant with waxy, shiny leaves such as holly, rhododendron or ivy. Do not eat brightly coloured berries such as whitethorn or lords-and-ladies fruit. Do not eat plants with milky sap and avoid plants with umbelliferous flower heads like the hog weeds. I might add that unless you have an established authority to consult as you learn, you would be well advised to leave fungi alone. So much for the do's and don'ts; now for a method that helps you to discover what you can eat and what you cannot eat without having any substantial plant identification knowledge.

The method is called test eating. Very simply it involves taking a small sample of the plant material under test and chewing it over in your mouth to get the full flavour. If you do not feel sick or the taste is not just plain revolting, swallow the sample and wait six to eight hours. If at the end of this period you have not experienced sickness, diarrhoea or stomach cramps you can then proceed to eat a few mouthfuls. Again wait six to eight hours, which is the time it takes the digestive tract to process food, and if there is still no ill effect try a full meal of the plant in question. If all is still well you can assume that the plant is safe to eat.

If at any stage in your trials you discover some ill effects try cooking, as this often breaks down the toxins in the plant that gives rise to the problem. You can try test eating with any part of the plant. The roots invariably need cooking while the leaves need very little cooking on the whole. Stems and shoots do not require much cooking either, as over-cooking of the more succulent parts of a plant destroys all the minerals and vitamins that are urgently needed by your body. The fruit, nuts, seeds, and even flowers from many plants are also worth trying. If one part of a plant is inedible try the other parts to see what the reaction is before writing the whole plant off as inedible. However, remember that the reverse is also true. Just because one part of a plant is fine to eat do not assume that the rest of it is also edible. The secret of finding out what is good safe plant food and what should be avoided is curiosity mixed with caution and much patience.

Plants are an excellent source of nourishment and energy. In the spring, summer and autumn they can provide you with a progressively better diet as the months roll on. The winter is, to say the least, a little barren and you will be lucky to find much to eat at this time of the year.

Plants can also be used as bush medicines. Boiled oak bark for diarrhoea, willow for aches and pains, fern shoots as an emetic, are just a few of the many examples that can be found.

Having just read the last few paragraphs, you are probably thinking to yourself that it is very time-consuming to produce any sort of meal from the wilds. The more so when you consider that you can only test-eat one part of one plant at a time if you are to be certain that the reaction you are getting is from your plant sample and not from something else you have eaten. For this reason the responsible outdoorsman always carries some kind of emergency ration pack.

This ration pack should see you through your emergency period, which in the UK rarely exceeds 48 hours. If you are stranded in a more remote area the pack will give you a breathing space in which to get your test eating and hunting organised.

Emergency ration packs should contain sugars and starchy carbohydrates plus some brew-making materials. Sugars are the short term instant sprint energy foods that you need to cope with a crisis. The brews of tea or coffee will give you very little in the way of energy, but as a psychological pick-me-up they are invaluable. The starchy carbohydrates give you longer term sustaining energy. You can buy ready-made expensive ration packs but I find that it is much better to make your own to your specific requirements. Barley sugar sweets, Kendal mint cake, Mars bars, oatmeal biscuits, potato powder and the ingredients to make a pan-boiled rice pudding are all ideal ration pack foods.

It is vital to learn how to use a compass and OS map correctly.

Wayfinding

Getting lost is one of the more common reasons for calling out the rescue services in this country. The responsible outdoorsman does not go any further into the hills than his navigation skills will safely allow. This includes being able to navigate in misty conditions or at night, even if you only go for short 'day' walks. The weather can change so rapidly that you may easily find yourself out on the moors at night or in the mist unintentionally. The confident use of a Silva-type compass and a 1:50,000 scale OS map is a must for any outdoor traveller. Apart from the safety factor your map is a wonderful source of information about local features. On our courses you will learn how to navigate with standard equipment as well as how to navigate using more unusual methods. Our students navigate with sun compasses, make their own maps and use the topography and flora to help with orientation. The stars can also be used to assist with navigation. A great deal of confidence is gained from being able to find your way in the wilds and, as confidence is one of the major factors that contributes to the survival attitude of mind, we are rather keen on teaching navigation skills at W.E.S.T.

Signals

Being able to signal for help is a much misunderstood skill. It amazes most people how difficult it is to attract someone's attention when you need help. The effective use of whistles, the voice, torches and pyrotechnics should be known by everybody who ventures out into the hills, forests or mountains.

The international distress call of six long blasts/flashes/shouts, followed by a minute's silence before repeating the call, is recognised by all outdoorsmen on land. The reply on hearing the signal is three long blasts/flashes/shouts followed by a one-minute interval. Pyrotechnics are fireworks that can be used to attract attention. A red colour is used to signal for help. A white colour is used to mark a position or reply to a red signal. For daytime use, smoke-producing pyrotechnics are the most effective. At night flares are used, a big Roman candle if you like, that can be seen over some distance. During the day a flare can be difficult to pick out. Star shells and rockets with flares that come down on a parachute can be used at night when they are most effective, or during the day when they can show up quite well against the background of the sky. Everybody on a W.E.S.T. course gets a chance to use some sort of pyrotechnic. We also teach you how to use signal fires, ground-to-air signal panels and other improvised means of attracting attention.

Setting off a smoke-producing pyrotechnic, more effective for daytime use than a flare.

First Aid

Field first aid is something we should all know about. We have a responsibility to ourselves and to those with whom we go into the hills to be able to cope with an accident involving bodily damage. It would take up too much space here to go into field first aid in the detail that the subject deserves. Go to a first-aid class. I think that the Red Cross run the most practical courses for the outdoorsman. Then, if you can, supplement this with a course on the subject of first aid as it is applied in the field, run by one of the outdoor pursuits schools. I am not saying that the Red Cross courses are not good enough. They are very good. But they are courses designed with urban man in mind, where hospital casualty departments are a very short space of time away from an accident scene. In the wilds you might be at best six hours or at the worst six days away from professional help. This means that your knowledge has to be greater to cope with your casualty over a longer period of time before help arrives to relieve you of the responsibility. On modern first-aid courses you are told not to give liquids to patients suffering from clinical shock. This is because the fluids drunk would cause problems to the anaesthetist at the hospital. In the field, because of the time it takes to get the patient to hospital, you must give fluids or risk the patient dying on you. In the case of an unconscious patient you may have to give the fluids by improvised rectal drip, and this is not the sort of subject taught on the average first-aid course. Doctors who have attended our survival courses have said that they learned a great deal from us about how to cope with a wilderness emergency without all the sophisticated tools they would normally have at their disposal.

Having learned all the basic skills that would help you to survive a wilderness survival situation, you now have to learn how to formulate a plan of action and do something positive about your predicament.

IMMEDIATE ACTION DRILLS

What to do as soon as disaster strikes? First, move yourself and your companions away from any further danger. This may mean that you have to move a badly injured person whom you would ordinarily leave lying where he fell. Then apply first aid where necessary to those who need it badly, leaving minor injuries until later. Check and safeguard food, water and stores. Construct a temporary shelter. Place signalling equipment close at hand. Deal with minor injuries. Get a brew on, get into warm dry clothes if you have them. Sit down and rest, recover from the shock and work out your position.

Now you can formulate a plan for the longer term. What you decide to do will vary so much that it is not practical to discuss the problem in great detail. Every survival situation is different because the people, the accident, the weather, the stores available, the location and the injuries involved are always different. As a rule, however, you should remain in the area in which the accident occurred. Send a party of two to get help with all the relevant details of what has happened, but only if you know where you are and where they are going. Stay with injured members of the party. Make your base camp as established as you can. Get a fire going, give everybody who can work something to do, even if it is only making a record of events. Make a more permanent shelter and find your source of water and firewood.

Make permanent signals and organise a watch-keeping rota. Keep your spirits up and sit it out. Believe it or not, your worst enemies will be boredom and the thankless hard work involved in being a survivor. Your will to survive must prevail at all times.

WHERE TO GO

Most of the land in Britain is owned privately and that which is owned by the community usually has by-laws governing it which prohibit the practising of bushcraft skills. I have found, however, that landowners are quite amenable to the idea of bush camping provided you can assure them that you are not going to burn down their woodland or rustle their sheep! If you act responsibly about the issue you will almost invariably get a favourable reaction. Photographs and diagrams of what you intend to do will help greatly to allay the fears felt by landowners.

Having secured the right to practise your pursuit on a suitable piece of land, hopefully broadleaf woodland with a stream, you must continue to be a responsible bushman. This means always leaving the site in a clean, tidy condition as you found it. Never fell or use green wood, that is, live trees, except for the odd basha pole or cooking spit cut from an unobtrusive branch. Once they are prepared I keep my poles for up to six months.

Decimation of woodland is damaging to good public relations and equally for conservation. There are enough adverse pressures on our wild places without adding any more. It gave me great pleasure to be told by one of our farmer landlords, "I haven't seen any sign of your students for some time", when I knew that we were on his land the week before while he was rounding up his sheep. Only the dogs knew we were there.

I have bushcamped on Exmoor, which is not renowned for its remoteness, and also as far away as the Scottish Highlands which is as removed from civilisation as you are able to get in the UK. However, you do not have to go very far to find isolation. Dunkery Beacon is swarming with people for most of the year, and yet I can take you to a woodland valley site not three miles distant and the only signs of life will be the deer and other woodland animals. With most of our training sites I have yet to see many people passing through. So, if you are a long way from the traditional wilderness areas of Britain, take heart! There is a small oasis of quiet woodland not very far from your home just waiting to give you a refuge. But do not forget to contact the owner first and do follow the Country Code. Remember you will want to use the site more than once.

As a bushman you will be able to set up your basha in the most unlikely situations. Some of our sites are on 45-degree slopes, one is in a bog (not the most pleasant, but it proves interesting!), and some are on exposed hilltops. So you are not restricted, as are most conventional backpackers, to 'ideal' level even ground. If you can, find a site with plenty of broadleaf trees which produce dead wood in abundance and offer an aesthetically pleasing setting, rather than a conifer wood which tends to be rather barren in terms of ground flora and animal life. Finding a site can be good fun. Arming yourself with the local OS map and enough cash to buy landowners the odd pint or three can lead you to many an interesting encounter with local characters, and eventually to that much-sought-after basha site.

COURSES AVAILABLE

Paulette Agnew has found a good basha-site on an exposed hillside.

Having, I hope, whetted your appetite for bushcraft I would not be surprised if you feel a little apprehensive about going out on your own straight away. Perhaps a little advice is needed, with some personal tuition. It helps greatly if someone actually shows you how to exercise the basic skills involved. Descriptions taken from books as often as not do not match up to practical application. So how about going on a course?

There are several organisations which run survival courses. The three major schools are all run by ex-Special Forces personnel, including ours. That is not to say that they are military courses run for soldiers by soldiers. You may perhaps be pleasantly surprised by what you find in these ex-Special Forces instructors. We take what is best from our military training, adapt it and then apply these skills to civilian situations. We are concerned about the relationship between man and his environment. Perhaps we are a little too keen at times to point out to the average urban man just how detached he has become from his rural roots, but I make no apologies for this attitude. Look at the selfish mess urban man is making of our world and you will see why. Much of the pleasure and philosophy behind bushcraft is about living in harmony with nature.

Our own courses at W.E.S.T. are very practical. Only four hours are actually spent in a classroom. The rest of the time you are out in the field learning and putting into practice the skills which will transform you into a bushman. The mixture of people that come to us is amazing. They include design engineers, dustmen, doctors, storemen, company directors, teachers, labourers, ballet dancers, lab. technicians and an accountant. One of our female survivalists is, at the moment of writing, on a Royal Geographic Society sponsored expedition to the Sahara. There have been husband and wife teams; father and sons; brothers. In short these courses are for anyone with a spirit of adventure. The normal barriers of class, creed, sex or nationality break down, allowing people to concentrate on themselves and their companions with no social inhibitions to get in the way.

It just does not matter who you are, or where you are from, or how well-educated you are, when you find yourself up to your neck in cold water crossing a lake. The important matters are: can you swim the distance? Is your pack leaking? Has your analysis of the opposite bank been correct? Is your companion OK? I find the variety of people who come fascinating and greatly admire their motives and pluck in doing so. One learns never to pre-judge a person, as the most unlikely of characters make very

good bushmen.

The courses we run are graded. They run from basic weekends, followed by an intermediate long weekend leading to a seven-day course. The climax of the week course is a 36-hour solo expedition to test the skills that you have learnt. Many people who come initially just for a weekend eventually end up coming on a full week course. Once the bug bites, you will be a confirmed survivor and bushman to the end!

CONCLUSION

By now you must appreciate that bushcraft and survival covers a multitude of different subjects, each of which can be seen from more than one angle. No two people will see the pursuit in the same light; you can make it just what you want for your own enjoyment and no one can say that you are wrong or that you are not a true devotee. It is the new outdoor pursuit for the individualist, for the person who wants to do his own thing with as little support from others or material equipment as possible.

Bushcraft is not just a way of gaining practical training in how to cope with a wilderness emergency. It is a means of throwing aside the restrictions of modern industrial society and finding spiritual and physical freedom in the wilds. It is a means of building self-confidence and self-reliance, of testing ourselves and coming to terms with our limitations, strengths and weaknesses. Not least of all, it is great fun. There are so many things to learn and do, with benefits for all concerned.

I hope this chapter has sparked off your interest. Perhaps one day our paths will cross and I will be able to share your experience of the outdoors as I sit with you and your family around a camp fire.

Photographic Acknowledgements

Frontispiece: Mr and Mrs Drake

Walking

Page 12 Peter Evans; page 15 Roger Smith; page 16 Roger Smith; page 17 Reg. Lowe; page 18 Mike Edwards; page 19 Reg. Lowe; page 21 courtesy of Silva (UK) Ltd; page 23 Reg. Lowe; page 27 Reg. Lowe; page 28 Mike Edwards.

Backpacking

Page 32 Christine Roche; page 34 Geoff Gadsby; page 35 top, Geoff Gadsby; page 35 Steve Ashton; page 39 Geoff Gadsby; page 42 Geoff Gadsby; page 50 Steve Ashton; page 53 Geoff Gadsby.

Cycling and Cycle Touring

Page 54 Peter Knottley; page 56 Peter Knottley; page 57 Peter Knottley; page 59 Peter Knottley; page 61 courtesy of Alex Moulton; page 63 Peter Knottley; page 64 Peter Knottley; page 67 Peter Knottley; page 59 Peter Knottley.

Youth Hostelling

Page 72 courtesy of the Youth Hostels Association of England and Wales; page 75 Steve Ashton; page 76 Steve Ashton; page 79 Steve Ashton.

Mountaineering

Page 82 Steve Ashton; page 85 Steve Ashton; page 86 Steve Ashton; page 88 Steve Ashton; page 89 Steve Ashton; page 90 below, Steve Ashton; page 91 right, Steve Ashton; page 92 Steve Ashton; page 95 Steve Ashton; page 98 Steve Ashton; page 105 Steve Ashton; page 106 Steve Ashton; page 107 Steve Ashton; page 111 Steve Ashton.

Cross-Country Ski-ing

Page 112 Neil Wakeling; page 114 Iain Hudson; page 115 Ann Wakeling; page 117 courtesy of the *Westmorland Gazette*; page 119 Ann Wakeling; page 120 Ann Wakeling; page 121 Ann Wakeling; page 123 Ann Wakeling; page 125 Steve Ashton.

Riding, Trekking and Owning a Family Pony

Page 128 Sue Gibson; page 130 Sue Gibson; page 132 Anne-Marie Edwards; page 133 Sue Gibson; page 135 Campbell Goldsmid; page 137 Mike Edwards; page 138 Sue Gibson; page 141 Mike Edwards; page 143 Mike Edwards; page 146 Mike Edwards; page 149 Simon Rowley; page 150 Mike Edwards; page 153 Sue Gibson.

Caving

Page 154 Rob Palmer; page 157 Rob Palmer; page 159 Rob Palmer; page 160 Rob Palmer; page 165 Rob Palmer; page 169 Rob Palmer.

Treasure Hunting

Page 170 Greg Payne; page 183 Greg Payne; page 174 Greg Payne; page 177 Greg Payne; page 178 Greg Payne; page 180 Greg Payne; page 182 Greg Payne; page 183 courtesy of the *Irish Press*; page 184 Greg Payne.

Windsurfing

Page 188 David Eberlin/*On Board*; page 192 David Eberlin/*On Board*; page 193 David Eberlin/*On Board*; page 194 David Eberlin/*On Board*; page 195 David Eberlin/*On Board*; page 195 David Eberlin/*On Board*.

Dinghy Sailing

Page 196 Fitzpatrick; page 199 Fitzpatrick; page 200 Fitzpatrick; page 202 Fitzpatrick; page 203 Fitzpatrick; page 206 Fitzpatrick; page 207 right, Fitzpatrick; page 211 courtesy of PGL Holidays.

Cruising under Sail

Page 212 Bernard Harrison; page 215 courtesy of the Island Cruising Club; page 216 Bernard Harrison; page 220 Bernard Harrison; page 223 Bernard Harrison; page 224 Bernard Harrison; page 226 courtesy of the Island Cruising Club; page 229 Bernard Harrison; page 230 Bernard Harrison; page 235 Mike Edwards.

Canoeing

Page 236 David Train; page 238 Steve Ashton; page 239 Steve Ashton; page 241 David Train; page 245 Steve Ashton; page 246 courtesy of the British Canoe Union; page 251 David Train.

Cruising Inland Waterways

Page 252 John Gagg; page 255 John Gagg; page 256 John Gagg; page 261 John Gagg; page 264 John Gagg; page 265 John Gagg; page 269 John Gagg.

Sub-Aqua

Page 272 Bernard Parker; page 275 Ashley Dobbs; page 276 Horace Dobbs; page 277 Horace Dobbs; page 281 Horace Dobbs; page 282 Horace Dobbs; page 286 Horace Dobbs; page 288 Horace Dobbs; page 289 Horace Dobbs; page 291 top, Ashley Dobbs; page 291 Horace Dobbs.

Bushcraft and Survival

Page 294 Stephen Doughty; page 296 Stephen Doughty; page 298 Stephen Doughty; page 299 Stephen Doughty; page 301 Stephen Doughty; page 302 Stephen Doughty; page 305 Stephen Doughty; page 307 Stephen Doughty; page 308 Stephen Doughty; page 311 Stephen Doughty.

Maps

Page 77 courtesy of the Youth Hostels Association of England and Wales; page 78 courtesy of the Scottish Youth Hostels Association; page 109 Steve Ashton; page 267 John Gagg.

Illustrations

Page 37 Maurice Roche; page 190 David Eberlin/*On Board.*